MICHIGAN GHOST TOWNS

Of The Lower Peninsula
(Formerly Michigan Ghost Towns I & II)

MICHIGAN GHOST TOWNS

Of The Lower Peninsula
(Formerly Michigan Ghost Towns I & II)

Published by
Glendon Publishing
P.O. Box 80807
Las Vegas, NV   89180-0807

ISBN 0-932212-64-6

Cover by Diane Tedora
Lithography by
Avery Color Studios
Au Train, Michigan   49806

DEDICATIONS

This book is dedicated to those hardy pioneers of "York State," New England, Canada, and many countries of the world who blazed the trails, "swamped" the tote-roads, built the railroad grades, and founded the hundreds of towns that lined the tracks.

Also to my daughter, grandchildren, nephews and members of the younger genertion who may someday wonder what it was like in the days when a trip to town was a exciting as landing a man on the moon is today.

Also to my father, Lake Frost Dodge (August 10, 1895-August 10, 1968) and to all the generations of Frosts and Dodges since their arrival on the shores of America in the 17th century and who joined the early pioneers of Michigan and helped make America the great land it is today.

VOLUME I
TABLE OF CONTENTS

VOLUME II
TABLE OF CONTENTS

INTRODUCTION

The words "ghost town" conjure up a picture of coyotes howling in an abandoned silver mining town on the side of a lonesome Nevada hill, or tumbleweeds blowing through the empty streets of a California town called "Calico" - the falsefront, wooden buildings still standing as they did in the 1800s. In most of the ghost towns in the West, the people, the gold, and the silver are gone, but the buildings and the towns remain intact.

This is a different story. Prior to this date there is no record of the former towns that existed in Michigan but the number runs into the thousands. Most ghost towns in Michigan have disappeared completely, due to ravages of nature or by the many fires that swept over northern Michigan after the timber was harvested. All evidence of many others lies buried beneath expressways and waters of rivers dammed up to obtain water power for electricity or to create artificial lakes.

Some of the former places listed in this book were not a town or even a settlement. They were named, either by someone who lived in the area, by a logging company, railroad company, or by the Post Office Department. There is not an area in the State, especially in northern Michigan, but where some person will invariably say, "Right over there in Section 6 of so-and-so township used to be a town called 'Belly Button,'" or some such name. The person who knows will go into detail about the number of saloons, either 22 or 27, and other business places once located on the site. During more than 15 years of casual research on ghost towns, and the past four years of intensive research, I have followed up hundreds of such leads. About one in a hundred prove to be true, for which I am grateful. For this reason I am listing every place located that was shown on a map or given a name. It is still possible that some of them have been missed.

Many people living in or near some of the ghost towns may resent their village listed as a ghost town. Some of the towns were deserted many years ago, then revived with the advent of the automobile and tourism. Other villages may at one time have had a population of several hundred people, places of business, and industries and are today occupied by summer homes and residences, but still retain the name of a village formerly located on the site. Others, such as *Jennings* in Missaukee County, at one time had a population of more than 2,000. Today there are only a few permanent residents.

The ghost towns described in this book were left in the wake of the lumbering industry, the settlements and villages that often sprang up in a matter of days from the 1860s to the early 1900s. They often disappeared as suddenly as they appeared. Any evidence that many of the towns ever existed is now hidden by second growths of poplar and birch trees, covered with piles of blowing sands, or eradicated by pipelines, oil wells, and other endeavors of modern progress.

Only blackened stumps remain where pines once towered in all their majestic splendor, before the coming of the white man. Pine stumps don't tell tales. Some of the thousands of old railroad beds that wend their way through nearly every county of northern Michigan sometimes do. In this book I have followed some of these trails to discover something about the towns and the people who lived in them.

Why are they so hard to find?

It is difficult to understand, especially by our younger generation and persons born since 1920, that our present road system in Michigan has been constructed since that time.

Anyone who expects to drive down a paved or blacktop highway and locate more than one of every one hundred ghost towns described in this book will be disappointed. It is nearly impossible to direct anyone to a former ghost town site in terms of today's roads. These towns were located either on a railroad, probably removed years ago, and with only parts of the old grade visible, or at the end of wagon trails through woods that ended somewhere near a river or lake.

First transportation in the State was by water. A brief period of road building occurred prior to the Civil War in the southern part of the State and an attempt was made by the State Legislature to construct a road from Lansing to the Straits of Mackinac by authorizing the construction of a road now known as the "Old State Road." Other State roads were authorized but many stretches were never completed and those that were consisted mainly of clearing the right-of-way of trees. With the coming of railroads, road building projects were abandoned as there was no need of other transportation, except for short distances.

No major attempt was made at road building again until the bicycle craze of the 1890s when some improvements were made, mostly in the area of large cities. Most roads, as we see them today, were built since 1930 and after World War II.

A 1925 road map looks quite impressive with heavy blue lines marking "main highways" of that era. These main highways were at best short stretches of blacktop near cities and narrow, gravel and sand roads through the counties covered in this book.

As an example, a heavy, blue line designates "Highway 10" beginning at *Detroit*, through *Pontiac, Flint, Saginaw, Bay City*, and north to *Mackinaw City* along a route roughly paralleling present day US-23 and M-65 highways.

"Highway 14" was a sand and gravel road extending north from Lansing to Houghton Lake, replaced by paved US-27 in the 1930s, and by a new 4-lane expressway in the 1960s. Autos travelling at the breakneck speed of 20 or 25 miles per hour could barely pass each other on most sections of the old road. On the few occasions two cars met, which could be told well in advance by the cloud of dust, one car was forced to find the widest spot in the road and wait for several minutes until the other auto passed before proceeding. Drivers were very considerate and the occupants of the oncoming car waved and yelled words of thanks to the motorist who waited for them to pass.

Although many roads in the *Bay City* area were at one time stone roads and believed to be the best since the days of ancient Rome, in the 1920s the main road north from *Bay City* (now US-23) narrowed down to a sand trail near *Kawkawlin*. Each side of the road from *Linwood* to *Pinconning* was lined with blowing sand and stump-covered fields, with an occasional abandoned house or log cabin. The 25-mile trip was nearly a ½-day journey. There was one pump near an abandoned house along the road with a rusty tin cup hanging on a wire from the spout and was the only available place along the road to get a drink of water.

In 1925, and until many years later, there was no M-55 west from *West Branch* to *Houghton Lake*. The area between consisted of impassable hills, swamps, and stump lands crisscrossed with wagon trails and tote roads.

Until 1940 there was no M-61 between *Gladwin* and *Harrison*, and then only 6 miles of the 40-mile stretch to *Standish* was paved.

M-115 between *Clare* and *Cadillac* was unheard of and there was no direct road west from *Cadillac* to *Manistee*.

Most towns, now only 15 or 20 miles apart, were separated by 40 or more miles of dirt roads, sand trails, or no roads at all and required a day's drive by automobile.

For these reasons very few ghost towns over 50 years old can be located along main roads and highways.

Winter months are the best to go "prospecting" for old railroad grades and trails that eventually lead to a former ghost town site. Many of these roads and trails that are impassable during spring thaws are frozen during the winter. Traffic on side roads is negligible, allowing more freedom to gaze while driving, and there is no dust to restrict vision while looking for locations. Trees are bare of leaves, weeds that grow waist-high in summer have died, and in most areas there is a visual distance of ½ mile or more through usually dense woods and brush. Old railroad grades and foundations, invisible in spring or summer, are clearly outlined and stand out in bold relief when covered with a layer of snow.

A winter excursion by auto on the side roads of any county in northern Michigan can be very rewarding. When covered with snow many abandoned buildings and foundations appear that were hidden from view in warm weather.

Most northern county roads are now marked with name signs. Keep a clipboard or notebook at your side and draw a rough map and make notes as you drive. When a railroad grade or possible ghost town site is observed make more detailed notes and mark the spot on your map to use as a guide for next summer's exploration with a metal detector.

How To Find A Ghost Town

Ghost town sites can be identified by the following signs:

(1)   A straight row of 100-year-old pine trees more than 12 inches in diameter that stand out among smaller oak, birch and poplar trees. These pines usually have low-hanging branches beginning 8 or 10 feet above the ground because they grew out in the open and were planted or preserved when small.

(2)   A straight row of Lombardy poplar trees, usually dead with only the trunks standing. Some of these stately trees may be 100 feet high with a trunk circumference of 20 or more feet. Lombardy poplars are not native to

Michigan but grow rapidly and were probably the only seedlings that survived without care while being transported long distances. They thrived in the poor, sandy soil of northern Michigan with little or no care. Traces of these tall, short-lived trees on a site prove that a dwelling once stood near the spot.

Straight rows of mature maple trees also determine a site, although few people took the pains to plant them outside of more permanent towns and cities. Old apple orchards determine inhabitants in an area, but usually only a single farmstead or dwelling.

(3)   Lilac bushes in any form. Dense growth of worn-out lilac bushes show that the site was abandoned more than 30 years ago and probably 50 years or more have passed. These bushes too were imported and planted the first year a house was built, usually in the front yard and close to the street or wagon trail.

Yellow roses were also a favorite of early settlers but were short-lived and without care very few remain.

(4)   A concentrated area of tag alder bushes covering an area approximating the size of a house or barn foundation may also disclose an old foundation or shallow basement of a building.

(5)   Any opening in the ground from 2 to 4 feet square with rotten pieces of boards among overgrown weeds is invariably the remains of a well pit. Nearly every well was dug by hand and ranged in depth from 8 to 10, or at the most, 14 feet deep. Over the years they became filled with blowing sand and debris but can be identified. These hand-dug wells often went dry and were later used as a depository for junk, bottles, tin cans, and refuse.

(6)   Any of these signs combined with a railroad grade or wagon trail are certain proof that an area was at one time inhabited. Also pieces of tarpaper or lath may indicate where a building once stood. Thin and flimsy as it was, tarpaper was practically indestructible except by fire and even then many pieces escaped the flames and were carried some distance from a burning building where they still remain, if not plowed under.

Other possible signs are old cemeteries, posts and pilings in streams, concrete sidewalks, and tanks. Cemeteries may help in locating former ghost town sites but were usually located a mile or more from the village. Oldest dates on tombstones can help determine the date of early settlement of an area but allow another five years prior to this date. First burials in most old cemeteries were made of necessity and without ceremony or fancy funerals. Graves of family members were marked with a wooden cross but most trappers, lumberjacks, and early settlers had no one to place even a simple marker.

If an old cemetery shows noticeable hollows overgrown with sweet-smelling, blue or purple flowers in an area with no grave markers, these are unmarked graves of probably first burials. Many northern cemeteries still contain wood cross markers. Large stones also marked many graves around lumber camps.

Old pilings in lakes, rivers, and streams often mark the site of a power dam for a saw or gristmill but can also be misleading. There were at least four major dams in a 20-mile stretch of the Tittabawassee River above Sanford. These wooden dams controlled the level of the river during the logging drives and had no connection with a town or settlement in the immediate vicinity. Dams such as these were built along nearly every stream or river in northern Michigan during days of the spring log drives.

Any type of concrete tanks ranging in size from 2 feet by 4 feet on up to 20 or more feet long are signs of a logging camp, banking site, railroad siding, or nearby settlement. Many of these watering troughs remain today along roads and trails. Some of them now lay in the midst of recently-planted tree plantations and can be found only by accident. These tanks, although usually filled with sand, weeds, and debris, are still in good condition and reinforced with steel rods or bolts.

Although board and plank sidewalks were the order of the day in newly-settled villages it is surprising how many former towns had concrete sidewalks, especially along the main street and in the business section. It is also surprising how soil has a tendency to "grow up" rather than to sink down over the years. Many times when an apparent small slab of concrete is uncovered near a foundation beneath a solid layer of sod, an hour's work with a shovel will uncover a hundred or more feet of unbroken concrete sidewalk placed there 75 years ago.

————

MICHIGAN GHOST TOWNS
Of The Lower Peninsula

Volume I

When a trip to town was as exciting as landing a man on the moon is today.

Chapter One

FIRST SETTLERS AND HOW TOWNS WERE NAMED

After the treaty with the Indians on January 14, 1837, The Regions of The Saginaw, which also contained the Midland Territory, Midland, Clare, part of Roscommon, Gladwin, Isabella, Bay, Saginaw, Gratiot, and Arenac counties became the Territory of Midland.

The first white people in these counties were for the most part transient hunters and trappers. Prior to 1860 the only permanent villages were established mainly on the shores of the Great Lakes. Many of these counties were set off as early as 1831. Except for Indians, trappers, and traders, there is no record of a settler as such until the 1850s.

Most northern Michigan towns were so isolated during the lumbering days that unknowingly, the founders often named several villages the same. Other towns were given the same names as those the first settlers moved from in lower Michigan to make it seem more like home. When post offices were established the postal authorities used a different name to avoid confusion in mail delivery. When the lumber companies moved in to clear the country of its pinelands, the lumberjacks gave an established town or post office another name of their own choosing. They might refer to it after the name of a popular saloon, such as *Red Keg* instead of *Averill* in Midland County. They often named a town after some geographic prominence, such as *"Maggie's Flats"* or *"Big Rapids,"* instead of *"Leonard,"* the official name chosen for *Big Rapids.*

With the coming of the railroads in the 1870s more confusion regarding names and locations of towns was created. Many times the railroad would locate its tracks within a short distance from an established town, a station would be located at this point with the railroad name of the station appearing on their timetables.

For these reasons a town often became known by three or four names: the name of the station which was its shipping point; the original name chosen by the townspeople; the name assigned by the postal department; and the name used by the lumberjacks or owner of the lumber camp.

Many lumbermen moved their families to the area of the lumber camps. Churches, schools, and stores were built and post offices established. A few

1

years later the mills were moved or destroyed by fire and never rebuilt. Sometimes people moved with the camp and others returned to their former homes. A few might stay on for a time but with the source of employment gone and no workers to support the community, the town eventually became deserted. Only huge piles of sawdust and slabs remained, along with the buildings. Thus another ghost town was created. They are as difficult to number or categorize as the stumps that dot the countryside.

From the 1920s until the 1950s, some of the ghost towns revived to accommodate the growing tourist trade. Gasoline stations, restaurants, and tourist cabins sprouted up along the main traveled roads. Many more such settlements acquired names, most of them designated on highway maps. With the coming of the expressways in the 1960s more towns and settlements were again deserted when the new highways bypassed them.

During the years aspen, poplar, and white birch trees appeared where the fires had burned over the land. Millions of trees were planted in the 1930s by the Civilian Conservation Corps. After the depression this was continued by the Michigan Conservation Department (now the D.N.R.) and private land owners. Now more sawmills have appeared in these northern counties. Most of them manufacture loading pallets for factories. The manufacture of plywood has also become a major industry in many areas. The pulpwood industry has also been developed to supply the constant and increasing demand of paper mills.

———

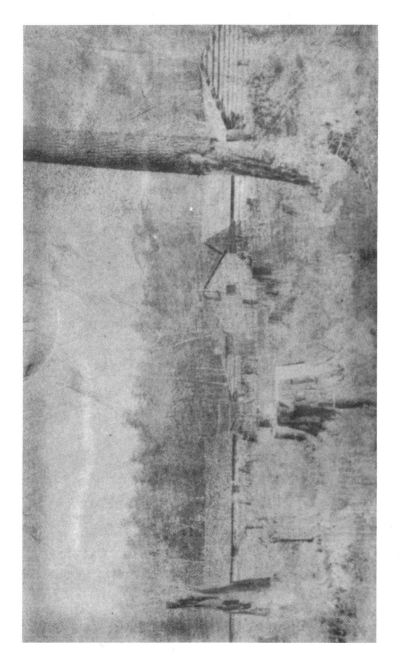

First settlements in the northern counties of Michigan were lumber camps and fishing villages. McEwan's lumber camp on site of Clare where main street is today—taken about 1868-69.

3

Chapter Two

GROWTH AND DECLINE OF POPULATION
HOW TO IDENTIFY GHOST TOWN SITES

There were three ways to travel from *Detroit* to *Chicago* in 1821. One by horseback along the Sauk Indian trail, now US 12; across the Lower Peninsula; and by sailing vessels through Lake Huron and Lake Michigan, and up the Maumee River, then by portage to the Wabash, across Illinois to *St. Louis*, then up the Mississippi and the Illinois Rivers along the Des Plaines River and to the head of Lake Michigan. *Fort Wayne* then consisted of 18 log buildings and the fort, with a population of 100. Three thousand Indians lived on the banks of the Chicago River near Fort Dearborn.

In 1843 the "Comet," pride of the Michigan Central Railroad was operating between Hillsdale and Monroe, a 5-hour run. In the same decade (1840-50) most of the log buildings were replaced with frame or brick structures.

The peak rural population of the Maumee basin in Michigan was reached about 1880. At that time, *Camden* (formerly called *"Henpeck"*) had a population of 200. *Montgomery* (formerly called *"Frog-Eye"*) had a population of 300, about 75 less than today (1969).

The population of the entire State in 1840 was 212,267 or the same as present-day city of *Grand Rapids*. Indians were not counted in the population. In that year there were approximately 500 sawmills in the State, most or all of them in the southern half of the lower peninsula. In 1900, six decades later, the population of Michigan was 2,420,982.

In 1875 there were 1,140 towns, cities, villages, sawmill settlements, flag stations, and corners where one or more people lived in the entire State.

The 1910 Rand McNally map and shippers guide of Michigan names and lists 3,823 cities, villages, settlements, corners, crossings, and railroad junctions; 190 railroad lines operating under 31 major companies in the entire State; and 18 electric railroad companies (inter-urbans) serving metropolitan areas in both the Lower and Upper Peninsulas.

The official Michigan highway map for 1940 listed 1,295 villages, hamlets and corners, or less than ½ as many listings as in 1910.

In the 30-year period, from 1875 to 1910, the number of cities, villages, and designated communities increased from 1,140 to 3,823. During the next 30 years, from 1910 to 1940, the number dropped to 1,295. Somewhere along the line 2,528 towns disappeared.

Between 1940 and 1969, not quite 30 years, there was a gain of 317 towns, making a total of 1,457 designated places on the 1969 official Michigan highway map. Most of this increase was in the suburbs of metropolitan, down-state areas around *Detroit, Grand Rapids, Flint*, and large cities. During this time settlements and villages in the northern counties above Highway M-20 continued to vanish.

————

First settlements in the northern counties of Michigan were lumber camps and fishing villages. Material for the necessary camp buildings, bunk houses, cook shanties, horse barns, storage buildings and "van," or camp store, were hewn from the forest by crews with cross-cut saws and axes. The buildings were made of logs, usually unhewn, and a miniature village, housing from 40 to 200 men, arose in the forest.

These buildings, although temporary and built to serve for the one or two winters it would take to clear the surrounding timber, often remained standing for years. Some of the camp buildings, erected about the time of the Civil War, were taken over by settlers or "squatters" in the late 1880s and 1890s and used for homes. Other camps eventually became villages. Each was given a name, and as they became more extensive and one company established many camps, they were numbered. Such as Wilson Camp No. 1, Mitchell Camp No. 3, etc.

A camp in Arenac County on the Rifle River became known statewide. It was called *"Rifle River Camp"* and was the jumping-off place for lumberjacks going north from Bay City and Saginaw enroute to other camps in the north. This camp was erected before the Civil War. It eventually became the village of Omer, located on US-23, a few miles north of Standish.

The present village of *Edenville* near the Gladwin-Midland county line on the Tittabawassee River was known as "Camp 16" for many years.

Most camps were eventually abandoned and many of the buildings remained as late as the 1940s. Thousands of these old sites remain in northern Michigan and would yield many artifacts and valuable tools if located.

5

Many logging tools and farm tools that were not considered of any value a few years ago are now classed by antique dealers as "primitives." This includes cross-cut saws, wagon parts, hand tools, and a multitude of utensils, etc. used on farms and in lumber camps and sawmills. One item of particular value is a log-marking hammer. These were made, many of them by hand, in the form of a sledge or hammer with a number, letter, or design embossed on one or both ends of the hammer head to identify the owner of logs. A few years ago they were considered to be worth up to $5. Today they are a rare collector's item and can't be purchased from a dealer for less than $45 and bring from $60 each and up at antique and farm auctions.

Old depot sites are also a good source for artifacts. Cecil Hubel of *Lake George* found several cross-cut saws in nearly new condition on the site of the old *Lake George* depot near the Scott Gerrish railroad. This was the first logging railroad in the world and operated from about 1876 to the late 1800s. One of the saws was dated to the 1870s from the type of set screws used for attaching the handles.

Most villages grew around the site of a sawmill. When the first settlers arrived, the sawmill was already operating and most of the timber had been cleared in the immediate area. For this reason there was no need of building log cabins, with huge piles of lumber on hand selling for from $3 to $7 per thousand board feet. Window sash costs about 50 cents each, and a 20 x 24 foot, 1½-story house could be built for less than $100. This was about two months wages in the mills or lumber camps in the 1870s.

Most mill towns, such as *AuSable, Michelson, Jennings*, and *McKinley*, consisted of company-built houses lining the main street. These were usually 16 by 20 foot cottages, erected on posts rather than foundations. Each was exactly the same size and painted the same color. Only married couples were allowed to rent them.

Other private homes sprang up around the company houses, called boardinghouses. Most of the workers were single so there was a demand for this type of housing.

Usually a cluster of shacks would be built near the mills and invariably called "slab town." With the coming of the railroads, beginning in the 1870s in northern Michigan, another section was added to villages fortunate enough to be served by the railroad. This was a district of shacks and shanties on "the other side of the tracks," housing the section and train crews. Due to a shortage of labor railroad contractors brought their own workers. Most of them were newly-arrived immigrants who could speak only their native tongue. Germans, Czechs, Irish, Italians, and natives from all parts of Europe disembarked at Port Huron, Port Austin, or Bay City and were taken to some newly-established village along the line. After the railroads were completed the majority of these immigrants took up land and remained in the area.

Even though most of these settlements, many of them reaching a population of 1,000 or more, disappeared 50 or 75 years ago, the site can still be identified. Very few had concrete or stone foundations but noticeable hollows remain where the houses once stood. Former sidings and railroad spurs still show signs of coal and cinders from the trains. Usually what appears to be black sand in northern Michigan along old trails and grades indicates a coal yard or bin near the site of a town, station, or siding.

Every logging camp and most villages required a water trough for oxen and horses. These were usually made of concrete and even though the buildings were destroyed by fire or the elements the water troughs remain.

No sawmill could operate without water. Water-powered sawmills were of necessity located on a stream. Steam-powered mills needed a large supply of water for the boilers and also to wash logs before entering the sawmill. Bark on trees hauled for long distances through dirt and sand contained stones and dirt that caused damage to saw blades and could hold up production if not removed before sawing. For this reason the mill had to be located by a stream or pond so the logs could be washed. Many mills built huge tanks of concrete and hauled water to fill them. These were reinforced with steel and usually had steel bolts imbedded in the concrete. Even though grown over with brush and covered with soil they could be located with a metal detector, and where there was a mill there was a camp or settlement.

———

7

Scene at a "flea market" near Lake City, Michigan, today a common sight all over the U.S. Many farm tools, logging tools, and household utensils that only a few years ago were thrown away are now valuable and sought-after items at antique shops, secondhand stores, and flea markets. Note glass insulators, old "sad irons," bottles, kerosene lamp parts, etc. on display table.   Photo by Roy L. Dodge

Chapter Three

THE GHOST COUNTY OF "MANITOU"
RESTORATION OF GHOST TOWNS

Before attempting to list the hundreds of ghost towns I must make mention of a "ghost county." This county was organized by an Act of the Legislature on February 12, 1855 and named Manitou, probably by Henry Rowe Schoolcraft after the Manitou Islands, which formed part of the county. Its county seat was the town of St. James on Beaver Island. The island, and the county for that matter, was a part of the kingdom of King James Jesse Strang. Through his efforts while serving on the Legislature from 1853 to 1855 the county was set off.

Much has been written about the Mormon King and would make a book in itself. I will limit this chapter to the history of the county.

After the untimely death of King Strang, Peter McKinley of St. James was elected representative and served from 1857 to 1859.

While the rest of the State was suffering from growing pains due to the great demand for its "inexhaustible" supply of white pine, the expansion of the railroads, and the ventures of land speculators luring new immigrants to settle on the stump lands of northern Michigan, Manitou continued its lawless existence all but unnoticed for a period of 40 years. During this period few records were kept so most of the happenings are merely conjecture.

During the logging days law in the camps was regulated by the camp boss, who answered only to the timber owners. Most of the land outside the lumber camps was owned by the railroad companies, over which they were the law. This left very little of the territory of northern Michigan under the jurisdiction of elected sheriffs and local law enforcement officers.

Apparently all the United States Marshalls were busy farther west in the newly-opened territories. Saloon keepers, camp bosses, and railroad agents were about the only law existing outside of police in large cities. Even there the police gave the lumberjacks a wide berth, staying clear of their usual haunts.

One thing can be said in favor of Manitou County. The populace was not two-faced about it. They went their lawless way for nearly a half century seldom making an effort to elect county officers. Conditions that existed during the lumbering days were expressed quite clearly by Governor John J. Bagley in his retiring message in January of 1877: *"Many of the counties and municipalities of the State have suffered heavy losses by the defalcation of their treasuries. There is something wrong in a system that allows these officers first to perpertrate, and then to conceal for a long time, such frauds as some of these have been guilty of."*

He then went on to propose new laws to deal with such cases and stated: *"They (the voters) had to wait until the end of their term of office to do anything, then merely not to re-elect them! ... If the words 'defaulter' and 'defalcation' could be stricken from our vocabulary, and the old-fashioned plain English, 'thief' and 'stolen,' substituted, it would tend to make these crimes less common.*

I submit herewith certain petitions and correspondence relative to the affairs in the county of Manitou. They show that the laws of the State and the United States are violated with impunity, and that there is no safety or protection to persons or property in portions of this county. No courts have been held for years. The county offices are vacant a large portion of the time, there is no jail, debts cannot be collected by process of law, nor are any of the forms of law complied with - I recommend that the county organization be discontinued and the territory be attached to the county of Charlevoix."

His warning fell on deaf ears. Nearly 20 years later on April 4, 1895, the following act was passed by the Legislature. *"To repeal Special Act No. 92 approved February 12, 1855, titled 'An act to organize the county of Manitou' and attach the territory comprising said county to the counties of Charlevoix and Leelanau, and to apportion the property and debts of said county of Manitou."*

By the time the county was disbanded the lumbering boom had ended and the population had dwindled to 917. The buzzards had picked the corpse clean and left for greener pastures. The territory was divided between Charlevoix and Leelanau as stated in the Act. Seven hundred forty of the population went to Charlevoix, and 177 went with the territory ceded to Leelanau.

Nothing remains to show that the County of Manitou ever existed. A historical plaque is erected to the memory of King James at the city park in Charlevoix and tells some of the history. It reads as follows: *"About 20 miles northwest of here is Beaver Island. In 1847 James Strang set up a colony for his followers, dissenters from the main body of Mormonism. Strang crowned himself 'King James' in 1850. Hatred of the sect by non-Mormons led to the Battle of Pine River in 1853 at present day Charlevoix. On June 16, 1856, because they hated his authoritarian rule, some of Strang's subjects mortally wounded him. Later in the summer, mainlanders drove the Mormons from Beaver Island."*

Another county, Wyandotte, was originally set off in the survey of 1840-43 but was never organized as a county government. It later was incorporated within the boundaries of Cheboygan County.

During the past few years there has been a trend all over the U.S. to rebuild ghost towns, mainly as tourist attractions. Ten years ago an Ohio resident, Edward Galitza, bought a deserted village near *Findlay, Ohio* and restored the 20 buildings as they were in the 1880s during an oil boom.

The buildings included a cobbler shop, barber shop, fire house, and a newspaper office and printing plant. Galitza named it "Ghost Town" and in 1969 it was designated on the Ohio State map.

From 1898 until the winter of 1912, *Kendall, Montana* was a village of 1,400 residents, with an opera house, a hospital, two schools, a church and eight saloons. $35 million in gold had been shoveled out of the hills from three gold mines. The miners left and within a few years only one man was left, Glenn C. Morton. He is now 81 years old. For 40 years he kept buying up its lots and parcels of real estate until he now owns the town. Last year (1969) he gave the town to the Boy Scouts' North Central Montana Council. The town is being restored for a tourist attraction.

Former residents of thousands of ghost towns all over the country hold reunions at the former site of their village. Each year in August about 100 people, who were residents of *Michelson* in Roscommon County, Michigan, meet at the Reedsburg Dam campgrounds for two or three days to reminisce and talk over old times when *Michelson* was a booming mill town.

Many ghost towns are not old. The village of *Scanlon, Florida*, formerly located 35 miles southeast of *Tallahassee*, was founded in 1923 near the Gulf of Mexico but died in 1938. Each year former residents meet at the site and recall how they worked in *Scanlon's* sawmills for 15 and 20 cents an hour.

11

Chapter Four

LAKE COUNTY GHOST TOWNS AND THE ONLY NEGRO GHOST TOWN IN THE HISTORY OF MICHIGAN

A historical plaque near the courthouse entrance in *Baldwin*, the county seat, gives most of the recorded history of Lake County. It reads: *"This county was originally set off in 1840 and first named "Aishum" after a well known Potawatomi Indian Chief. In 1843 the name was changed to "Lake" (for no particular reason). For three decades it was attached to neighboring counties until 1871 when settlement was sufficient to warrant organization. Baldwin, the county seat, was settled in 1872. The county's forests helped make Michigan a leading lumbering state. Farming and the tourist industry are the chief activities. Wild life is abundant."*

The first recorded population of Lake County in 1870, was 548. The county reached its peak of population in 1884 with 7,539 inhabitants. In 1960 Lake County ranked fourth of the lowest populated counties in Michigan, with a population of 5,338, a little less than in 1890, averaging 9.3 persons per square mile. A large percentage of the population is Negro.

Baldwin was described in 1875 as: *"A village of some 200 inhabitants and is the new seat of justice for Lake County. (Chase was the first county seat). It is on the line of the Flint & Pere Marquette Railroad about 7 miles southwest of the center of the county and 30 east of Ludington. Excellent water power is derived from the Pere Marquette River, at present not utilized. The place has a steam sawmill and other business interests."* These included a drug store, general store, meat market, boot and shoe store, two hotels, hardware, two saloons, a blacksmith shop, and railroad station.

RAILROADS

Railroads serving the county were:

1890–the Flint & Pere Marquette. Beginning at *Monroe* and entering Lake County at *Chase*, going west: *Monroe*, 0 miles; *Chase*, 211.6 miles; *Nirvana*, 215.6 miles; *Forman*, 220.1 miles; *Baldwin*, 222.6 miles; *Wingleton*, 225.2 miles.

1900–Pere Marquette Railroad entering Lake County at *Olivers*, going west: *Saginaw*, 0 miles; *Olivers*, 93 miles; *Chase*, 96 miles; *Nirvana*, 100 miles; *Ungers*, 102 miles; *Baldwin*, 107 miles; and *Wingleton*, 111 miles.

Wayland, in Allegan County, was called *"Brady"* until 1869.

Whitehall, in Muskegon County, was named *"Mears,"* after the name of its founder until 1869.

Yale, St. Clair County was *"Brockway Center"* until 1889.

Lowell, in Kent County, was originally *"Dansville."* The name was changed February 4, 1857.

Clio, in Genessee County was *"Varna"* until March 20, 1867.

Caro, in Tuscola County, was *"Centerville."* Changed February 13, 1869.

Almont, in Lapeer County, was *"Newbury"* until March 13, 1846.

"West Bay City" was formerly *"Wenona," "Banks,"* and *"Salzburgh"* until 1879. Today it is a part of *Bay City*.

"East Saginaw" was consolidated with *Saginaw* city in 1889.

Many towns that people believed actually existed in the 1800s were merely "paper towns" created by land speculators who owned huge tracts of land. These cities were highly advertised all over the nation to draw settlers to the area. Thousands of city lots were sold to people, most of who never visited the State. Many of these ficticious cities claimed to have a bank and issued their own money or "script." This was during the era of "wildcat banks," when banks were allowed to print money as long as it was backed by gold or silver. Many of them, on investigation, turned out to be a hollow stump in some deserted area miles from civilization.

Prior to the Civil War the only post offices or mail service in northern Michigan were along the lakeshore. By 1872 there were 1,111 post offices in the 73 counties of Michigan. Only 233 were located in the northern part of the Lower Peninsula. Southern Michigan and the thumb area had a total of 878 post offices. Many of these were located in trappers' cabins near a trading post, in a country store, or in a farmer's house. In 1965 more than 3,000 post offices had been discontinued. In 1969 there were 773 post offices listed in the State. Many of these are located at airbases, veteran's hospitals, and other military installations. This number also includes all postal sub-stations in large cities.

Chapter Four

SPECTACULAR GHOST TOWNS OF EARLY 1800s

One of the ghost towns of note in areas other than the counties covered in this book was *Superior*, located on Macataw Lake in Ottawa County. It was referred to as *"Point Superior"* for many years after it disappeared. The village was plotted and recorded at *Kalamazoo* on July 2, 1836. There were 122 waterfront lots and 465 back lots laid out by the company which consisted of Cyron Burdick, Elisha Belcher, Caleb Sherman, and Captain Edward Macy, who was manager of the enterprise.

The company soon set up a sawmill, blacksmith shop, and even a shipyard to build and repair ships. In October, 1839, a post office was established under the name *"Tusearara."*

The first white child born in Holland Township was born in the village.

In 1838, two years after the founding of the city, Captain Macy was killed in a horse-drawn streetcar accident at *Kalamazoo*. Soon after his death the expansion of the village was halted and ceased to exist. The people moved away one family at a time. Nothing remains on the site today to show that a town ever existed.

————

PORT SHELDON was located on Pigeon Lake, 10 miles south of *Grand Haven* and 5 miles southeast of *West Olive* in Ottawa County. This was one of the first, and probably most spectacular, ghost towns in the history of Michigan, rivaled only by some of the fabulous paper cities.

Founded by Alex H. Joudon of Pennsylvania and several wealthy men who formed the Port Sheldon Land Company with the purpose of founding a town in the area where Reverend William H. Ferry formed the present town of *Grand Haven*.

Ferry refused to sell out so they purchased 600 acres of timberland at Pigeon Lake on the shores of Lake Michigan. In the fall of 1836, Joudon, along with a party of 40 surveyors, engineers, etc., arrived on the site of their land purchase. Among other things necessary for the construction of a new town they brought with them what were probably the first "pre-fab" houses in the history of Michigan. The houses were built in sections ready for erection.

They laid out 142 blocks with 24 lots in each block. Their plans called for churches, a fish market, railroad station, and schoolhouses. They cleared the timber for streets and laid board sidewalks along what was to be the business section.

One building completed was a $40,000 hotel (comparable to $100,000 or more today), called the "Ottawa House." The hotel was fronted by eight Gothic pillars and ornately furnished at a cost of $30,000. An office building cost $10,000. They also erected a steam sawmill, general store, and lighthouse at the harbor entrance at a cost of $20,000. A pier for shipping and receiving goods via the Great Lakes was built. The lighthouse was maintained for two years. A beautiful yacht, named the *Me-mee*, was purchased and anchored at the pier.

In 1838 a railroad charter was obtained and 2 miles of railroad bed was built. It was to connect with Port Huron and extend across the State to that point.

The expectations of the company were never realized. The speculators went broke during the bank failures and panic of 1837 caused by the wildcat banks, and the city was abandoned.

———

A historical marker near *Saugatuck* in Allegan County tells the story of *SINGAPORE*. "*Beneath the sands near the mouth of the Kalamazoo River lies the site of Singapore, one of Michigan's most famous ghost towns.*" Founded in the 1830s by New York land speculators, who hoped it would rival *Chicago* or *Milwaukee* as a lake port, *Singapore* was in fact, until the 1870s, a busy lumbering town. With three mills, two hotels, several general stores, and a renowned "Wildcat Bank," it outshone its neighbor to the south, *"The Flats,"* as *Saugatuck* was then called. When the supply of timber was exhausted the mills closed, the once bustling waterfront grew quiet. The people left, most of them settling in *Saugatuck*. Gradually, Lake Michigan's shifting sands buried *Singapore*.

———

GRINDSTONE CITY in Huron County, located on M-25 at the tip of the thumb, was established about 1872. In 1884 the population was 560 and remained about the same until demand ceased to exist for the stone after which it was named.

15

At one time it became world famous for grinding wheels and whetstones. In 1905 it was on the Pere Marquette Railroad, Port Austin Township, 5 miles east of *Port Austin*. There was a Methodist church and a daily stage to *Huron*. In addition to a gristmill and cooper shop (barrel factory), it was served by two hardwares, two grocery stores, a meat market and other business places. John Wallace Jr., postmaster.

The village is now a summer resort and fishing and boating center.

On August 16, 1969, a few miles west of *Grindstone City*, the Port Austin Marine Museum was dedicated in memory of men of the U.S. Life Saving Service and its successor, the U.S. Coast Guard. The plaque was presented by Edward Korn, president of the Port Austin Village Council, to Lt. Commander Piner on the 90th anniversary of the sinking of the screw steamer *Jacob Bertschy* off *Grindstone City* in 1879, and was fashioned from timber of the *Bertschy*. Surfmen of the station saved all hands in the shipwreck.

———

MELBOURNE, once a mill town located a short distance north of where the present Consumers Power Zilwaukee steam plant near *Saginaw* now stands, was destroyed by fire August 3, 1877. Thousands of persons were left homeless in the blaze, the mills were razed, and the town was never rebuilt.

Melbourne was created by Wellington R. Burt, the richest man in *Saginaw* history, who made his fortune from timber. Here was located the largest and most complete lumber manufacturing establishments in the world, as well as the largest salt block.

It had a shingle mill, stave and heading mill, barrel factory, carpenter shops, blacksmith shops and the salt works. The plant occupied 10 acres of land, with docks for lumber barges and tugs, and fine boom facilities for the sorting and handling of logs.

It also included about 50 company houses for married workers and their families. There were two large rooming houses for single men, a schoolhouse, and a public library. Two hundred fifty men were employed in the mills.

The fire was believed to have been set by arsonists as the watchman said he discovered fire in three different places. The fire loss was estimated at $200,000, of which $90,000 was insured.

Chapter Five

ALCONA COUNTY GHOST TOWNS
AND THE "LOST GOLD MINE OF MICHIGAN"

RAILROADS

In 1890 the county was served by the Detroit-Bay City & Alpena Railroad, extending from the *AuSable-Oscoda* station on Lake Huron to *Alpena*. The stations were: *AuSable-Oscoda*, 0 miles; *Handy*, 11 miles; *Black River*, 7 miles; *Ossineke*, 10 miles; ending at *Alpena*, 55 miles.

POST OFFICES

During its 100 year history the county has had a total of at least 17 post offices. Eight remain today.

GHOST TOWNS

ALCONA–was a one-time lumbering village near US-23 on the shore of Lake Huron, Haynes Township, 8 miles north of *Harrisville*, the county seat.

Although it is designated on the 1969 Michigan highway map, very little remains to reveal it was once a thriving village, lasting from about 1875 to the turn-of-the-century. William Culling was the first white man to visit the site about 1836, and called it the *"Cove."*

In 1877 the population was 125, and as most logging towns, it consisted of two general stores, two hotels, a saloon, large lumbermen's supply building, harness and blacksmith shop, and boat docks. F. E. Beard was postmaster. By 1890 the population had increased to 250.

With the introduction of rural free delivery, shortly after the turn-of-the-century, the post office was discontinued and the village became deserted. In 1918 only one store, operated by F. C. Cook, was doing business.

———

ALVIN–in 1918 described as in Mikado Township, 18 miles southwest of *Harrisville* and 5½ from *Mikado*, the nearest banking and shipping point. RFD *Mikado*.

17

CURRAN–in 1918 population 150. Located on the D. & M. Railroad, Mitchell Township, 14 miles north of *Glennie*. Daily mail. E. J. Burleigh, general store. *Curran* is shown on the 1969 Michigan highway map at the intersection of M-65 and M-72. No population given.

––––––––

CURTISVILLE–in 1905 a country post office in Curtis Township, 8 miles north of *South Branch*. In 1918 population 125. *South Branch* was its shipping point. Mrs. Eva Heilig, postmistress.

The first school was built in 1898. Laura Hanson was the second teacher at the *Sinclair* school in 1908. Selig Solomon operated the now vacant store on the corner of M-65 and West Bamfield Road.

Harper Hayes had the "Red Store" where a Shell gas station stands (1969). Another early merchant was Uncle Johnny Redman who was also postmaster at one time.

One of the many lumber camps in the area was located on the Albert Saymn farm. (*Bay City Times*, May 26, 1968, written by Mrs. Stanley Regier.)

––––––––

GUSTIN–had a population of 25 in 1905. A station on the Detroit & Mackinac Railroad, Gustin Township, 8 miles southwest of *Harrisville* and 3 from *Mikado*. Daily stage to *Killmaster*. Tina Smith, postmistress. L. D. Atkins, railroad and express agent. 1910 population 28. Had a general store. In 1910, mail RFD *Mikado*.

––––––––

KILLMASTER–1905 population 150. Shown on 1969 highway maps. On the east branch of the Pine River, Gustin Township, 2½ miles from *Gustin* on the D. & M. Railroad, its station. F. A. Becker, postmaster and general store. Daily mail. Hotel and livery. 1918 population 75. RFD *Harrisville*.

––––––––

MUD LAKE–1910 population 40, Hawes Township, 18 miles west of *Harrisville* and 12 west of *Lincoln*, nearest shipping point. RFD *Barton City*.

––––––––

SPRUCE–shown on 1969 highway maps, was a post office in 1905 located in

Caledonia Township, 8 miles from *Ossineke*. D. A. Hecox, postmaster. Two general stores and a sawmill.

1918 population 100. E. J. Gillard, postmaster. In addition to the general stores, had a creamery, wagonmaker, blacksmith shop, and other business places.

———

VAUGHN–is not listed as a post office and was not the name of a village. Was the railroad name for *Glennie* in Curtis Township, 23 miles from *Oscoda*. In 1905 J. H. Haynes, postmaster. Also a sawmill. In 1912 *Glennie* had a population of 125. C. H. Anderson, postmaster. Hotel, livery, bank, drugstore, elevator, general store, etc.

———

Other stations and flag stops on the AuSable & N. W. Railroad were:

CODE–1910, mail *Curran*.

GROULEAU–in 1918, a discontinued post office 7½ miles northwest of *Harrisville*, the mailing point.

HANDY–the railroad name for *"Roy,"* on the D. & M. Railroad, 12 miles south of *Harrisville*. In the approximate location of *Mikado*.

HAWES–in 1918 a discontinued post office in Hawes Township, 4½ half miles from *Lincoln*, RFD *Kurtz*. In 1910 RFD *Glennie*.

KURTZ–in 1918 population 50. On the A. S. & N. W. Railroad, Mikado Township. Samuel F. Hetzler, general store.

LODGE–in 1910 a discontinued post office, RFD *Harrisville*.

FLAT ROCK LODGE–in 1910, mail to *McKinley*.

ROY–1905, mail to *Mikado*.

———

Although there are records of at least two gold mines in the Upper Peninsula, Alcona County had the only gold mine in the Lower Peninsula of Michigan.

THE GHOST GOLD MINE OF MICHIGAN

This mine was located in Haynes Township, Alcona County. Gold was discovered on the Fleming Farm near *Harrisville* in November, 1912. The next year a mine shaft was sunk to a depth of about 100 feet. About a year later an explosion occurred in the mine, killing four Domke brothers, and the shaft filled with water. The site of the mine hasn't been located to this date.

According to Frank Jozwiak of *Harrison*, who has the deed to the former Fleming farm on which the mine was located, and directions to the location given to him by his father, John Jozwiak, the discovery of gold in Haynes Township was kept secret for several months until a stock company was formed to establish a mining company.

Old newspaper accounts tell that Indians, years ago, sold large quantities of silver and copper in *Bay City* and *Saginaw*. They claimed to have found it in the immediate vicinity of *Harrisville* but never revealed the exact source of the minerals.

When gold nuggets were discovered in the same area in 1912, a mine shaft was sunk and tons of Alcona black dirt processed for gold. The venture ended in disaster when the steam-operated equipment blew up.

The elder Jozwiak, who lived to be 89 years old and died at his home in *Bay City* in 1956, said an old man lived in a shack near the creek and while everyone was involved in the excitement of the gold discovery and busy sinking a mine shaft, the old man started shoveling dirt along the creek banks and hauling it to his house. He worked during the summer hauling dirt to his property in a wheelbarrow then worked all winter panning for gold.

Jozwiak said the old man made his living from the gold for years, and it was rumored that he made a fortune in gold long after the gold mine was abandoned. Deeds to the property describe it as in the northwest quarter of Section 8, Haynes Township. Frank made a trip to *Harrisville* in the summer of 1969 in an attempt to find the abandoned mine shaft but was unsuccessful.

Chapter Six

ALPENA COUNTY GHOST TOWNS
AND THE LOST SHIP *PEWABIC*

This county was first named "Anamickee" after a Chippewa chief, meaning "thunder." Henry R. Schoolcraft later changed the name to Alpena, meaning "partridge country." Laid out as a county in the survey of 1840, the county government wasn't organized until 1857. The land area was taken from Cheboygan County.

Alpena, the county seat, in 1877 had a population of 5,000. The 1960 census recorded 28,566 residents. It was first called *"Fremont."*

In 1958 a historical marker was dedicated and placed near the *Alpena* city limits that reads: *"World's largest cement plant. Portland cement - so called because it resembles in color stone from the Isle of Portland in the British Isles, was first produced in the United States in 1871, in Michigan in 1896. Because of Alpena's location in the midst of immense limestone deposits, the Huron Portland Cement Co., founded in Detroit in 1907, chose this site for its plant. Cement production began here in 1908. Able management and skilled workmen made this the world's largest cement plant. From Thunder Bay ships of the Huron fleet deliver cement to all parts of the Great Lakes region."*

POST OFFICES

Of at least 15 post offices that existed in the county, only 5 remain today. The locations of 10 towns or villages are designated on 1969 Michigan highway maps. Several of these are merely four-corners, with little or no population.

RAILROADS

In 1890 the county was served by the Detroit-Bay City & Alpena Railroad extending from *Alger* in Arenac County, east to *AuSable* and north to *Black River, Ossineke*, 10 miles; *Alpena*, 12 miles.

GHOST TOWNS

THUNDER BAY ISLANDS–off the north point of Thunder Bay in Lake Huron

22

lies a tiny group of islands that are tied in with the history of Alpena County, and *Alpena* in particular. Jack E. LaForest of *Bay City*, formerly with the U.S. Coast Guard, wrote a history of these islands in 1969. *Sugar Island* is the largest, covering 100 acres.

J. W. Paxton established a gill net fishery on *Thunder Bay Island* in 1840. He placed his nets on North Point Reef and the Thunder Bay Shoals, the resting place of the German freighter, *Nordmeer*, which ran aground November 19, 1966.

The first lighthouse was erected on *Thunder Bay Island* in the summer of 1841. It was built of wood and in 1857 was replaced with a more substantial structure, still standing today.

In 1858, Paxton moved his fishing headquarters to *Sugar Island*. The islands reached their peak population at this time with 150 residents and a fleet of 31 fishing boats.

On August 9, 1865, the year-old steamer *Pewabic*, listed as one of the ten Great Lakes disasters, sank in 180 feet of water and claimed 125 lives. Thirty-four years later John D. Persons aided in locating the wreck of the *Pewabic* for a salvage crew. He descended to the floor of Lake Huron in a diving bell with his wife and daughter to view the ship. The *Pewabic* was located for the last time in 1917.

Thunder Bay Island is the only one of three islands inhabited today and contains only the U.S. Coast Guard facilities, a lighthouse, radio beacon, life boat, and other equipment.

BOLTON–located in Maple Ridge Township was a post office as early as 1890. In 1905 population 250, on the D. & M. Railroad, 11 miles northwest of *Alpena*. Daily mail. N. J. Dowling, postmaster. The village contained a general store, saw and shingle mill, saloon, and school.

In 1910 population 150. In 1918, 30. Mrs. S. M. Fox, postmistress. Contained a grocery, dry goods, and general store.

Shown on 1968 Michigan highway maps. No population given.

CATHRO–in 1905 population 125. On the D. & M. Railroad, Maple Ridge Township, 9 miles northwest of *Alpena*. Elspeth Cathro, postmistress.

At one time had a church, blacksmith shop, general store, and shingle mill. In 1918 population 65. John Mellville, postmaster.

The post office was established in 1894 and named after Elijah Cathro, the first postmaster.

––––––––

DAFOE–named after Lemuel G. Dafoe, early settler and later became State Representative. Was a post office in 1900. In 1905 a country post office in Wilson Township, 12 miles west of *Alpena*. H. Wise, postmaster.

In 1918, A. M. Shell, postmaster. Contained a shingle mill, two blacksmith shops, sawmill, general store, and grocery.

––––––––

EAST SIDE–was a post office in Alpena Township, 9 miles north of *Alpena* in 1877. Lumber camps and mills were located in the area. Mrs. Ellen Roberts, postmistress.

––––––––

FLANDERS–was a post office in 1890. Located in Green Township, 16 miles west of Alpena. Population about 200 in 1905. In 1893 W. H. Pushor, postmaster. Also had a grocery and sawmill.

In 1905 S. W. Flanders, postmaster. Contained two sawmills, two blacksmith shops, and a general store.

1918 population 100. *Lachine* was the nearest shipping point. RFD *Hillman*.

––––––––

HOBSON–was a post office in Wilson Township, 12 miles west of *Alpena*. Named for Richard Pearson Hobson of Spanish American War fame who sank the *Merrimac* at Santiago Harbor in 1896. In 1910 population 25. Mail to *Dafoe*.

––––––––

LEER–was named by early settlers after their home town of that name in Norway. In 1905 a country post office in Long Rapids Township, 22 miles northwest of *Alpena* and 6 from *Posen*. Carl Alfson, postmaster. Martha Alfson, schoolteacher. Had an orchestra, flour and sawmill, blacksmith shop, etc.

1918 population 25. George Christopherson, postmaster. *Leer* is shown on the 1969 Michigan highway map. No population.

————

LONG RAPIDS–is one of the first settlements in the county. Was first called *"Merrillsville."* In 1877 listed as a post office on Thunder Bay River, 18 miles west of *Alpena*. Settled about 1870.

1905 population 100. Daily mail stage to *Bolton*. D. R. Martindale, postmaster. Contained a boot and shoe store, saw and shingle mills, hotel, general store, etc.

————

ORCHARD HILL–was a post office 13 miles northwest of *Alpena* on the Thunder Bay River and 9 miles south of *Bolton*. Was a post office in 1890 and until about 1910. 1912, RFD *Cathro*.

In 1953 an Orchard Hill school was standing and a bridge over the river.

————

SPRATT–in 1905 a country post office in Green Township, 24 miles southwest of *Alpena*. Melville B. Spratt, postmaster. 1910 census listed the population as 18.

In 1918 seven miles from *Lachine*. Martha G. Marshall, postmaster. A sawmill, grocery store, and other buildings were located there.

Shown on 1969 Michigan highway maps, located on M-65 near *Fletcher's Pond*. No population given.

————

WALBURG–listed in 1918 as a discontinued post office, RFD *Dafoe*. Contained a flour mill, wagon shop, general store, blacksmith shop, and other buildings.

SALINA, EMERSON, PAXTON, and *KERSTON*–were flag stations on the D. & M. Railroad between *Alpena* and *Hillman.* In 1910 each of these stations (except *Salina*) received mail from *Dafoe.*

––––––––

   Fletcher's Pond, or flood waters, was flooded before the railroad tracks were removed in this area. Alvin (Ben) Bartow, now of *Harrison,* Michigan, who was raised near *Hillman* in Montmorency County, said he heard a train whistle one morning about 1932 and rushed to see where the sound came from. The tracks had been abandoned years before, he said, and when they went outside to see where the engine was a crew had moved in with equipment to remove the tracks. *"There was a train engine in water four feet deep tearing up the tracks,"* he said.

Chapter Seven

ANTRIM COUNTY GHOST TOWNS

After the survey of 1840 Henry R. Schoolcraft named this county "Meegesee," after a Chippewa Indian chief. When the county government was organized in 1863, the name was changed to "Antrim," after the county of that name in Ireland. The county borders Grand Traverse Bay, and Torch Lake, within its borders, is known as the sixth most beautiful lake in the world.

First the home of the Indian, then a part of the great fur trading district in the Northwest Territory during the 17th century, Antrim County became a center of the logging industry during the lumbering era, beginning with the end of the Civil War and lasting through the first part of the 20th century.

In 1877 *Elk Rapids* was the county seat, vying with *Bellaire* for the honor. *Bellaire* later became the seat of government.

Peak population was reached during the lumbering era. In 1894 it was 12,427. Today (1970) it has again reached about 11,000 after a sharp decline after the timber was removed.

POST OFFICES

During the history of the county there have been at least 24 post offices. Of these, eight remain.

RAILROADS

In 1890 the east side of the county was served by the Grand Rapids Indiana Railroad, extending from *Antrim* to *Mancelona*, 4 miles; *Alba*, 6.6 miles; *Simons*, 3.8 miles; and to *Elmira*, 4.9 miles.

GHOST TOWNS

ANTRIM CITY–established in 1863. In 1877 described as located in Banks Township, 22 miles north of *Elk Rapids*, the county seat. James N. Sickles, postmaster. The village also contained a general store, gristmill, and several other buildings.

27

The name was changed to *"Mancelona"* in 1899 and became a village.

————

ATWOOD–in Banks Township, 22 miles north of *Elk Rapids* and 4 miles from *Norwood* on Traverse Bay. 1905 population 75. Samuel K. Bagley, postmaster. Had a flour mill, general store, and other buildings.

In 1910 a discontinued post office, RFD *Central Lake*. Henry E. Klooster, general store.

————

CASCADE–in 1877 eighteen miles south of *Boyne Falls* in Forest Home Township. A flag station on the G. R. & I. Railroad.

Until 1920 there were two other towns by this name. One in Kent County and one on the C. & N. W. Railroad in Marquette County, 10 miles from *Ispeming*.

————

CLAM LAKE–in 1905 a country post office in Helena Township, 7 miles southwest of *Bellaire* and 5 from *Alden*. Andrew F. Anderson, postmaster. The place had a general store, hotel, and other buildings.

In 1918 RFD *Helena*.

————

CRESWELL–in 1877 a post office in Milton Township, 8 miles north of *Elk Rapids*. Archibald Cameron, Sr., postmaster.

In 1905 listed as a discontinued post office, mail to *Torch Lake*.

————

ECHO–was a post office in 1890 on Intermediate Lake, Echo Township, 9 miles north of *Bellaire* and 4 from *Central Lake*. Eber Dingman, postmaster in 1905. Had a store, sawmill, and gristmill.

1910 RFD *East Jordan*.

————

ELGIN–in 1877 in Milton Township, 7 miles north of *Elk Rapids*. Charles Russell, postmaster. Not listed as a post office in 1890.

Another *"Elgin"* was located in Ottawa County, 10 miles west of *Grand Rapids.*

––––––––

FINKTON–was a post office in 1890, Echo Township, 2½ miles from *Chestonia.* In 1905 German Button, postmaster. Had a general store, blacksmith shop, and other buildings. Discontinued about 1906.

In 1918 RFD *East Jordan.*

––––––––

GREEN RIVER–on the D. & C. Railroad, Chestonia Township, 8 miles east of *Bellaire.* Was a post office in 1904. Discontinued about 1906. After that RFD *Mancelona.* Had a general store and other buildings.

––––––––

HELENA–was a post office in 1927. Not listed in 1912 railroad guide.

––––––––

HITCHCOCK–was a post office from 1902 until about 1909. In 1905 a country post office on the P. M. Railroad, 6 miles northeast of *Bellaire.* The East Jordan Lumber Company operated sawmills and a lumberman's supply store and general store there.

After 1909 mail *Bellaire.* Designated on 1968 county maps in Kearney Township. No population given for any year.

––––––––

JORDAN–in 1877 a post office and 50 inhabitants, Jordan Township, 11 miles west of *Boyne Falls.* Settled in 1874. Gilbert E. Green, postmaster.

In 1887 incorporated as a village, located on Pine Lake (now Charlevoix Lake) in South Arm Township. Name changed to *"East Jordan."* Incorporated as a city in 1911 with a population of 2,516.

––––––––

KEARNEY–in 1877 a settlement in Kearney Township, 22 miles east of *Elk Rapids.* George Palmer, postmaster and general store. Sheridan Hill, mail contractor. Also contained a sawmill. No record of this place after 1877.

KEWADIN–shown on 1969 highway maps and has a post office. Was a post office in 1890. In 1910 population 38. In 1918 population 150.

On Elk Lake, Milton Township, 3½ miles from *Elk Rapids*. J. Fred Roof, postmaster. Had two stores, a shingle mill, machine shop, and a restaurant.

LAKE SHORE–in 1877 a village in Kearney Township, 15 miles from *Elk Rapids*, the county seat, and 10 northwest of *Mancelona*. Located on Intermediate Lake. Calvin C. Cutler, postmaster. Had a population of more than 200 but business places were not listed. Was a good-sized village at that time. No record of this village after 1877.

In 1905 a town by this name was located in Erin Township, Macomb County.

ROOTVILLE–located in Helena Township, 10 miles northeast of *Elk Rapids* in 1877. Situated between Clam and Grass Lakes (now Thayer Lake). Henry W. Stewart, postmaster. No record after 1877.

SOUTH MILTON–in 1910 listed as RFD *Rapid City*.

SPENCER CREEK–in 1877 located in Helena Township, 8 miles east of *Elk Rapids*, population 30. Reuben W. Coy, postmaster. Had a general store, gristmill, sawmill, and hotel. Also other buildings. Listed as a post office until 1890. After that name changed to *"Alden."*

There was also a *"Spencer"* in Kalkaska County, shown on some maps in 1969; and a *"Spencer's Mill"* in Kent County near *Trufant*.

SIMONS–was a post office in 1890. A short-lived flag station on the G. R. & I. Railroad, about midway between *Alba* and *Elmira*. In 1910 mail to *Alba*.

WETZELL–in Mancelona Township, was a post office in 1890 and until 1912.

In 1905 population 250. On the G. R. & I. Railroad (now the Pennsylvania) 12 miles from *Bellaire*, and 2½ from *Mancelona*. George F. Beckstein, postmaster.

In 1918 RFD *Mancelona*. Mrs. J. W. Lauterman, general store.

———

MT. BLISS–in 1910 mail *Chestonia*.

———

Chapter Eight

ARENAC COUNTY GHOST TOWN
AND THE D. B. C. & A. RAILROAD

Arenac County was named by Henry R. Schoolcraft during the survey of 1840. The name is of Latin origin meaning "sandy place" due to its sandy soil. Many of the towns and villages settled at an early date have the distinction of having been located in two different counties. It was first set off as a county in 1831. In 1847 it was combined with Bay County and in 1883 made a separate county again.

The only written history of Arenac County was compiled by Calvin Ennes of *Omer*. Ennes, a former superintendent of schools, is over 80 years old. He moved to the county with his parents in 1896. His history has not been published in book form. Parts of it were published in the *Arenac County Independent* as a series in 1966-67, and excerpts were published in *Michigan Heritage Magazine*.

POST OFFICES

At least 17 post offices existed during its history. Seven remain today.

RAILROADS

The Detroit-Bay City & Alpena Railroad and the Mackinaw Division of the Michigan Central served the county in 1890. The D. B. C. & A. Railroad started at *Alger* and extended to *AuSable, Oscoda* and *Alpena*. Stations within the county were: *Alger*, 0 miles; *Moffat*, 4 miles; and *Shearer*, 7 miles. It entered Ogemaw County at *Prescott*, 4 miles distant.

The Michigan Central, extending from *Bay City* to *Mackinaw City*, entered the county from the south at *Worth*; *Standish*, 4 miles; *Deep River*, 6 miles; *Sterling*, 2 miles; *Alger*, 40 miles; and *Summit*, 44 miles.

GHOST TOWNS

ARENAC–a village by that name was settled about 1865. At one time the village contained sawmills, several stores, and a dry goods store.

This wood trestle across the Rifle River near *Alger*, Michigan, served the Detroit-Bay City & Alpena Railroad from about 1880 until the turn-of-the-century. One of the largest trestles in Michigan in 1895, it was deteriorating rapidly and passengers were requested to walk across while the train crew took the engine across. Note millions of feet of logs in the river on their way to the mills of *Bay City* and *Saginaw*.   Photo Courtesy of Neil Thornton.

The hotel in *Shearer* on the D & M Railroad, Clayton Township, Arenac County, 14 miles north of *Standish* in 1889-90. Nothing remains of the village except the old railroad grade and some worn-out lilac bushes. Was located on the Ogemaw-Arenac County line.   Photo courtesy of Dan Berry.

34

In 1877 five miles east of *Standish* in Hampton Township, Bay County. Has a sawmill, shingle mill, a store, and several hotels. J. G. Payne, postmaster.

In 1905 population 150 in Arenac Township, 5 miles northeast of *Standish* and 3 from *Omer*, on the D. & M. Railroad. In 1910 population 130. In 1918 RFD *Standish*. Two general stores, no population given.

———

CULVER–in 1877 population 127, in Moffat Township, Bay County. Settled in May of 1872. Alvin N. Culver, postmaster. The village contained a general store, lumberman's supply, two planing mills, shingle mills, sawmills, and a box factory. Not listed as a post office in 1890. In 1910 another *"Culver"* is listed on railroad timetables in Kalkaska County.

———

DEEP RIVER–in 1877 population 200, on the Michigan Central Railroad in Deep River Township, Bay County, 3 miles north of *Standish*. Settled in 1870. T. E. Haskins, postmaster. The village had hotels, a general store, blacksmith shop, and a sawmill. There was also a train station or depot and several other buildings. Listed as a post office in 1893 but not in 1899. In 1905 a discontinued post office, RFD *Standish*.

———

MAPLE RIDGE–was settled in 1869. In 1877 population 100. In Clayton Township on the northern line of Bay County, 12 miles from *Deep River* station. Has a Methodist Church, sawmill, district school, etc. Stillman Smith, postmaster.

In 1905 population 150. Located in Mason and Clayton Townships, 4 miles from Prescott. C. Briggs, postmaster. The village contained a blacksmith shop, grocery and general store, drug store, bicycle shop, grain elevator, several other business places, and sawmills.

In 1918 population 150. Anna B. Cross, acting postmistress. A farm implement store, doctor and dentist offices were added, and a photo studio was doing business. Today the place is a four-corners. The post office was discontinued about 1920.

———

MELITA–in 1905 population 300. On the Rifle River in Clayton Township, 11 miles north of *Standish* and 6 north of *Sterling*. Two churches. Jesse A. Hamlin,

35

postmaster. Contained several stores, two barber shops, blacksmith shop, and other places.

In 1910 listed as RFD *Sterling*, population 50.

In 1918 only two business places listed: a blacksmith shop and general store.

Melita is designated on 1969 Michigan highway maps but in the 1960s the only remaining building, formerly the town hall, was moved to another location.

––––––––

MOFFAT–4 miles east of Alger near the Rifle River was a flag station on the D. B. C. & A. Railroad in 1890. A sawmill was located there.

––––––––

PINE RIVER–in 1877 two miles south of Arenac and 5 east of *Standish*, in Granton Township, Bay County. *Arenac* is its post office.

In 1905 population 150. On the D. & M. Railroad, on the Pine River, in Standish Township, Arenac County, 4 miles from *Standish*. William Major, postmaster, land-looker, and logger. Also contained a railroad station, blacksmith shop, grocery, feed mill, and bean elevator.

Population in 1910 was 31. In 1918 RFD *Standish*. Jesse A. Hamlin, general store. Shown on 1969 Michigan highway map.

––––––––

RIFLE RIVER CAMP–settled in 1866, was later named *Omer*, which is still a village. A tombstone in the cemetery on the grave of Daniel Fisher, died 1871, has an inscription which reads: *"Remember friend as you pass by, As you are now - so was I. As I am now - so you will be. Prepare for death and follow me"*.

1877 population 75. George Carscallen, postmaster.

––––––––

SAGANING–in 1877 described as an Indian village on the Saganing River in Standish Township, Bay County. Located 1 mile east of the M. C. Railroad. Population 140. Has a stave and shingle mill, an Indian church and school, and one store. E. H. Chamberlain, acting postmaster.

The post office was established in 1876 and in 1886 the name changed. In 1897 changed back to *"Saganing."* The post office was discontinued in 1914. The village remained an Indian village until 1871 when whites moved in from Indiana.

SANTIAGO–was founded during the Spanish American War (1898) and named after Santiago De Cuba, a name in the news at that time. A large lumber camp, called *"Moro Castle"* after a Spanish fort in Cuba, was located there.

Mrs. McIntyre of East Tawas said the village was about 5 miles south of *Twining*. *"My parents and two brothers and I walked to Santiago from Twining before the road was put through"*, she said. *"At that time it was just a trail through a swamp until we reached a small, sandy rise known as 'Vinegar Hill,' where there had been a logging camp."* She said the buildings were still there, about 1 mile from Santiago. They are still noticeable along the blacktop road of today (1968), she said.

In 1905 population 250. Ella McEwan, postmistress, on the AuGres River. Had hoop factory, general store, shoe and harness shop, sawmills, stave and heading mill, and a brick factory.

In 1918 population 100. Mail from *Twining*. A post office was there until about 1912. Fires burned the remaining timber and the village soon became deserted.

SHEARER–on the D. & M. Railroad, Clayton Township, 14 miles north of *Standish*. Post office established in 1889. Edwin F. Alexander was the first postmaster. In 1895 population 65. W. H. Judson, postmaster. Hannah R. Randall was postmistress until April, 1895. Discontinued September 7, 1898. The village was near Mansfield Creek, on the Arenac-Ogemaw county line.

The village was abandoned about 1903 or 1904 when lumbering in the area ceased and the railroad was discontinued. Buildings were either moved or torn down for the lumber. Archie Berry, a native of the area, said one building near the oil storage tanks on the Shephard farm is one of the original buildings.

The old railroad bed is still visible from the blacktop highway. By walking east down the grade lilac bushes that once grew in front of houses can be seen and there is other evidence of the one-time village.

37

TURNERVILLE–was the headquarters for Joe Turner, a lumberman, in the 1870s. Located in Turner Township, about 1 mile northeast of *Twining*, it contained a roundhouse and repair shop for Turner's logging trains. There were a dozen houses, a boot and shoe store, a general store, post office, and other buildings. The tracks were removed in 1886, Ennes said. Cedar Creek ran through the village and a dam and mill pond was formed there. The village was also on the site of Indian camps of the Ojibwa tribes.

––––––––

WORTH–in 1905 population 100. Formerly known as *"Saganing."* Josephine De Rosia, postmistress.

In 1910 population 45, mail RFD *Pinconning.*

In 1918 there were two general stores.

––––––––

Other flag stations and places were:

QUINN–in 1910 mail *Alger.*

LIMESTEAD and *SOUVENGNY*–flag stations on the D. & M. Railroad, located between *AuGres* and *Omer*.

UMSTEAD–in 1910 mail *AuGres*.

OGDEN–mail *Sterling*.

––––––––

Chapter Nine

BAY COUNTY GHOST TOWNS

Bay City is the central gateway to northern Michigan and was an important railroad center at an early date. In 1877 the manufacture of railroad equipment was a major industry. In that year the Bousfield & Company factory was the largest woodenware factory in the world, and the Michigan Pipe Company was the largest wooden pipe factory. As recently as 1969 some lengths of wooden water lines, made by this company, were uncovered and replaced in *Detroit*.

A historical plaque located in the East Michigan Tourist Association office in *Bay City* reads: *"Although French explorers had visited this area in the 1600s, a permanent white settlement occurred only in the 1830s. During the Civil War period the lumber industry developed reaching its peak in 1882. When the lumbermen left, coal mining, fishing, shipbuilding, and the production of beet sugar provided the basis for Bay City's economic growth"*.

In 1877 there were eight villages and settlements in the county in addition to *Bay City*.

GHOST TOWNS

BANKS–first called *"Bangor,"* was a village of 1,500 population on the west bank of the Saginaw River, 1½ miles below *Wenona* and 2½ from *Bay City*. Joseph Marchand, postmaster (1877). *Banks* is listed as a post office in 1890. After that date it became a part of *Bay City*.

———

BAYSIDE–in 1910 RFD *Bay City*. 1918 population 300. On Saginaw Bay, Bangor Township, 5 miles from *Bay City*. No railroad station, but the D. & M. and M. C. switches run in here. Three grocery stores and other business places.

———

BEAVER–shown on 1969 county map.

––––––––

BEDELL–in 1918 five miles from *Bay City* and 3 from *Kawkawlin*, whence mail is supplied rural delivery. Two stores.

In 1910 population 70. Mail to *Auburn*.

––––––––

BENTLEY–was a post office in 1890. Peak population at any one time was about 500. Buildings, a tavern, and one or two other business places remain in the village (1969), and it has a post office.

1905 population 200. In Gibson Township, 11 miles west of *Standish*. It was on the Michigan Central Railroad. Peter Edmuds, postmaster. Had hotels, sawmill and shingle mills, hoop factory, cheese factory, etc.

In 1918 population 400. N. E. Leffler, postmaster. Had a bank, grist-mill and elevator, drug store and doctor, restaurant and bakery, general store, hardware, "Traveler's Home," boardinghouse, a garage, hotel, and other buildings.

––––––––

BROOKS–listed in 1910 as on the Grand Trunk Railroad. Mail to *Bay City*. In 1918 another *"Brooks"* is listed in Holmes Township, Menominee County.

––––––––

COLDEN–listed in 1897 as a post office. In 1918 on the M. C. Railroad, Williams Township, 14 miles west of *Bay City*.

In 1905 C. B. Hubbell, postmaster and general store.

––––––––

COLFAX–in 1918 listed as a discontinued post office. In 1897 was a post office.

There was also a *"Colfax"* listed in Wexford County and one in Benzie County.

40

CRUMP–reached its peak population of 300 in 1910. In 1905 population 50. Garfield Township, 7½ miles from *Linwood* on the M. C. Railroad. L. N. Princing, postmaster. Had a general store, sawmill, lumber company, saloons, hardware, etc.

In 1918 population 150. Jesse S. Rhodes, postmaster. Also listed a bank, two hotels, hardware, sawmills, and other places.

———

CUMMINS–was a post office May 1, 1897, and as late as 1902. In Fraser Township, 15 miles north of *Bay City*.

After 1902 RFD *Linwood*.

———

DUEL–listed as a post office in 1897. In 1905 a country post office in Beaver Township, 19 miles northwest of *Bay City* and 11 from *Midland*. Mrs. E. J. Tobias, postmistress. Had a heading mill, blacksmith shops, general store, and a sawmill.

In 1910 population 150. RFD *Auburn*.

In 1918 no population. E. B. Owen, general store, and C. H. Stanley, heading mill (made lids, or heads, for barrels).

———

FISHERVILLE–a station on the M. C. Railroad 13 miles west of *Bay City*.

In 1910, send mail to *Auburn*.

———

FLAJOLE–a short distance east of *Fisherville* on the M. C. Railroad.

———

GARFIELD–listed as a post office in September, 1900. In 1910 population 50. RFD *Pinconning*. In 1918 located in Garfield Township, 22 miles north of *Bay City*, and 7 from *Pinconning*. Two general stores. No population.

GLENCOE–in 1877 on the line of Gladwin County, 11 miles west of *Pinconning*. Settled in 1873. Population 150. *"It is reached from Pinconning by the Glencoe-Pinconning & Lake Shore Railroad, a line extending from Glencoe east to the lakeshore, a distance of 14 miles. The railroad is owned and operated by George Campbell & Co. for transporting lumber from their mills."* Daily mail. George Campbell, postmaster, and owns the only business.

———

GLOVER–listed as a post office in 1900. 1910 population 12. In 1918 a discontinued post office, RFD *Bentley*. O. M. Clows, grocer.

The *Glover* school was standing in 1953, a short distance south of M-61 and north of *Bentley*.

———

HAMBLEN–a post office in December, 1890 and in 1902.

In 1918, RFD *Auburn*.

———

LAREDO–a post office in April, 1893. In 1905 on the M. C. Railroad, 11 miles west of *Bay City* and 7 miles east of *Midland*. Henry Turner, postmaster, and general store. Also a blacksmith shop and other buildings.

In 1910 population 23. RFD *Auburn*.

———

LENGSVILLE–was a post office April, 1893. In 1905 population 300. On the Grand Trunk Railroad, Fraser Township, 12½ miles north of *Bay City*, on Saginaw Bay. F. Hebinger, postmaster. Had several fish markets, a saloon, grocery stores, general store, and stave mill.

In 1910 population 70. On the D. M. & M. C. Railroad; RFD *Linwood*.

In 1918 population 200. D. F. Rockwell, postmaster and general store. Had a cooperage and cedar post factory, stave and heading mill, and J. L. Trombley, fisherman.

LOEHNE–a settlement and post office 14 miles northwest of *Bay City* and 8 from *Kawkawlin*. Was a post office in May, 1897.

In 1905 RFD *Auburn*.

In 1918 Edwin Loehne operated a general store, sawmill, and feed mill.

———

MAXWELL–in 1877 in Fraser Township, 15 miles above *Bay City*. Settled in 1870. On the Mackinaw division of the M. C. Railroad and listed on the time cards of the railroad as *"State Road Crossing."*

In 1877 William Mitchie, postmaster. Several shingle, saw and lumber mills were located there. Also a hotel called the "Royal Oak House."

This town had three names: *"Maxwell," "State Road Crossing,"* and a postal name of *"Michie."*

In 1910 a discontinued post office, 4 miles from *Pinconning*, whence mail is supplied by rural delivery.

———

MICHIE–see *Maxwell*.

———

MONITOR–a post office in May, 1897. In 1910 population 100. In 1918 on the M. C. Railroad, 7 miles from *Bay City*. RFD *Auburn*. Had two hotels, a general store, and other buildings.

———

MOUNT FOREST–was a post office in December, 1890. In 1905 population 50. On the M. C. Railroad, 18 miles northwest of *Bay City* and 12 from *Standish*. Irene Bouers, postmistress. Three general stores and a saw and shingle mill.

1910 population 60. In 1918 population 50. Eight miles northwest of *Pinconning*. Had a hotel, two hardwares, blacksmith shop, two grocery stores, and an elevator.

The town is designated on 1969 highway maps.

––––––––

NINE MILE–was a flag stop on the Gladwin Division of the M. C. Railroad (removed about 1965). No record as a post office.

In 1953 the *Nine Mile* country school building remained on the site.

––––––––

NORTH WILLIAMS–was a post office located about 2 miles north of *Auburn* in 1893, but lasted only a few years.

In 1910, RFD *Auburn*.

––––––––

PORTSMOUTH–in 1877 described as: *"Now an integral part of Bay City, but lately a separate village. It still maintains a separate post office."* Was listed as a post office in 1890.

––––––––

SALZBURG–in 1877 described as a lumber and salt manufacturing village on the left bank of the Saginaw River opposite *Portsmouth*. In Bangor Township, on the M. C. Railroad, 1 mile southwest of *Bay City*. Has between 500 and 600 inhabitants, five or six large sawmills, a flouring mill, three salt companies, and two breweries. Settled in 1854. George Staudacher, postmaster. Later incorporated with *Bay City*.

––––––––

SKINNER–in 1877 described as a village of 250 in Williams Township, 9 miles west of *Bay City*. Has two sawmills and a Methodist church. Ships lumber, hoops, square timber, and produce. Ira Swart, postmaster. Also had hotels, a doctor, general store, etc.

It is likely the name was changed to *"Fisher"* a few years later. It is doubtful that a village of 250 population disappeared within a year or two after its founding, and the location coincides with that of *"Fisher"* on the M. C. Railroad.

STATE ROAD–see *Maxwell* or *Michie*. Also known as *"State Road Cross-ing."*

––––––––

TOBICO–on the D. & M. Railroad in 1910, north of *Bay City*. Mail to *Bay City*.

––––––––

TEBO–in 1918 a discontinued post office. RFD *Pinconning*.

––––––––

WENONA–was platted as *"Lake City"* but the Post Office Department re-quested a name change and accepted *Wenona*. In 1877 an incorporated village of 2,600 on the left bank of the Saginaw River, opposite *Bay City*, with which it is connected by a bridge. The Saginaw division of the M. C. Railroad passes through it. It is also the eastern terminus of the Bay City-Midland and Grand Rapids Railroad, now in course of construction.

It has the largest sawmill in the State, H. W. Sage & Company (made up of Henry W. Sage, William Sage, and a Mr. Dean).

Platted in 1864 and incorporated in 1865. Henry H. Alpin, postmaster.

In 1877 *Wenona* became a part of *West Bay City*, along with *Banks* and *Salzburgh*.

In 1903 *West Bay City* was in turn consolidated with *Bay City*. At that time the population of the three combined villages was 12,197.

––––––––

WHITE FEATHER–in 1877 a post office and station on the Mackinaw Di-vision of the M. C. Railroad, in Pinconning Township, 23 miles north of *Bay City*. Settled in 1872. Average population 100. W. G. Clark, postmas-ter; J. M. Root, deputy postmaster. The only interests are the White Feather Lumber Company.

––––––––

Other places were:

AMELITH–a post office in 1900 and population 60 in 1910, RFD *Bay City*.

ARN–10 miles east of *Bay City* on the M. C. Railroad. In 1910 RFD *Munger*. The *Arn* school was standing in 1953.

BERTIE–in 1910 RFD *Pinconning*. Population 12.

———

Chapter Ten

BENZIE COUNTY GHOST TOWNS

RAILROADS

In 1893 three railroads served the county. The Manistee & North Eastern served the southwest, extending through *Lake Ann* and *Cedar Run*. The Chicago & West Michigan served *Thompsonville* and *Alden*.

The Toledo-Ann Arbor & North Michigan served *Thompsonville, Homestead, Benzonia*, and *Frankfort*.

POST OFFICES

In 1890 there were 15 post offices in the county. Only three remain today.

GHOST TOWNS

ALMIRA–in 1877 had a population (township) of 350. The village was 14 miles west of *Traverse City* and 16 miles north of *Frankfort*. Mostly a farming area. *"The Platte River affords waterpower for a sawmill and one gristmill."* Stages to *Traverse City* and *Glen Arbor*. Mail three times a week. Reverend Elihu Linkletter, postmaster. The place had a church, general store and stage stop, shoemaker, and blacksmith shop, in addition to the mills.

In 1953 the *Almira* school and cemetery was all that was left.

———

ALLYN STATION–see *Pratts*.

———

ARAL–listed as a discontinued post office in 1905. Mail to *Platte*.

———

BENDON–formerly known as *"Kentville."* 1905 population 125. On the P. M. Railroad, Inland Township, 18 miles northeast of *Frankfort*, and 10 from *Thompsonville*. Arthur Allen, postmaster. There was a sawmill, blacksmith shop, two general stores, express office, and two boardinghouses.

1918 population the same. Eight miles from *Grawn*. Had two general stores, grocery, produce company, hardware, hotel, and auto garage.

––––––––

CEDAR RUN–in 1877 a post office in Long Lake Township, Grand Traverse County, 10 miles west of *Traverse City*. Steam saw and shingle mill, a cooperage, general store, and blacksmith shop. Two hundred residents in the immediate area.

In 1905 population 200. On the M. & N. E. Railroad, Almira Township, Benzie County. Two churches. Mrs. A. H. Crain, postmistress. The "Transient House Hotel," several stores, mills, etc.

By 1918 the population had dropped to about 50. Sixteen miles by rail northeast of *Honor*, the county seat. Sadie B. Loomis, postmistress. Three grocery stores and the hotel remained.

––––––––

EDGEWATER–in 1905 a country post office in Lake Township, 13 miles northeast of *Frankfort* and 8 from *Honor*. Henry Wrede, postmaster. Not listed in 1910.

––––––––

GILMORE–in 1877 described as: *"Located in Blaine Township on the shore of Lake Michigan, 12 miles south of Benzonia. Settled in 1850. Wood and logs shipped. Tri-weekly stage to Frankfort and Pier Point. George B. Farley, postmaster and general store."*

––––––––

GRANT HOUSE–see *Homestead*.

––––––––

HOMESTEAD–in 1877 also known as "Grant House." In Homestead Town-

48

ship, 5 miles west of *Benzonia*. *"It contains two sawmills, gristmill, and a shingle factory. Sugar is also shipped. Tri-weekly stages to Traverse City and Frankfort. T. M. Wakely, postmaster and proprietor of the 'Grant House' hotel."* Had several lumber and gristmills.

In 1905 a discontinued post office, RFD *Benzonia*. Shown on the 1968 highway map.

———

HONOR–is a "semi-ghost town." In 1905 population 550. Today is only one-half that number. In 1905 on the M. & N. E. and the P. M. Railroads, Homestead Township, 18 miles northwest of *Frankfort* and 6 from *Benzonia*. J. W. Van Blaircom, postmaster. Rensselaer Brundage, proprietor of "Brundage House" hotel. Also "Hotel Chessir." The place also had saloons, saw and planing mill, boardinghouses, a saw and veneer mill, another hotel "The Robinson," livery, etc.

A few original buildings remain and only a few old-timers, who reminisce about the "good old days" when the town was booming. With recent introduction of coho salmon the village shows some signs of revival.

———

INLAND–in 1877 a post office in Inland Township, 15 miles north of *Benzonia*. Stage to *Benzonia* and *Traverse City*. E. P. Alpin, postmaster and hotel. Also had a general store and other buildings.

In 1905 a discontinued post office, 2¾ miles from *Bendon*.

———

JOYFIELD–in 1877 a post office in Joyfield Township, 10 miles south of *Benzonia*. *"It is located in a fruit belt, mail by stage four times weekly. Amazia Joy, postmistress and Pastor of the Baptist Church"*.

In 1905 a discontinued post office 6 miles south of *Benzonia*. 1910 population 72.

———

MELVA–in 1905 located in Almira Township, 15 miles from *Benzonia*.

Population 85. E. E. Rhinehart, postmaster and railroad agent. On the M. & N. E. Railroad. Railroad name *"Platte River."* Mail *Honor*.

———

LAKE ANN–had a population of 250 in 1905. The 1960 census listed 106. In 1905 on the M. & N. E. Railroad, and on Lake Ann, Almira Township, 18 miles from *Traverse City* (west). S. S. Burnett, postmaster. Had saloons, the "Douglas House" hotel and livery, carriage and wagon works, flour mill, school, etc.

In 1918 population 175. One church and a school. George T. Valleu, postmaster. Hotel, general stores, and hardware store.

———

OSBORN–in 1905 a country post office on the E. & S. E. Railroad in Platte Township, 19 miles from *Traverse City* and 10 from *Lake Ann*. Issac Huff, postmaster and general store. Two stores, school, and other buildings.

1910 population 10, mail to Empire.

———

OVIAT–1905 population 60. Fifteen miles west of *Traverse City* and 4½ from *Cedar Run*. H. C. Pettingill, postmaster. Has stores, a hotel, two blacksmith shops, church, etc.

1910 population 54, mail *Empire*.

1918 population 50, in Almira and Kasson Townships. One store.

———

PLATTE RIVER–see *Melva*.

———

PLATTE–in 1877 a post office in Platte Township and on Platte Bay. Thirteen miles north of *Frankfort*. The country has been mostly timbered off. Stages to *Frankfort* and *Glen Arbor* twice weekly. Leroy Morgan, postmaster. Had several buildings, a wagon shop, blacksmith, etc.

1910, RFD *Honor*.

PRATTS–also known as *"Allyn Station,"* on the M. & N. E. Railroad and on the Platte River, Inland Township, 29 miles east of *Frankfort*, the county seat (1918), and 6½ from *Honor*. Mail to *Melva*.

———

SOUTH FRANKFORT–in 1877 population 400, located 1 mile south of *Frankfort*, the former county seat of Benzie County, is the location of the "Frankfort Furnace," has a sawmill and broom handle factory. Wood, lumber, handles, bark, and pig iron are shipped. Daily mail. E. B. Fletcher, postmaster.

———

STORMER–1905 population 40, on the M. & N. E. Railroad, 15 miles northeast of *Frankfort*, and 10 from *Benzonia*. A. D. Kempt, postmaster and railroad agent.

1910 RFD *Honor*, 16 miles north.

———

SUCCESS–didn't live up to its name. In 1877, a post office in Almira Township on *Lake Ann*, the head of Platte River, 16 miles northeast of *Frankfort*, and 14 west of *Traverse City*. *"Has a sawmill and a gristmill."* Semi-weekly mail. A. P. Wheelcock, postmaster.

No record after this date.

———

WALLIN–1918 population 100. On the P. M. Railroad and on the Betsie River in Colfax Township, 14 miles east of *Beulah*, the county seat, and 4½ from *Thompsonville*. Caroline M. Bauer, postmistress. Had a church, general stores, produce store, hotel, and opera house.

———

WELDON–in 1918 a discontinued post office in Weldon Township, 14 miles southeast of *Frankfort* and 6½ from *Benzonia*. RFD *Benzonia*.

———

51

Other places in the county were:

CLARK–about 1 mile south of *Allyn*

CLARY–near *Grass Lake*, about 3 miles southwest of *Bendon* on the P. M. Railroad (in 1910, mail to *Bendon*)

MARO–shown on 1920 maps

TURTLE LAKE–in 1918 a discontinued post office, RFD *Thompsonville*

RICE–on the Betsie River about 1 mile above the Homestead Dam.

———

Chapter Eleven

CHARLEVOIX COUNTY GHOST TOWNS AND TREASURE ON LAKE MICHIGAN ISLANDS

High Island is now uninhabited and in public ownership but at one time was a thriving community of 800 persons. As late as 1910 a sawmill was in operation. Deane E. Weston of *Trout Creek*, Michigan, said his cousin Lynn Brownell worked at the mill. Walter O'Donnell, park ranger in charge of the Bay City State Park said his parents lived on the island at one time. Today only tumbledown buildings and a few crumbling stone foundations can be found at the site.

There is a legend of a vast treasure in Mormon gold buried in Fox Lake on *Beaver Island*. It is said that when a dissident sect of Mormons was expelled from the island by King James they took their share of the riches and buried it in Fox Lake.

It is also possible that other treasure may be hidden on the island. Mrs. Williams, in her book *A Child of The Sea*, said King James appointed men, called "the band of 40 thieves," to plunder the mainland and rob visitors coming to the island. *"The two men who headed the band were brothers and were large and powerful men, Isaac and John Pierce. They were well suited to do such work. The place they chose to secrete their stolen goods was a long point at the lower end of Beaver Island, distant about three miles from the harbor. This place was called by them 'Rocky Mountain Point.' Being an out-of-the-way place they would not be seen secreting much of their plunder."* Many vacant houses, all in a state of decay, remain on the island where artifacts may remain buried. The island was also the site of ancient Indian mounds before 16th century Indians moved to the island.

POST OFFICES

There were at least 29 post offices during the history of the county.

RAILROADS

In 1906 the county was served by the Boyne City-Gaylord & Alpena Railroad. Beginning at *Boyne City*, 0 miles; *Doyle's Siding*, 3 miles; *Cushman*, 4 miles; *Moore*, 6 miles; *Boyne Falls*, 7 miles; *Project*, 11 miles; *Camp 10*, 12 miles; *Orville*, 13 miles; then to *North Elmira*, 15 miles.

––––––––

ADVANCE–settled in 1865. In 1877 on the shores of Pine Lake (now Charlevoix), Eveline Township, 12 miles from *Charlevoix*, the county seat, and 11 miles from *Boyne Falls*. On the G. R. & I. Railroad. Population about 10. Had a saw and gristmill, blacksmith and wagonmaker, general stores, etc. A. E. Hayes, post-master.

In 1905 population 175. Three-and-one-half miles from *Boyne*, on the B. C. & S. E. Railroad, its shipping point. Daily mail. A. B. Steele, postmaster.

Last registered as a post office in 1907. In 1910, population 62.

––––––––

BARNARD–in 1877 six miles south of *Charlevoix*, in Marion Township, on Burns Creek. Population 50, settled in 1866. Bernard Burns, postmaster and sawmill owner. Other buildings also.

1910, mail to *Charlevoix*.

––––––––

BAY SPRINGS–had a post office in 1890. In 1905 population 525. A summer resort at the head of Pine Lake (Charlevoix), 1 mile north of *Boyne*. L. R. Chase, Jr., postmaster. Had a chemical works, iron foundry, bicycle factory, tower clock repairer and machinest, large general stores, a photographer, and other busi-nesses.

In 1910, RFD *Boyne City*.

––––––––

BOYNE–in 1877 described as a post office at *Spring Harbor*, in Evangeline Township, 15 miles southeast of *Charlevoix*. Settled in 1874. John Miller, postmaster. Had two general stores, hotel, and lumber camps. Was a post office in 1890.

––––––––

BURGESS–in 1905 a discontinued post office, in Hayes Township, RFD *Charlevoix*.

In 1910 population 40.

––––––––

CLARION–shown on 1968 highway maps. In 1905 population 200, on the G. R. & I. Railroad, Melrose Township, 25 miles east of *Charlevoix* and 7 from *Petoskey*. William H. Ransom, postmaster. "Robinson House" hotel, had a dairy, sawmill, planing mill, shoe, drug and hardware store, railroad station, two churches, etc.

In 1918 population 100. Ruth A. Colden, postmistress. Auto livery, dairy, hotel, and saw and planing mill.

––––––––

DWIGHT–in 1905 a discontinued post office, mail to *Advance*.

––––––––

EMBO–was a village on the mail route between *Charlevoix* and *Petoskey*, 4½ miles east of *Charlevoix*. Received mail in 1877. Not listed as a post office after 1902.

––––––––

HAMMERS–was a flag stop on the G. R. & I. Railroad in 1877, twelve miles south of *Petoskey*.

––––––––

INTERMEDIATE–in 1877 in South Arm Township, 12 miles south of *Charlevoix*, and on Intermediate Lake. Sawmill and church. On the stage line to *Boyne Falls* and *Acme*. Daniel Isaman, postmaster. Had a hotel, wagon shop, and sawmill.

Post office discontinued in 1905 and mail to *Ellsworth*.

––––––––

INWOOD– in 1905 a discontinued post office 7½ miles southwest of *Charlevoix*.

––––––––

NORWOOD–in 1877 located in Norwood Township, on the shore of Lake Michigan at the mouth of Grand Traverse Bay, 11 miles southwest of *Charlevoix*. Fred J. Meech, postmaster. Had general store, sawmill, two shoe shops, and a blacksmith.

In 1905 population 300. Daily mail. William Harris, postmaster. Several stores, a doctor, general store, and a "last block" manufacturer (used to form shoes).

Post office discontinued between 1913 and 1918. In 1910 population 150.

––––––––

SOUTH ARM–in 1877 postal name was *"Nelsonville,"* at the head of Pine Lake (Charlevoix), 14 miles south of *Charlevoix*. S. G. Isaman, postmaster.

1890 population 115.

In 1905 population 450. On the D. & C. and East Jordan & Southern Railroads, at the mouth of Jordan River on Pine Lake, South Arm Township, about ¼ mile from *East Jordan*. C. A. Brabant, postmaster. Shipped piles (posts used in harbors and docks), had a blacksmith shop, and other business places.

––––––––

SPRINGVALE–was a post office in 1890, discontinued between 1918 and 1923. In 1905 population 50. In Chandler Township, 25 miles southeast of *Charlevoix* and 14 from *Petoskey*. *Boyne Falls*, 12 miles away was shipping point. A. J. Crago, postmaster. This was mainly a settlement formed for the Cobbs & Mitchell Lumbering Company. In 1910 population 60.

In 1918, *Wolverine*, 9 miles distant was the banking point. W. R. Allen, postmaster. Also a hotel and lumbermen's supply store.

––––––––

TALCOTT–name changed to *"Walloon Lake."*

––––––––

WALLOON LAKE–formerly known as Talcott. 1905 population 300. On the G. R. & I. Railroad, Melrose Township, 18 miles southeast of *Charlevoix*. On Walloon Lake and is a summer resort. I. E. Tillapaugh, postmaster. Had three hotels, boardinghouse, depot and railroad station, general stores, cottages, bath house, and the Eclipse Boat Works (manufacturers of small gasoline launches and clinker row boats). Also livery stables, ice cream manufacturer, photographer, and school.

1918 population 100. A. J. Crago, postmaster. Also a saw and planing mill.

In November 1968, Ernest Hemingway's former cottage, "Windemere," near *Horton Bay* on Walloon Lake was designated as a national historic landmark. Hemingway brought his first bride here and was married in the church at *Horton Bay.*

Horton Bay in 1905 was described as a post office on Pine Bay in Bay Township, 12 miles southeast of *Charlevoix*, and from *Bayshore*, its shipping point. Conrad Schneider, general store.

In 1910 population 60.

1918 RFD *Boyne City*. Has Evangelical and Methodist Episcopal churches; J. H. Dilworth, wagonmaker; and Lester Fox, general store.

In 1965 the store was boarded up and a "For Sale" sign tacked on the building. The main road on that side of the lake is far back from the lakeshore and all the summer homes are between the road and the lake. Most of these homes are barred by gates and not open to the public.

———

'Big wheels,' such as these, up to 14 feet in diameter, helped in harvesting timber and clearing many a town site in northern Michigan during the late 1800s. A set of original wheels today are as scarce as wild buffalo on the western plains. Metal hoops, or parts from one of these, would be a valuable asset to any museum. There is only one recorded instance of a set of big wheels in Clare County. They were shipped by train, minus the long tongue, were 8 feet high, and cost $80 new, plus $2.74 freight. Any color could be ordered, but they were painted red only.

58

Chapter Twelve

CLARE COUNTY GHOST TOWNS
AND THE WORLD'S FIRST LOGGING RAILROAD

Clare County played an important part during the lumbering era of northern Michigan, furnishing lumber and logs to *Bay City* and *Saginaw* via the Tobacco River, and to *Muskegon* via the Muskegon River, both of which lie within the county.

In 1874 Winfield Scott Gerrish, a young man from *Hersey*, Michigan, purchased 12,000 acres of timber on the west side of the county in partnership with E. H. Hazelton, T. D. Stinson, and others. In January, 1877, Gerrish introduced the first logging railroad in the history of the world, called the "Lake George & Muskegon Railroad," and revolutionized the logging industry. It extended from Bertha Lake to Lake George. Most of the old grade can still be walked or driven. A historical plaque is erected on Old US-27 midway between *Clare* and *Harrison* commemorating the railroad. Clare County probably has more miles of old railroad grades than any county in the State.

By 1890 the entire county had been stripped of its virgin pine forests. Fires soon swept over the barren country and for many years most of the area was covered with blackened stumps. Very few roads were constructed until the advent of the automobile. During the 1920s many tourists and sportsmen were attracted to the county to visit the many lakes and streams. Today tourism is the main industry of the county.

In 1969 a Clare County Historical Society was formed to preserve some of the landmarks and railroad grades. They now own the old *Dover* school, the first in the county, and it is being restored as a typical country school. Visitors are welcome, and the school is open to the public weekends, or by appointment. *Dover* is one of the few ghost towns in Michigan with original buildings still standing. It is located 1 mile east of Old US-27 and 5 miles north of *Clare*. In addition to the school is an old country store and a sawmill is again in operation on the site.

RAILROADS

Principal railroads in the county were the Flint & Pere Marquette-Meredith Division and the Toledo, Ann Arbor & North Michigan. In 1890 the F. & P. M. Beginning at *Clare*, 0 miles; *Moore's Siding*, 4.17 miles; *Atwood's Siding*, 7.83 miles; *Hatton*, 9.11 miles; *Mann's Siding*, 12.76 miles; *Harrison*, 16.83 miles; *Arnold*

Lake, 22 miles; *Levington Siding*, 25.08 miles; *Frost*, 26.04 miles; *Eke*, 28.04 miles; ending at *Meredith* on the Gladwin County line, 31.70 miles.

The T. A. A. & N. M. Beginning at *Shepherd* in Isabella County to *Clare*, 0 miles; *Farwell*, 5 miles; *Clinton's*, 3.2 (called *"Clintonville"*); *Lake George*, 6 miles; *Temple* (*"Campbell"* on Maps), 8.3 miles; *Pennock's*, 1.6 miles.

The F. & P. M. branched near Wilson State Park and extended to *Leota*, 12 miles north on the Muskegon River. Another wide-gauge track branched east from *Hatton*, across land now owned by the Mid-Michigan Community College, through *Mostettler's Siding*, and north to *Dodge City*. There were also miles of narrow-gauge track, most of which it is almost impossible to trace.

POST OFFICES

Clare County had at least 29 post offices during its history. Today there are 5 remaining.

GHOST TOWNS

ALWARD–13 miles southeast of *Harrison* and 10 from *Gladwin*, in Sections 14 and 15, Arthur Township. 1905 Theron Eddy, postmaster and sawmill. There was also a general store, blacksmith shop, etc. In 1910 located on M-13, RFD *Gladwin*, population 20.

––––––––

AUSTA–1905 had a general store and two or three buildings. William Dykestra, postmaster. This was a Holland Dutch settlement founded by John Vogel, early surveyor and settler of Missaukee County. William Dykestra built his home 20 rods or more off the wagon trail, which in some way conflicted with red tape in the post office department. To overcome it and receive mail delivery by the stage that ran from *Marion* to *Houghton Lake*, he agreed to carry the mail sacks from the road, which he did until a rural route was established.

––––––––

BROWN'S CORNERS–George Kanar opened the first store in 1898-99. In Section 36, Hatton Township. Had a store, church, and school. In 1910 a discontinued post office, RFD *Clare*.

––––––––

CLARENCE–only a few foundations remain to show the village once existed in Redding Township, about 10 miles west of *Harrison* on the Ann Arbor Railroad (tracks remain and used). In 1890s had a sawmill and banking grounds for logs shipped by rail. 1905 population 100. Daily stage to *Harrison.* Two lumber companies operating, general store, and W. W. Cross, postmaster.

In 1918 population 40. C. L. Apel, postmaster. Had a sawmill, implement sales, and general store. The store stood vacant for years. The old post office safe remained in the building and someone dragged it out and blew it up with dynamite. The safe was empty. The building burned in the 1930s.

———

COLONVILLE–five miles northeast of *Clare*, Sheridan Township, was one of the first settlements in the county. First called the *"Bradley Settlement"* after an early settler. First post office in 1896 in a general store owned by Curtis Palmer. Had a post office until 1905. After that RFD *Clare*. 1910 population 45.

One of the few, two-story, original log cabins in the State stands vacant on Colonville Road. This cabin, made of hewn logs, was built about 1870 by David Smalley, the first settler. Smalley was a Civil War veteran and became the first township supervisor. He held other township offices and was a highly-respected man and good citizen.

The log cabin, still in good condition, is now owned by one of David Smalley's descendants. The last resident of the cabin was David Robart, a nephew or grandson. The present owners said they plan to raze the old building sometime soon (1969).

Robart said the cabin was at one time the hideout of John A. Smalley, Michigan's notorious train and bank robber of the 1890s. John Smalley died in a hail of bullets from a sheriff's posse August 25, 1895 in *McBain* where he was buried.

———

CROOKED LAKE–in Garfield Township, 7 miles southeast of *Farwell*, has three names. *"Lake"* is the postal name and is listed on railroad timetables as *"Lake Station."* First settled in 1875. In 1905 population about 300. Thomas Maltby, postmaster. At one time had large mills around Crooked Lake, Perch Lake, Gray Lake, and other lakes in the area. Is now a resort village and most buildings were erected since 1950 on old foundations of buildings that had burned. Many foundations remain.

In 1918 population 200. On the Pere Marquette Railroad (now C. & O.). Thomas Maltby, postmaster. Hotel, drug and hardware stores, general stores, blacksmith shop, etc.

This 100-year-old log cabin is one of only a few two-story cabins remaining in good condition in Michigan. Was once the hide-out of Michigan's notorious train and bank robbers of the 1890s.   Photo by Roy L. Dodge.

DODGE–now a resort settlement called *"Dodge City."* Founded about 1884 when the Lansing Lumber Company set up lumber mills. Was served by a branch of the F. & P. M. Railroad until destroyed by fire in 1890.

1893 population 300. Telephone and Western Union telegraph. W. H. Dodge, postmaster. Had two saw and shingle mills, barber shop, railroad station, etc.

By 1905 the timber was exhausted and the mills that burned were never rebuilt. Described as a country post office in Hamilton Township, 11 miles from *Gladwin*. Elizabeth Robbins, postmistress. Had a blacksmith shop, school, post office, grocery, etc.

Post office discontinued 1906-08. In 1910 listed as RFD *Gladwin*, population 40. In 1918, Charles Hersee, general store.

From 1920 until 1936 only two houses remained near the four corners of *Dodge*. About 1950 Lee Swallow, a present resident, purchased 700 acres including the former site of *Dodge*, and developed it as a resort. Many of the streets bear the names "Sawmill Road," "Wagon Road," "Railroad Street," etc. Now contains several stores, a large sawmill and crate works, lumber yard, and other business places.

———

GRANDON–1905 population 90, Winterfield Township, 17 miles north of *Harrison*, and 5 from *Marion*. C. Howard, postmaster. (1905 atlas says Mrs. C. Howard.) Only the old, stone school building stands empty on the site, and a huge house that could have been a hotel. The place contained a lumber and lath factory. Had stores, logging camp, and a photographer. Was served by a daily stage.

1910, RFD *Marion*.

———

HATTON–8 miles south of *Harrison* and 2 miles west on Hatton Road, was established by Whitney & Remick Lumber Company in 1881. Fire destroyed most of the buildings and two lumber mills in 1910. After that time had a siding and shipping yard for cattle until about 1940.

1890 population 350, contained a hotel, post office, two stores, two restaurants, and a drug store. At one time had a general store and bazaar. Also a schoolhouse (still standing), a depot, and three saloons. The Hatton Cemetery is still maintained about ½ mile north of the school. The railroad grade and its branches are clearly visible, also remains of the stockyard.

In 1905 a rural post office on the P. & M. Railroad, Hatton Township. William Goodknecht, postmaster. Anna Goodknect was at one time postmistress.

Many fires plagued residents of the town, after the fire of 1910 most people moved away and it was never rebuilt.

––––––––

LONG LAKE–in Frost Township, 7 miles north of *Harrison*. In 1905 had three saw and shingle mills, hotel, grocery, clothing store, blacksmith shop, etc. R. T. Whaley, postmaster. In 1910, population 31.

Village founded by Hackley & Hume Lumber Company who had camps in the area and put in a narrow gauge railroad to haul logs to Long Lake.

Post office discontinued in 1912 and RFD *Harrison*. Today is a resort district. Part of the old hotel is now the Long Lake Grocery.

––––––––

LEOTA–12 miles north of *Harrison* in Summerfield Township, was named after the daughter of A. E. Rhodes, who erected a sawmill at the site. Leota (Rhodes) Green is now 76 years old and in the Masonic Home in *Alma* (1970).

A. E. Rhodes employed 200 men in his lumber camp and mill. He built the first store on the "bayou" below the dam. The village was served by the F. & P. M. Railroad extending from *Harrison* to Russell's store, about ½ mile from *Leota*. People came there to pick up their mail and the station was known as *"Sunrise."*

In 1905 M. C. Johnson, postmaster and general store. Population 100. Had a sawmill, stave mill, several stores, and a blacksmith shop. Most of the buildings were moved away from the site. One concrete block building, once a store, remains and is lived in.

At one time there were three saloons, a town hall, and several stores. By 1930 the place was deserted.

Leota was at one time headquarters for rivermen on the logging drives on the Muskegon. Many stories of drownings and rough-and-tumble fights during the logging days are connected with the village. Link Jones, who has descendants living in the area, quit the river drives and set up a saloon at *Leota*, where he was killed in a fight while still a young man.

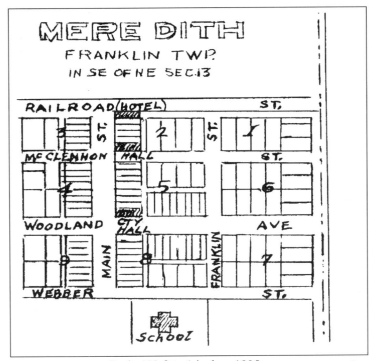

Scale 400 ft to 1 inch   1905

Meredith was platted as a city August 20, 1885, and soon reached a population of 500. Isolated from the rest of the world at the terminus of the F. & P. M. Railroad that ran from *Harrison* to *Meredith* in the midst of vast pine forests. This town won the reputation as the "Toughest Town in Michigan."

By 1890 the timber was depleted and only 100 residents remained. On April 18, 1892, two subdivisions were platted adjacent to the town and divided into 3,990 lots measuring 25 x 100 feet. The Wilson-McNally Tobacco Company of Ohio advertised lots in the city of *Meredith* to be given as premiums with the purchase of their brand of plug chewing tobacco. Tobacco users could redeem a certain number of metal tags and receive a deed to one of these lots. Apparently none of the new owners ever took possession of a lot but more than 2,000 deeds were issued to people in every state of the union. *Meredith* was the only city on record that was ever "traded for tobacco coupons."

On April 18, 1899, these plats were vacated and the town became deserted.

In the past few years a grocery store, laundromat, and a tavern have been built on the site, and there are many cottages in the area.

MEREDITH–so many stories have been written about this one-time roaring logging town that it is difficult to describe it in less than a large volume. During its short existence, from 1883 to about 1900, it became known as the "Toughest Town in Michigan."

In 1884 population 283; 1885, 300; 1887, 500; and in 1895 dropped to 100 and only two saloons remained. At one time it contained several saloons (one owned by the infamous Jim Carr), three hotels, and opera house, city hall and jail, railroad station and roundhouse, and a three-story school. Most of the buildings were torn down and moved. The old opera house, seating 700, was moved to Arthur Township and rebuilt for a church. The church burned. Residents of *Prudenville*, during the Depression of the 1930s, drove there and hauled bricks from the only remaining building, the schoolhouse, and used them to build chimneys.

In 1945 Herbert McIntosh purchased the site of *Meredith* at a State land tax sale for $12.57. He later sold it. At one time he offered it for sale for $2,800, but the prospective purchaser said it wasn't worth that much.

Residents of the present village, about 150 in the area, resent *Meredith* being called a "ghost town." All of them moved there since 1946 and 1950. The present stone store is on the site of the old railroad station. Other store buildings extended south along the street, many of them on the site of the present drive-in-theatre. The abandoned cemetery lies about ½ mile behind the theatre.

Many lumberjacks were unsavory characters, and were held in low esteem by village residents and "respectable citizens." *Meredith* had many upstanding, church-going families (although the village had no church). When a lumberjack was killed in a saloon brawl or by accident in the woods, these people often refused to allow his burial in the Meredith Cemetery.

Thomas Garrity had set off a small plot in one corner of his farm, in Hamilton Township, for a private cemetery. When citizens of *Meredith* refused a departed jack a last resting place, the story is told that several of his pals built a rough box, chipped in to buy a few bottles of liquor, and held their own private funeral for the deceased.

By the time the funeral procession reached the cemetery all the pallbearers and mourners were in a very jovial mood. After digging the grave and lowering the deceased, one of their members removed his hat and with bowed head recited these lines: *"Ashes to ashes, dust to dust. If Meredith won't have him, then Garrity must."*

––––––––––

MOSTETTLER or *"Mostettler Siding"*–was located 5 miles east of *Harrison* on what is now Mostettler Road. In 1885 W. H. Mostettler established a saw and shingle mill on the site, built huge storage sheds, and stored the production from several shingle mills in the area to be shipped by rail. This siding was a post office from 1885 until 1890.

W. H. Mostettler died from gunshot wounds to the head in March of 1889. There are several stories about his death. Some old-timers say he was murdered by his wife, while lying in bed. Others say he committed suicide. The latter story is the most plausible.

Mostettler entered into a business agreement with the Corey Brothers, who owned a shingle mill at *Dodge* in 1885. From that date until his death he became deeply indebted. When he died he owed the Wilson Brothers of *Harrison* $3,289.99 for supplies for his camp and mill, in addition to notes in amounts ranging from $500 to $1,000.

Shortly after that time the post office was discontinued.

––––––––––

PENNOCK–on the Ann Arbor Railroad, Redding Township, 5 miles east of *Marion* and 17 from *Harrison*, was a short-lived post office and station, lasting from about 1900 to 1908. In 1905 population 60. J. C. Albertson, postmaster and general store. The place also had a station and blacksmith shop. After 1908, RFD *Marion*.

Several old houses and what appears to be the remains of the old shingle mill remain on the site today, along with an auto junkyard.

––––––––––

PRESTEL–in 1892 the F. & P. M. Railroad was extended from *Harrison* to a lumber camp owned by Neff Prestel and his son, Gordon. At one time the population was more than 200. Was a post office April 1, 1893; April 1899; and September 1, 1900. Not listed in 1902.

The Prestels moved to Idaho and the post office was moved to the Chaffee store on Old State Road. Charlie Budd, Wallace Harper, Reverend A. F. Light, and Clyde Pifer were mail carriers over the years. In 1905 Thomas G. Adams ran a saw and shingle mill on the site. There was also a schoolhouse. Located in Summerfield Township.

Typical of thousands of former general stores scattered all over northern Michigan until the 1950s with the advent of tourism and paved highways. Until the spring of 1970, this store stood vacant on M-61 near *Temple* in Clare County. Last operated about 1946. *Bay City Times* - Photo by Richard Hardy.

Once the main street of *Campbell City*, now *Temple*, the terminus of the Lake George and Muskegon River Railroad, Michigan's first logging railroad and the first in the world.   *Bay City Times* - Photo by Richard Hardy.

REMICK–one of the first settlements in the county, located about 2 miles south of Lake on the then P. M. Railroad. It is one of three places shown on the 1873 county map. The other two are *Clare Station* and *Farwell*.

In 1877 described as: *"A hamlet on the F. & P. M. Railroad, 4 miles west of Farwell, the county seat. Andre Alexander operates a mill on this site."*

Not listed as a post office in 1890. In 1910 listed on the Rand McNally map and railroad guide as being in Isabella County. Mail to *Wyman*.

————

TEMPLE–was plotted as *"Campbell"* and is listed on maps as such. In 1899 Mrs. Mary Campbell donated 80 acres in Section 16, Redding Township, to be used for a town. It was platted into 27 blocks along the Ann Arbor Railroad. A few years later another addition of three blocks was added to the north called the Dewey & Store addition. Today this is built up with tarpaper shacks and old busses and trailers.

When the post office was established the name was changed to *"Temple,"* after W. M. Temple, the first postmaster.

At one time, the village contained two hotels, a depot, city hall, several saloons, grocery stores, sawmills, shingle mill, and a hame factory. Two abandoned school buildings remain; one former hotel is now lived in. The old, wood-frame church was moved in December, 1969 a few miles east on M-61, and a new church built. There is a large, two-story town hall, and one grocery store is still in business. The depot and old mills have been removed.

In 1905 population 400. Had shingle, stave and heading mills, and a Methodist church. W. M. Temple, postmaster.

1918, E. E. Farnham, postmaster.

As the vast acreages of pine dwindled in the area, the mills moved out, leaving their buildings vacant. A huge hame mill was located north of town on the Muskegon River and a railroad spur extended to it. This was approximately on the site of the present State forest campgrounds. Reverse twists in the Muskegon River were so sharp at this point that at one time an engineering feat changed the course of the river at this point to take some of the "kinks" out.

Joe Russell moved the large dry kiln building from its location ° mile west on the river, next to the railroad near the depot and opened a huge grocery store. William Barber was the last owner. He closed shop about 1920.

Scenes such as this were a common, everyday occurrence in northern Michigan after the introduction of rural free delivery in 1898. From that date until about 1910 thousands of post offices were closed. This post office is for sale. Located at *Temple*, Michigan in Clare County, discontinued in 1966. *Bay City Times* - Photo by Richard Hardy.

Until 1927 there was no business place in town, although the post office was continued. In 1927 Anna Crawford opened a store in the old hotel formerly owned by her father, Thomas Crawford, a former riverman during the logging days. She purchased equipment from the vacant Apel store at *Clarence*, 4 miles east. In 1935 she became postmistress, replacing Mrs. Rouse. About 1940 she razed the old hotel and saloon and erected a cement block store building. Shortly after World War II the Ann Arbor Railroad discontinued passenger service and mail was delivered by truck. In 1966 Miss Crawford retired and the post office was discontinued. About 40 people live there today.

––––––––

TONKIN–several residents of Clare County remember *Tonkin* as a sawmill town on the Middle Branch of the Tobacco River in Section 32, Arthur Township. The site of the former village lays ½ mile east of Rogers Road and a short distance north of Poplar Road, on land owned by Glen Blystone (1970).

Alfred Toushe, a Frenchman from Canada, set up a mill on the site in 1891-92, which lasted until the timber was logged off about 1898.

Tousche operated a general store and lumberman's supply, and for one year (1893) had a post office in his store. Before and after that date mail was picked up at *Dover*, about 5 miles southwest.

S. T. Darey and the Tobacco River Lumber Company operated in the area. They purchased logs from local farmers and jobbers. The logs were stamped with the letters "T-O-B-A-C-C-O," one of the few full-name log marks used during the logging days.

A huge dam, 30-feet high, with two sluices was erected on the site and made a small lake above the dam. In 1910 the dam was blasted out to drain the pond.

After Tousche returned to Canada about 1898, the 15 or 20 houses and camp buildings stood vacant. About the turn-of-the-century an immigration of home-steaders from Ohio and Indiana moved into the vacant buildings until they built houses of their own.

Only a few mounds and hollows from the houses and a few rotted pilings of the dam remain today.

––––––––

UPTON–in 1893 on the Muskegon River, Summerfield Township, near the Missaukee County line. Population 100. Mrs. G. Cole, postmistress. Was on the stage line to *Harrison*. Had a hotel, lath and lumber mill, blacksmith shop, machine shop, school, and a store.

_____

WINTERFIELD–in 1883 a post office and settlement established in 1871. Located in Section 16, Winterfield Township, 15 miles north of *Harrison*. The post office was across the road, south of other buildings in Section 21. Located at the junction of the Clam and Muskegon Rivers. Eunice Brewer, postmistress. Had a grocery store, post office, sawmill, blacksmith shop, and other buildings.

_____

Other locations were:

CHAFFEE'S CORNERS–Greenwood Township, E. S. Chaffee & Company, general merchandise.

GREENS–on the P. M. Railroad, 1910 mail *Leota*.

PAGES–7 miles north of *Harrison*. 1910 mail *Harrison*.

ROBINSONS–on the P. M. Railroad. 1910 mail *Lake*.

SUMMITT–on the Ann Arbor Railroad. Mail *Farwell*. In 1910 had a grocery and general store and a hotel.

ARNOLD, *FROST*, and *MARK*–were flag stations on the P. M. Railroad, Meredith Division, north of *Harrison*. Had an unlicensed saloon, etc.

RISKE'S SIDING–was in Franklin Township on the Meredith Railroad.

WHEATLEY–a country post office in Arthur Township. J. Wheatley, postmaster November 15, 1887. Post office discontinued January 31, 1914. In 1905 George Bryan, postmaster.

McKAY–was a flag station on the P. M. Railroad. 1910, mail *Hatton*.

MANN'S SIDING–a station 5 miles south of *Harrison*. In 1900s a boxcar was located on the siding and used for a station.

CAIRNS–listed as a post office in 1890.

MOORE'S SIDING–located about 1 mile north of Lake 13, near present Surrey Road. Log camps of Green & Harter were located there.

Engine and logging train of F. & P. M. Railroad at *Moore's Siding* near *Farwell* in Clare County. Logs from camp of Green & Harter of *Saginaw*. In the 1890s, an average of 20 trains of logs per hour were hauled between *Harrison* and *Clare*. Picture taken in 1896.

74

HACKLEY–a flag station north of Long Lake, in Frost Township.

HENDERSON–was a half-way house and stopover for travelers on the stage between *Marion* and *Houghton Lake*. Near the present Marion Oil Fields and near the Osceola county line.

CLINTONVILLE or *"Clinton"* on railroad timetables–was a short-lived village 10 miles northwest of *Clare*. Daniel Clinton of *Mt. Pleasant* set up a saw and gristmill at the intersection of two creeks in 1883. The main stream is Littlefield Creek. The Ann Arbor Railroad ran a spur to the site. Within a year 25 families had built homes near the mill, where 20 men were employed. In the summer of 1885, 2½ million feet of lumber was piled near the siding.

On Sunday morning, July 3, 1885, while the population made the 4-mile trip to attend church in *Farwell*, the buildings caught fire from a brush fire.

L. L. Kelly, who later became a doctor and moved to *Lansing*, piled women and children on a handcar and went to *Farwell* to get assistance. By the time help arrived it was too late to save anything. No attempt was made to rebuild the settlement. In 1932 Willis Dunlop, who had purchased 80 acres in Section 10, Surrey Township, plowed the site of *Clintonville* under. The farm is owned today by Donal Arts and is located on Harding Avenue, about 1 mile south of Dover Road, and west of the Ann Arbor Railroad.

—————

Picture of *Mitchell Camp #3* in Clare County about 1898 after the big timber had been cut off. Note the narrow-guage track and steam log loader.

Chapter Thirteen

CRAWFORD COUNTY GHOST TOWNS
AND MICHIGAN'S ONLY STAND OF VIRGIN PINE

Mrs. Edward Hartwick of *Ann Arbor* donated the only virgin stand of pine left in Michigan to the State in memory of her husband, Major Edward Hartwick, who was killed in World War I. He was a descendant of Mike Hartwick, one of the original settlers and hotel owner in *Grayling*. Hartwick Pines, a few miles east of *Grayling*, is now a major tourist attraction. It has been developed as a park and museum dedicated to the lumbering industry in Michigan under the direction of Wendell Hoover of the Department of Conservation.

RAILROADS

In 1893 the county was served by the Michigan Central Railroad, Mackinaw Division. *Cheney (Pere Cheney)*, 0; *Grayling*, 8 miles; and *Frederic*, 9 miles.

Another railroad called the G. T. L. & N. extended northeast across the county from *Grayling* to a point near Bear Lake in Montmorency County.

POST OFFICES

Only two post offices remain in the county today, *Grayling* and *Frederic*, which at one time had a population of 500.

GHOST TOWNS

BUCKS–of *Buck's Siding,* was a settlement on the Grayling-Lewiston logging railroad. Logging was in progress in the late 1800s. In 1905 a station on the Twin Lakes Branch of the M. C. Railroad, 11 miles northwest of *Grayling*. Mail to *Lovells*.

———

CHENEY–the railroad name for *"Pere Cheney,"* the postal name of the first county seat, and probably the first settlement. Settled about 1869-70. In 1877 a station on the M. C. Railroad, 28 miles south of Otsego Lake. Population 60. Stewart Hutt, postmaster. G. M. Cheney, sawmill. Had a hotel, wagon shop, blacksmith, grocery store, etc.

In 1905 a post office in Central Plains Township. Population 30. Abner J. Stillwell, postmaster. In 1918 population 18. Mail RFD *Roscommon*, 6 miles south.

Only a few hollows in the ground and a cemetery mark the site.

————

DEWARD–the village was founded and named in honor of David Ward for the sole purpose of timbering off the remains of virgin pine timber after his death in May of 1900. This and one stand in the Upper Peninsula was the last big stand of virgin pine in the State.

Many biographies and stories have been written about David Ward, who at the peak of the lumbering industry owned most of the choice timberlands in the five counties of Crawford, Kalkaska, Antrim, Charlevoix, and Otsego, extending from *Deward* on the south to *Boyne Falls* on the north, and from *Frederic* and *Vanderbilt* on the east, to *Mancelona* and *East Jordan* on the west, an expanse of nearly 50 miles in either direction.

In addition to a school, church, community hall, boardinghouse, hotel and stores, there was a roundhouse, depot, warehouse and other facilities connected with the Detroit & Charlevoix railroad yards over which eight engines steamed day and night delivering nearly ½ million board feet of lumber, the daily output of the sawmills.

The post office was established in 1901; George K. Root, postmaster. At one time the population reached 800. In 1905 it was 25, and contained only a sawmill, store, and hotel.

The village made a comeback for a short time in 1917, and had a population of 191. Had a telephone; S. G. Sedgman, postmaster. The hotel and other business places were open.

After 1918, mail to *Frederic*. Only a few foundations and the old railroad grade remain today.

————

ELDORADO–also known as *"Jackpine,"* was a settlement on McMaster's Bridge Road in the southeast corner of the county. First called *"Jackpine"* and a post office by that name. In 1918, J. F. Crane, postmaster. Mrs. Grace Finch is a native of the area, still living, and the original log cabin of her family remains on the site (1969).

————

HARDGROVE–in 1905 a country post office, 14 miles northeast of *Grayling* and 7 from *Frederic*. Telephone. A. A. Geister, postmaster and general store. 1910 population 50. 1918, located in Forest Township.

JACK PINE–also known as *"Eldorado,"* in 1905 a country post office in South

JACK PINE–also known as *"Eldorado,"* in 1905 a country post office in South Branch Township, 22 miles southeast of *Grayling* and 14 from *Roscommon*. George Hartman, postmaster and farmer.

––––––––

JUDGES–was the post office at Lovell Station on the M. C. Railroad, and on the north branch of the AuSable River. Located on the opposite side of the river from Lovells. Settled about 1881. Mainly a post office, stage stop, and the site of the "Douglas Hotel" (still standing).

In 1905 in Maple Forest Township, 18 miles northeast of *Grayling*. M. A. B. Simms, postmaster. Hotel, boardinghouse, sawmill, etc.

––––––––

LOVELLS–was first settled in 1870 when Charles S. Brink set up a lumber camp on the site. By 1900 had a population of more than 500.

In 1918, population 200, on the M. C. Railroad, Lovells Township, 19 miles northwest of *Grayling*. M. A. B. Simms, postmaster. T. E. Douglas ran a hotel and the North Branch Outing Club.

A large, two-story, well-kept hotel, grocery, gas station, tavern, and barber shop are located on the site of Lovells. The old Douglas Hotel, across the river, is lived in.

––––––––

SIGSBEE–on the North Down River Road, about 10 miles east of *Grayling*, was a post office and settlement from 1900 until about 1930. Was orginally called *"Appenzel"* after a Swiss immigrant. Shown on 1893 railroad maps as *Appenzel*.

In 1918, described as a summer resort. Hugo Schreiber, postmaster. Had a hotel, grocery, and was a headquarters for fishermen. In 1910 the population was 40.

People in the area are latecomers, most of whom moved in since the tourist industry boom of the 1950s. A grocery store and school is near the location.

––––––––

WELLINGTON–in 1905 a country post office in Beaver Creek Township, 8 miles southwest of *Grayling*, and 6 west of *Pere Cheney*. Population 40. H. G. Benedict, postmaster.

In 1918, RFD *Grayling*. Alton Brott, sheep breeder lived there. Nothing remains today.

––––––

Other flag stops and corners were:

ALEXANDER–1910 mail *Grayling*.

AUSABLE RIVER–1910 mail *Frederic*.

HANSON–on the M. C. Railroad, mail *Grayling*.

HARRIGAN–1910 mail *Grayling*.

KNEELANDS–*1*918, a station on the M. C. Railroad, 8 miles northwest of *Grayling*. 1910 mail *Frederic*.

MOOTS.

SMITH'S SIDING–1910 mail *Frederic*.

LONGS.

FORTY PINES.

FORBUSH CORNERS.

KINSLAND SIDING.

RED BRIDGE.

TALBUTS.

BURKES.

FOXTOWN.

STRANGER'S BANKING GROUNDS–site of a lumber mill in the logging days.

––––––

Chapter Fourteen

EMMET COUNTY GHOST TOWNS
AND FORT MICHILIMACKINAC

A historical marker is erected at Mackinaw dedicated to Fort Michilimackinac. *"This fort, built about 1715, put French soldiers at the Straits for the first time since 1701. French authority ceased in 1761 when British troops entered the fort. On June 2, 1763, during Pontiac's uprising, Chippewa Indians seized the fort, killing most of the small force, and held it a year. When the British moved to Mackinac Island in 1781 this old fort soon reverted back to the wilderness."*

Since this plaque was erected in 1958, the fort has been restored under the direction of Dr. Eugene Petersen of *East Lansing*. It is now a major tourist attraction at the foot of Mackinaw Bridge.

RAILROADS

In 1893 the county was served by the Grand Rapids & Indiana Railroad. Beginning at *Petoskey*, 0 miles; *Bay View*, 2 miles; *Conway*, 4 miles; *Oden*, 2 miles; *Alanson*, 3 miles; *Brutus*, 3 miles; *Pellston*, 4 miles; *Levering*, 6 miles; *Carp Lake*, 4 miles; and *Mackinaw City*, 8 miles.

POST OFFICES

During its history the county has had a total of about 30 post offices. Thirteen remain today.

GHOST TOWNS

CROSS VILLAGE–once had a population of nearly 1,000 and today consists of only one store and gas station, a tavern and restaurant combined, and a few unpainted houses in addition to two churches. A town hall, souvenir shop, and post office make up the rest of the few remaining buildings.

The first priests were in the area in 1691. In 1775 the Jesuits abandoned the mission, and in 1799 a cross was erected on the bluff overlooking Lake Michigan.

The first buildings were erected in 1840. They were a frame church, and a log house and cooper shop built by Alexander Gascon, a French Canadian. About 1850 the first buildings were started, and J. C. Glenn a U.S. surveyor, laid out the streets and platted the village in 1859. It was named after the cross erected in 1799.

In 1905 the Holy Cross School was built and served 100 Indian families and 23 white families until it was razed in 1966. In 1918 a fire destroyed more than half the buildings. The present Presbyterian church was built in 1921. In February, 1970, fire destroyed the rectory and damaged the historic Holy Cross Church, built in 1895.

In 1877 the population was 800. In LaCroix Township, 22 miles north of *Little Traverse (Harbor Springs)*, to which it has weekly stage. In that year there were two sawmills, a gristmill, Catholic church and school. Fish, wood, and maple sugar were shipped. There were also three general stores, a shoe shop, blacksmith shop, and extensive docks. L. G. Metevier operated a sawmill in the village in 1847-48. Mary B. Shurtleff was postmistress in 1877.

In 1865 the first white family, that of Captain John Wagley, arrived. In 1869 he built the first dock. In that year the post office was established.

There are no historical plaques near the village. One old, dilapidated, weather-beaten house with the yard overgrown to weeds bears a small sign stating the house was built in 1848 by Chief Joseph Nawinashkote, who bought 80 acres in 1846.

The school was closed a few years ago and only a few children of school age live there; less than a dozen.

In 1905 there were three churches. Sarah King, postmistress. There was a fishing fleet, flour mill, blacksmith shop, lumber camp and supply store, saloon, and other buildings.

AYR–Maple River Township, 13 miles northeast of *Petoskey* and 3½ miles west of *Brutus*. In 1905 population 25. P. J. Burns, postmaster. Had one sawmill. 1910 population 60, RFD *Alanson*.

BLISS–in Bliss Township, 7 miles from *Levering*. 1910 population 75. In 1918, 31. Gideon Noel, postmaster.

CECIL–1905 population 150. In Carp Lake Township, 8 miles south of *Mackinaw City* and 14 from *St. Ignace*. Daily mail. W. W. Bruce, postmaster. General store, lumbermen's supply, saw and shingle mill. 1918 population 250.

ELY–the post office for *"Bogardus Station"* on the G. R. & I. Railroad in Center Township, 5 miles from *Pellston*. In 1905, Lena Yettaw, assistant postmistress. W. R. Kussel, mayor. Had a flour mill, school, blacksmith, grocery, etc. In 1918 send mail to *Pellston*. Discontinued post office in 1910.

———

EPSILON–Littlefield Township, 8 miles east of *Petoskey*. In 1910 population 30. RFD *Conway*. V. E. Talladay & Company, general store.

———

GOOD HART–in 1877 the post office at *"Middle Village,"* both shown on present day maps. In that year population 100 (three-fourths of which were Indians), in Cross Village Township on the shore of Lake Michigan, 13 miles north of *Little Traverse*, the county seat. Had a Catholic church, Indian school, and a store. Mrs. Julia Cole, postmistress. Two stores, a doctor, and blacksmith shops.

In 1905 population 100, all whites. Located in Redmond Township, 7 miles southwest of *Cross Village*. Stage daily to *Harbor Springs*. Lowell Lamkin, post-master, general store, meats, wholesale fish, saw and feed mill. Also a shoe shop. Additions to the directory for 1918 included the "Old Trail Tavern," and V. A. Pool, express agent.

Only one small store remains in the one-time village, which includes the post office.

———

LITTLEFIELD–in 1905 a farmer's post office in Springvale Township, 11 miles east of *Petoskey*. On daily stage route from *Wildwood* to *Petoskey*. Ernest J. Hyatt, postmaster. In 1910, mail to *Epsilon*.

———

LAKEWOOD–in 1905 population 150. On the G. R. & I. Railroad, McKinley Township, 24 miles from *Petoskey*. John R. Neilan, postmaster. Had a lumber company and general store. In 1910, RFD *Levering*.

———

LARKS–in 1905 a country post office in Center Township, 10 miles northwest of *Pellston*. Daily mail. In 1910, mail RFD *Pellston*.

———

LITTLE TRAVERSE –(name changed to *"Harbor Springs"*)–in 1877: *"The county seat, 10 miles north of Petoskey, the northern terminus of the G. R. & I. Railroad.*

Settled by Catholic missionaries in 1827. Population 400. The county is settled largely by Indians. Daily stage to Charlevoix. Andrew J. Blackbird, postmaster. Philo Christley runs the ferry between Petoskey and Little Traverse."

Today *Harbor Springs* is a resort center; has extensive boat marinas, shops, stores, and the old depot has been converted into an exclusive dress shop.

MOSSVILLE–was a post office in 1877.

PLEASANT VIEW–in Pleasant View Township in 1905, population 70. Settled in 1876, eight miles north of *Harbor Springs*. Daily stage. A. C. Willis, postmaster. In 1910, RFD *Harbor Springs*.

READMOND–in Readmond Township, 9 miles north of *Harbor Springs*. 1905, send mail to *Cross Village*.

WEQUETONSING–was and is now a summer resort on Little Traverse Bay. In 1905 Harriette L. Judd, postmistress. Now a branch of *Harbor Springs* post office.

WA-WAT-AM BEACH–in 1918 a summer resort on the Straits of Mackinaw, 1½ miles from *Mackinaw City*.

Other place names:

CANBY–in 1910 mail *Levering*.

CARPENTER–1910 a discontinued post office on the P. M. Railroad, 6 miles from *Petoskey*.

LAKE GROVE and *SUTTMANSVILLE*.

Chapter Fifteen

GLADWIN COUNTY GHOST TOWNS

RAILROADS

In 1890 the Gladwin Division of the Michigan Central Railroad ran from *Bay City* to *Gladwin*. It entered the county on the east, extending west from *Pinconning*: *Rhodes*, 0 miles; *Smiths*, 3 miles; *Hawes Bridge*, 6 miles; *Howrys*, 12 miles; and *Gladwin*, 17 miles.

The railroad was discontinued about 1951 and the tracks removed in 1965.

A branch of the Pere Marquette once connected *Coleman* and *Beaverton*. The train arrived in *Beaverton* each morning, coming from *Harrison* via *Coleman*, and returned each evening to *Harrison*.

At one time another railroad extended south from *Gladwin* to *Coleman*.

Many other narrow-gauge railroads, used for transporting logs, served the county. One line, owned by Wells & Stone Lumber Company, extended from *Meredith* to *Butman* in the north part of the county. Also a line from *Achill* and *Nester*, in Roscommon County, to the Sugar River.

GHOST TOWNS

ARBUTUS–was a settlement in Buckeye Township, 9 miles from *Gladwin* and 7 from *Beaverton*. The first grocery store was opened in 1890. In 1905 the post office was established. Oliver choose the name *"Sugar Town,"* but the postal department requested another name, so he chose *Arbutus*.

1910 population 25. Had a sawmill and a school. RFD *Beaverton*.

———

BARD–in Beaverton Township, 10 miles southwest of *Gladwin*. Settled in 1890. First school built in 1893. John M. Bard, postmaster, March 19, 1902. George Booth, general store and postmaster from November 23, 1903 until discontinued June 15, 1907. William Tubbs was first postmaster.

Bard was the site of a trading post for bartering between fur buyers and Indians until late 1800s. As late as 1905 one of several lumber camps was active. Also a sawmill, shingle mill, and barrel hoop factory on the Tobacco River.

A stone school building, that replaced the first one, still stands.

———

BOMANVILLE–in Sheridan Township, 18 miles northeast of *Gladwin*, had a large lumber mill, shingle and stave mill. Lumber was shipped out by train on the "Bomanville Line" until 1910 when the mills moved out and the tracks were removed.

Was a post office from 1908 to 1912. 1905, Lewis S. David, postmaster. Also a general store and a school, located some distance from the village.

———

BUTMAN–Wells & Stone Lumber Company ran a narrow-gauge railroad from *Meredith* to *Butman* in 1883. In that year population 100. In 1884 Amos Wagar, postmaster. Had sawmills, grocery, blacksmith shop, town hall (finished April 12, 1894), and a Gleaner's Hall. Railroad tracks were removed about 1912 and post office discontinued. Located in the northeast corner of Section 7, R2W, T20N.

———

ESTEY–in Bentley Township, 18 miles southeast of *Gladwin* and in the southeast part of the county, was settled about 1890. In 1895 the business district was two blocks long, lined with buildings. Estey & Calkins operated a large sawmill. Also a large barrel hoop factory.

1905 population 100. Church, stores, hotel, saloon, and blacksmith shop. In 1920 discontinued as a village. Post office closed about 1921.

In 1948 a new town hall was built. Now contains a grocery, gas station, and a supermarket.

———

GROUT–never got off the ground as a village, but was once considered for the location of the county seat. First settlers came in March, 1863. In 1886 a plank road was built from *Coleman* on the stage route to *Gladwin*. Had a half-way house and hotel for a stage stop.

Grout school and cemetery in Section 10, R2W, T20N.

———

HIGHWOOD–was first called the *"Oliver Settlement."* Later it was named *"Hawes Bridge"* after a man of that name who fell from the bridge and was killed.

In 1877 had a boardinghouse. In 1888 post office applied for and called *"Highwood."* Located in Buckeye Township until 1910 when Hay Township was organized. At one time had a hotel, school, and three large stores. Four passenger trains a day stopped at the village.

George Sprowl, who moved there in November 1887 and was the first postmaster, was kicked by a horse and died in April of 1900. The post office closed in 1912.

Located in Section 26, on the M. C. Railroad grade near the Tittabawassee River.

In 1905 J. L. Robbins, postmaster. Had a general store and shingle mill. 1918 population 200. Hotel, two general stores, shingle mill, etc. Julia A. L. Robbins, postmistress.

Became a resort called *"Whitney Beach"* near the site of the former village in the 1920s.

————

HOCKADAY (sometimes spelled *"Hocaday"*)–was a village in Butman Township, about 10 miles north of *Gladwin*. On County Road 584, two miles east of Butman School, District No. 3.

In 1901 post office established. Robert Hockaday, postmaster.

In 1905, R. M. Hockaday, postmaster. Had a general store, butcher shop, and saw and shingle mill, 1 mile east. Also a saw and gristmill in the village.

1918 population 50. Post office closed in 1912.

————

LYLE–in 1905 on the Pere Marquette Railroad, Beaverton Township, 14 miles southwest of *Beaverton*. Population 150. Fred Drake, postmaster. Aaron T. Bliss of *Saginaw* established a sawmill and lumber camp 1 mile south of the railroad, called *"Halfway"* in 1892.

Name changed to *Lyle* when the post office was established in 1905.

After 1910 mail received RFD *Beaverton*. Railroad removed in 1943.

————

McCLURE–7 miles northeast of *Gladwin*, in Gladwin Township. Named for a lumberman, William C. McClure. Store and post office established in 1889. The store burned in 1896, the following year another store was built across the road, using the old stables. This store stands today with living quarters in the rear. Present school built in 1891, still standing.

The post office was discontinued in 1901. Had a sawmill and hoop mill. In 1918 had a store, Methodist church, and school. Located in Section 15, four miles south of *Hockaday*, R1W, T20N.

––––––––––

NEW HEADQUARTERS–also called *"Millsville"* and *"Shotgun Corners."* Was on the corner of Grass Lake Road and Butman Road near Grass Lake. Settled in 1878. Had a post office until 1884 until other places were settled. Several families lived there at one time.

––––––––––

OBERLIN–is a four-corners on M-18 between *Skeels* and *Meredith*. Named by a Baptist minister after one of his friends. Post office established in 1902. Fred Reithel, Sr. had the store and post office for 45 years. Was a post office until 1949.

In 1918 a farmer's post office in Sherman Township. Had a store and sawmill.

––––––––––

SKEELS–shown on most road maps. Is four-corners on M-18, twelve miles north of *Gladwin*, in Sherman Township. First settled in 1887. When the *Meredith* post office closed in 1892 (see Clare County) Simon Skeels applied for a post office and became postmaster. At one time had a sawmill, store, church, and a stone school built in 1905.

In 1969 the old church was torn down and a new one built. A gas station remains on the corner and the school is now an antique shop.

––––––––––

WAGARVILLE–a grocery store, Methodist church, a few houses, and the weed-covered foundation of a former hotel are all that remain of this one-time village 4 miles north of *Gladwin* and 1 mile east of M-18, at Wagarville and Nickless Roads.

First called *"Ridgeville,"* was founded May 15, 1872. The church, still standing, was built in 1885. In 1905 contained a hotel, two large boardinghouses, a creamery, and a tall building shaped like a lighthouse that towered above the other buildings.

There was also a cheese factory, general store, saw and shingle mill, two black-smith shops, the Presbyterian church, and several homes.

In 1922 a fire destroyed most of the buildings. The livery stable was saved and used as part of the creamery, which was rebuilt.

————

Other places were:

DECATUR BRIDGE–in 1905, four miles southeast of *Gladwin*.

DALE–formerly *"Tobacco,"* in 1905 a discontinued post office, Tobacco Township, 4 miles southeast of *Beaverton*. Section 16 on the Tobacco River, R1W, T17N. Had a grocery store, sawmill, string band, and several buildings. Post office from 1900 to 1901. In 1910 population 50, RFD *Beaverton*.

SUGAR RAPIDS–in 1918 population 30, eleven miles north of *Gladwin*, mail to *Hocaday*. Was a post office in 1908. Sugar River Store is near the site today (1970).

SMITH'S CREEK–1 mile north of M-61 near Frost Lake was a sawmill town in 1880s. In 1881 had a sawmill. First school opened in 1886. Church built in 1904. Church abandoned and rapidly deteriorating (1970).

RHODES–although it has a modern post office, is a ghost town. One grocery and a tavern are in operation. Other old buildings, the hotel, large general store, and other business buildings are now either abandoned or used as residences.

In 1918 population 100, on the M. C. Railroad, Bentley Township, 16 miles southeast of *Gladwin*. Methodist church (still standing), bank, railroad station, black-smith shop, restaurant, hardware, hotel, livery stables, large elevator, and other buildings.

RAYMONDS–in 1910 mail *Sterling*.

WHEATLEY–Grout Township, RFD *Gladwin*. Had a general store in 1918.

CEDAR–name changed to *"Gladwin"* when the post office was established, due to so many villages using the name.

————

Chapter Sixteen

GRAND TRAVERSE COUNTY GHOST TOWNS AND THE TOUGHEST RAILROAD JUNCTION IN MICHIGAN

RAILROADS

Railroads serving the county in 1906 were the Elk Rapids Branch of the Pere Marquette: *Williamsburg*, 0 miles; *Angell*, 4 miles; *Elk Rapids*, 9 miles.

Grand Rapids to *Bayview* Branch of Pere Marquette: *Interlochen*, 0 Miles; *Grawn*, 4 miles; *Beitners*, 3 miles; *Boardman*, 6 miles; *Traverse City*, 1 mile; *Acme*, 5 miles; *Bates*, 4 miles; and *Williamsburgh*, 2 miles.

Manistee & Northeastern Railroad: *Manistee*, 0 miles; *Karlin*, 39 miles; *Wylies*, 5 miles; *Interlochen*, 1 mile; *Filer's Switch*, 2 miles; *Platte River*, 2 miles; *Lake Ann*, 3 miles; *Cedar Run*, 3 miles; *Solon*, 4 miles; *Fouchs*, 3 miles; *Hatch's Crossing*, 2 miles; *Grelickville*, 3 miles; and *Traverse City*, 3 miles.

Grand Rapids and Indiana Railroad-Northern Division: *Mackinaw City*, 0 miles; *South Boardman*, 97 miles; *Fife Lake*, 5 miles; *Walton Junction*, 5 miles.

Grand Rapids & Indiana Railroad-Traverse City Branch: *Walton Junction*, 0 miles; *Summit City*, 7 miles; *Kingsley*, 10 miles; *Mayfield*, 13 miles; *Slights*, 18 miles; *Keystone*, 20 miles; *Traverse City*, 26 miles; and *Hatch's Crossing*, 32 miles.

POST OFFICES

Grand Traverse County had at least 28 post offices during its history. Nine remain today.

GHOST TOWNS

ANGELL–in 1905 population 75. On the P. M. Railroad, Whitewater Township, 13 miles northeast of *Traverse City* and 4 miles from *Elk Rapids*. George F. Frink, postmaster. Had a lath mill and other businesses. In 1910 population 45. Mail to *Elk Rapids*.

BATES–in 1905 George Whitson, postmaster. Had an express agent and grocery store. 1918 population 25. J. E. Langworth, postmaster. On the P. M. Railroad, Acme Township.

———

CEDAR RUN (see Benzie County)–at one time in Benzie and another time in Grand Traverse.

———

EAST BAY–in 1877 a post office at the head of the eastern arm of Grand Traverse Bay, 4 miles east of *Traverse City*. Population 40. M. Mahan, postmaster. Had boardinghouse, shingle and sawmill, blacksmith shop, etc. Not a post office in 1890.

———

GRAWN–in 1905 population 300. On the P. M. Railroad, Blair Township, 9 miles southwest of *Traverse City*. H. C. Burt, postmaster. Had a depot, two sawmills, shingle mill, barber shop, drug store, three general stores, produce company, hardware and general store, meat market, saloon, hotel and livery, two livery and feed barns, and a millinery shop.

The remains of the village is on M-31, two miles west of M-37. When the M-31 pavement was built it bisected the village, leaving the Methodist Church on the north side of the road. Many of the old buildings remain, all badly in need of repair. The old hotel stands at the corner of State and Brook Streets, the main corners. Other than an occasional thin coat of white paint nothing has been done to alter the exterior. Each time it changed hands the new owner painted the name of his business over the last name. It is now a grocery and liquor store.

The old blacksmith shop and livery stable stands next to the former hotel, a wood-frame building, and hasn't been used for years. Across from the livery stable is an old, two-story frame house that contains the post office.

Another long, low wood building about 60 by 100 feet stands deserted, and looks as though it could have been a mill or lumber yard.

The town was originally laid out in about 20 blocks. The store, or old hotel, and the site of the former depot and express office now lie in a triangle, due to another blacktop road that cuts across to *Monroe Center* to the south.

The original Silver Lake Grange Hall still stands on State Street. There are probably 25 or 30 permanent residents.

––––––––

HANNAH–in 1918 a discontinued post office, Mayfield Township, 14 miles south of *Traverse City* and 6 west of *Kingsley*. Mail RFD *Kingsley*. Frank Koepel, general store.

The remains of what was the village lays along M-13, a blacktop road between *Kingsley* and *Fife Lake*. The old, two-story general store still stands, but looks like a slight breeze would blow it away. The huge frame building, about 60 feet wide and more than 100 feet long, is unpainted and weather-beaten. Adjoining the building on the east is a large, two-story house, nearly as big as the store. It too is in a rundown condition. (Note: These buildings were bulldozed and razed in June, 1970).

West of the former store stands an enormous three-story, square house built in the same style. Huge poplar trees, probably 100 years old stand along the road near the store building. The nearly dead trees and abandoned buildings give a forlorn and ghostly aura to the settlement. A small metal road sign marks the road at each approach to the village. The faded letters *"Hannah"* are visible.

By the time this is written the old house described above may also be gone. A complex of church and school buildings, all very modern, stand east of the store buildings and are operated by the St. Mary's Catholic Church Diocese. A short distance beyond the church is a farm with well-kept buildings. Adjacent to the farm drive stands an old cider mill painted red and kept in good condition.

––––––––

KEYSTONE–was a post office as early as 1901 until 1905. In that year population 100, a station on the G. R. & I. Railroad, Blair Township, 6° miles south of *Traverse City*. Charles Cedersten, postmaster. Had a sawmill, two grocery stores, shingle mill, brick yards, etc. 1910 RFD *Traverse City*. A Keystone Road and Keystone Pond are the only remains today.

––––––––

LAKE BREWSTER–in 1905 on Brewster Lake, Mayfield Township, 16 miles south of *Traverse City* and 3 from *Kingsley*, its mailing point. Was a post office in 1890.

––––––––

MABLE–platted in 1893. In 1905 on the P. M. Railroad, in Whitewater Township, 15 miles east of *Traverse City*. B. J. Hoyt, postmaster. Had a shingle mill, general store, shipped railroad ties, poles, etc.

The post office was discontinued shortly after 1912.

————

MAPLETON–shown on 1968 State highway map on M-37 between *Traverse City* and *Old Mission*. In 1877 was a post office on the point of land separating the eastern and western arms of Traverse Bay, 12 miles north of *Traverse City*. Was a post office in 1890. In 1905 discontinued. RFD *Traverse City*.

————

MAYFIELD–in 1877 a station on the G. R. & I. Railroad, 27 miles from *Walton*, and 14 miles from *Traverse City*. Located in Paradise Township, population 100. Settled in 1868. Charles A. Denniston, postmaster. Had hotel, store, and sawmill.

In 1905 population 100. L. K. Gibbs, postmaster. Had general store, saw and shingle mill, hotel railroad station, shingle mill, and other mills in the area.

1910 population 87. 1918, 75. Addie A. Gibbs, postmistress. Post office discontinued about 1927.

————

MONROE CENTER–in 1877 in Blair Township 12 miles south of *Traverse City*. Settled in 1859. Population 200. W. H. Brownshon, postmaster (could be Bronson). Had hotel, several sawmills, boot and shoe store, grocery, and church.

In 1905 in Blair and Green Townships, 3½ miles from *Grawn*. Charles B. Dye, postmaster. Blacksmith shop, feed mill, and boat livery had been added. Population 1910, 57. RFD *Grawn*.

————

NEAL–was a post office in 1890 and in 1901. In Long Lake Township at the north end of Long Lake, 8 miles west of *Traverse City*. In 1905 a discontinued post office. RFD *Traverse City*.

————

NE-AH-TA-WAN-TA–meaning "placid waters," was a summer resort between

93

Old Mission and *Traverse City* in Peninsula Township. In 1905 on the P. M. Railroad, address *Traverse City*.

———

OLD MISSION–in 1877 a post office in Peninsula Township, 20 miles north of *Traverse City*. Two churches. No manufacturing. George W. Hedden, postmaster. Had one general store.

———

PARADISE–name changed to *"Kingsley."* In 1877 was the post office at *Kingsley Station* on the G. R. & I. Railroad, 4 miles from the junction with the main line. J. W. Kingsley, postmaster. In 1884 an unincorporated village, population 156. Incorporated as a village in 1890.

———

SUMMIT CITY–in 1877 a station on the G. R. & I. Railroad, 19 miles southeast of *Traverse City*. In Paradise Township. Oscar P. Carver, general store and station agent. Had other stores and a sawmill.

———

WALTON–not much remains of this once important railroad station where passeners on the old G. R. & I. Railroad at one time disembarked to change trains for *Traverse City* on the line extending from *Cadillac* to *Petoskey*.

Walton is still shown on Michigan highway maps, but the bar, gas station, and few houses along US-131 are some distance east of where the giant Stornach Lumber Company built a company store in 1872 and a few years later Robert Knaggs built a hotel called the "Walton House."

In the 1870s there were three hotels. One owned by J. C. Church, another by Robert Knaggs, who was also postmaster, and the Brownson House. *Walton*, near the Wexford County line, was the only place between *Traverse City* and *Cadillac* where thousands of thirsty lumberjacks could buy a drink.

Some of the toughest lumberjacks and river hogs in the north celebrated at *Walton Junction*. On days during the winter when the jacks were unable to work in the woods, they came in by trainloads from *Traverse City, Cadillac*, and the Boardman and Manistee Rivers to see which camp could whip the other.

In 1905 surrounding land was opened to farming and the village, reached a population of 250. One hotel, the "Union House," was still open and Henry

Some of the toughest lumberjacks in Michigan met at *Walton Junction* during the logging days to see which camp could whip the other and who could hold the most liquor. These two jacks took time out from a binge to pose at the local photo studio for a picture dressed as a blacksmith and his helper. Note the phony chisel and horse-shoe welded together and bed sheet used as a backdrop.

Hoerl operated a saloon. Robert Waltz was postmaster. There was also a cheese factory and a factory that made potato and peach pit planters. Several other places were doing business.

Although the old siding rails remain in place, a huge iron rail locks the switch. Some of the tourists and summer residents fish in a small lake across the tracks where the depot once stood. Several foundations of old buildings remain, and a few old houses. Only a few people live in the one-time village.

––––––––

WHITEWATER–in 1877 a discontinued post office. Address *Acme*.

––––––––

Chapter Seventeen

IOSCO COUNTY GHOST TOWNS AND MICHIGAN'S MOST SPECTACULAR GHOST TOWN IN HISTORY

RAILROADS

In 1893 the county was served by the AuSable & Northwestern Railroad that extended from *McKinley* to *AuSable*: *McKinley*, 0 miles; *North Branch*, 4 miles; *Grams Crossing*, 6 miles; *Flat Rock*, 8 miles; *Bamfield*, 12 miles; *Chevrier*, 15 miles; *Vaughn*, 17 miles; *Batton*, 19 miles; *Bryant*, 21 miles; *Beadle*, 27 miles; *Doan*, 29 miles; *Tucker*, 37 miles; and *AuSable*, 40 miles.

The Detroit, Bay City & Alpena Railroad, extending from *Alger* to *Alpena* entered the county at *Whittemore*, 19 miles; *Emery Junction*, 23 miles; *Arn*, 25 miles; *Hale*, 29 miles; *East Tawas*, 35 miles; *Bristol*, 38 miles; *AuSable-Oscoda*, 49 miles.

POST OFFICES

Iosco county had at least 18 post offices during its history. Only 8 remain today.

GHOST TOWNS

AUSABLE–the story of *AuSable*, once a prosperous incorporated city of nearly 10,000 population, make this city the most spectacular ghost town in the State.

First settled in 1851, until 1857 all mail was addressed either to *Bay City* or *Tawas*. The first post office was established in 1857. Elijiah Grandy was the first postmaster. In 1879 the post office was moved to *Oscoda*, on the opposite side of the river. In 1877 it was again moved to *AuSable* and James E. Forrest appointed postmaster. George P. Warner, former postmaster, retained that position at *Oscoda*.

The first docks were built in 1868. The first sawmill was built in 1873 and four years later burned to the ground. In 1877 described as situated at the mouth of the AuSable River, incorporated as a village on October 15, 1872. *"The population at present numbers about 1,500. The lumber interest occupies most of the people. Six large sawmills are engaged in the manufacture of lumber, one sash and blind fac-*

97

tory, three stores, three hotels, three churches, a bank and other interests. During the navigation season shipments are made via Bay City. Lumber, timber, salt and fish are exported."

Some business listings for that year included the AuSable River Boom Company (sorting logs); Brady & Buhl, saloon; Cowie & Murphy, fish dealers; John Dempsey, billiard hall; John Egan, saloon; John W. Glennie, customs collector and banker; Mrs. M. McGarity, proprietor of "Hawkins House"; J. D. Holmes & Company, fish dealers; Peter Shien & Company, owners of the "Lee House"; and John C. Angus, Peter J. McDonald and McCormick had the rest of the extensive saloon and billiard business cornered. David Murdock, fish dealer; George Orth, boots and shoes; J. E. Potts & Company, sawmill; Mrs. Miliss Steward & Company, liquor dealers; and Philip Yakey, hotel.

Edna M. Otis, in her booklet *Their Yesterdays- AuSable and Oscoda, 1848-1948* said: *"Felix O'Toole was one of the most colorful characters who ever hit AuSable. He dressed like a 'dandy' but was well-liked by everyone. He was a natural-born leader and soon had a hand in every type of business there was at the time. He was a promoter, land speculator, horse trader, and business man. He hired many fishermen, paid fair wages and made a fair profit."*

In addition to one of the main streets named in his honor there was also the O'Toole block, O'Toole's Hall (which was the Masonic Lodge hall in 1868), his own general store on the main street, and several other business places.

In 1877 the Loud Company owned two sawmills, two salt blocks, a huge dock, several railroad lines, a line of tow barges, and large holdings of standing pine. Along with other lumbermen of their day enough lumber was cut at *AuSable* within a 30-year period to build a board fence 8 feet high that would encircle the world 20 times at the equator.

In that year the Loud Company had ten camps operating in the woods. In 1872, 400 men were employed in the mills at *AuSable*. During his two terms in Congress George A. Loud proposed a bill which established the Huron National Forest.

In 1891 the Louds ran seven log trains a day over their AuSable Northwestern Railroad. The Loud family practically built the eventual city of *AuSable*, and in the end were mainly responsible for its downfall and total disappearance.

By 1884 *AuSable* had taken on the shape of a city. The main street, O'Toole Street, was 1 mile long and lined on each side with business houses and boardwalks. Fishing in the Great Lakes was at its peak and the many mills were humming 24-hours-a-day. Fifteen saloons were bursting at the seams with business, not only from *AuSable* and travelers who came in by boat and train, but also the entire drinking population of Oscoda swarmed the town on nights and weekends. *Oscoda*, which wasn't platted until 1867, had a restrictive clause prohibiting spirits or intoxicating beverages. With only the river separating the two cities it is unfortunate they couldn't have joined. Today it would be a large metropolis.

The beginning of the end for *AuSable* began on a hot summer day in 1884. As one old-timer put it, *"If that dock-walloper had kept his kid home where she belonged everything would be hunky-dory!"*

The dockworker referred to was a Mr. Shippey, who came home for lunch every day from the nearby docks where he worked. One noon he arrived home at the usual time and his wife discovered there was no meat for dinner. She gave her 6-year-old daughter, Laura, some money and told her to run downtown to the meat market and buy some frankfurters. As the little girl neared the market she was skipping along on the walk when she tripped on a broken plank and broke her leg. A few days later her father appeared at the village council meeting and asked for $150 to pay for the doctor bill incurred from the accident. The city fathers said they would take it under advisement and he returned home.

Sometime later, after hearing nothing from the city council, he contacted a lawyer. The lawyer said he would gladly take the case on a percentage fee basis. He asked the city for $2,000 damages. About the same time, the city was in the process of improving the city waterworks.

After some time passed the case was taken to court and a Circuit Court Jury awarded the Shippeys $2,000 in damages. The city then requested a bond issue of $15,000, which was approved by the voters. This money was to include the price of improvements plus the damage award to Shippey.

Although *AuSable* was a booming city and there was no doubt that payments could be made on the bond issue, another unfortunate incident occurred. H. M. Loud conducted most of the lumber business in the area. His mills were a part of the city environs and produced much of the revenue to meet its operating costs. He successfully petitioned the State to have his landholdings removed from the city limits, therefore removing them from the city tax rolls. When the bonds became redeemable in 1980, the city was unable to meet their obligations.

A short time later, in July of 1911, another disaster struck the city. Fire raged through the city uncontrolled for several days. During the holocaust a lumber barge took 300 women and children aboard and docked out in Lake Huron to save them from the fire. At the same time the twin city of *Oscoda* was also caught up in flames. When the fire finally was brought under control only 12 houses and two school buildings remained in *AuSable*.

For every $1 of assessed valuation in the city, each person was assessed $9 for payment on the bond issue at compound interest. By 1929 there were only 50 residents within the corporate limits. They disorganized as a city to avoid suit.

An article in the *Kansas City Times*, dated December 31, 1929, stated that $90,000 was owed to the Union Trust Company of *Kansas City* by the City of *AuSable*. When a family gave up their property and moved from the city limits to avoid the enormous taxes, the property was immediately taken over by the AuSable Land Company, who eventually owned most of the property. This company was formed by the Trust Company as the only means to realize any payment on the huge debt.

Thus ended *AuSable* which had been a town for three-quarters-of-a-century. Settled in 1850, before the Civil War, incorporated as a village October 15, 1872, and as a city in 1889, died in 1920, and buried in 1929.

In 1917 *AuSable* still had a population of nearly 200. The business directory for that year listed Edward J. Betz, fisherman; Colbath Brothers, fishermen; Gillingham Brothers Fishing Company; Alexander Hagland, fisherman; Oscar Hurket, fish; Joseph Miller, fish; Winn Seeley, fisherman; and James and Jesse Spencer, fishermen.

AuSable, founded as a fishing town in 1848, once more became a fishing town. Frank Light and Louis LaVoie, operated grocery stores; W. H. Dickinson operated the Lake View Hotel; and Winn Seeley ran a general store.

The streets of *AuSable* today bear street signs with the same names as when the town was platted. US-23, a main, paved highway, runs parallel with the shore of Lake Huron and crosses a bridge overlooking the one-time city. Two original fishery buildings remain standing near the mouth of the river. Two or three boats still operate from there on the lakes, but most of the time the patched nets are left rolled on huge reels, overgrown with weeds.

One vacant store building stands near the river bank next to the old steel bridge that the city bonded themselves for in 1879 and crosses the river to *Oscoda*. An empty gas station, in a rapid state of decay, overhangs a curve on the "old highway" that once ran through the deserted city. Many of the lots are now graced with modernistic, ranch-style homes lining O'Toole Street, once lined with business buildings and boardwalks.

The rotted hull of a fishing boat stands lone sentinel of the great fishing fleet that once was. Blowing sand and reeds cover the site of the docks and mills that overlooked Lake Huron during the lumbering days. These are the remains of the once roaring, booming, proud city of *AuSable*.

––––––––

ALABASTER–shown on Michigan highway maps in 1877 *"on the west shore of Saginaw Bay, 5½ miles south of Tawas City and 35 miles northeast of Standish. Population 300. Gypsum and staves are the main exports. Daily stage to Standish during winter. George R. Beard, postmaster."* Had two hotels, a plaster works, and general store.

1905 population 600. Settled in 1863, in Alabaster Township and on the Detroit & Mackinac Railroad. Thomas G. McCausland, postmaster. Had three fisheries, wagonmaker, hotel, sawmill, plaster works, and general store.

1918 population 400. *"Settled in 1854. Has Catholic, Lutheran and Methodist churches. H. E. Miller, postmaster."* Two stores and a hotel.

One church and a few houses are located in the vicinity today. There are no business places.

––––––––

EDSON–was a sawmill settlement in Grant Township, 8 miles west of *Tawas City.* In 1905 a farmer's post office. E. M. Raymond, postmaster. Had blacksmith shop, two sawmills and a shingle factory. In 1918 a discontinued post office.

––––––––

EMERY JUNCTION–in Sherman Township, was a post office and important railroad center from about 1890 until about 1928, when the name was changed to *"National City."*

1905, six miles north of *Turner.* Q. C. Martin, postmaster. Had a brick factory, sawmill, hotel, livery, and shingle mill.

In 1918 population 100. On the D. & M. Railroad at the junction of the Rose City and Prescott Branches. Hotel, telephone company, general store, station agent, hotel, and livery.

ELLAKE–name changed to *"Long Lake,"* settled about 1880. In 1893 the "Turtle Route" of the D. & M. Railroad ran through the village. It was later called the *"Rose City Division."* A depot was built in 1905. The railroad was abandoned April 16, 1930. At one time large shipments of ice were shipped by rail, then via boat to southern cities.

First post office established about 1895. In 1908 Frank Eymer was postmaster. Name changed to *Long Lake* in 1924.

In 1918, 27 miles northwest of *Tawas City* and 5 from *Hale*. Three stores and a real estate dealer.

————

MCIVOR–1918 population 25. On the D. & M. Railroad, Sherman Township, 9 miles southwest of *Tawas*. G. A. Pringle, postmaster. Had general store, hotel, and livery.

————

OGEMAW–described in 1877 as a settlement in Grant Township, 8 miles west of *Tawas City*.

————

SILOAM–in Reno Township, midway between *National City* and *Hale*. In 1905 on a spur of the D. & M. Railroad. Population 100. J. P. Covin, postmaster. U. G. Colvin, general store. Had a shoe and harness shop and two schoolteachers.

1918 population 50. J. F. Sibley, postmaster. Two general stores. Listed on railroad timetables as *"Cooper's Crossing."*

————

WILBER–7½ miles north of *Tawas City* in Wilber Township. Was a post office in 1890 and township population was 299.

In 1905 A. Corner, postmaster. Two grocery stores, saw and feedmill, dentist, doctor, meat market, etc.

1918, population 20. Mrs. Clara G. Alder, postmistress. Had three blacksmiths, thresher, millinery shop, and grocery store.

————

Other places were:

DOAN–1910, mail *AuSable*.

FIVE CHANNELS–in 1918 a recently established post office.

TURTLE and *VAUGHN*–flag stations on the D. & M. Railroad.

ROBINSON–1910, mail *Alabaster*.

SLINGERLAND–mail *Alabaster*.

SERRADELLA–in 1918 a recently established post office 23 miles northeast of *Tawas* and on the D. & M. Railroad

SPENCER'S MILL–1877, a settlement in Plainfield Township, 10 miles northwest of *Tawas City*.

TAFT–a flag station on the D. & M. Railroad, mail to *Siloam*.

BAMFIELD and *BRYANT*–were stations or stops on the AuSable & North Western Railroad, a narrow-gauge track extending from *AuSable* to *Commins*, in Oscoda County. In 1908 Charlie Cote, a Frenchman, was the only inhabitant of *Bryant*. Orral A. Wardlow, now living at *Glennie* (1970), said Charlie could feed and sleep half-a-dozen people and his place was "modestly" famous for his pea soup.

Wardlow said Harry Garrett and Ray Rose were supervisors on the railroad. *"The train, which made one round trip daily, was made up of 20 to 25 bunk cars for hauling logs, and whatever boxcars were needed to haul freight, which was not much. The daily arrival of this train at Glennie was something to look forward to and greeted by the whole town."*

"Billie Ellis, the conductor, would go into Joe Solomon's general store and help himself to a smoked herring that was always handy on top of the counter," Wardlow said. *"I don't remember that he ever paid for one, and Joe never complained. It seemed to be a matter of course that Billie had his herring".*

Near the end of the logging era in the 1890s, many villages near lakes commercialized in harvesting ice for shipment to cities. This was before the days of modern refrigeration. Photo courtesy of Marie Bailey of Harrison.

Chapter Eighteen

ISABELLA COUNTY GHOST TOWNS
AND THE MAN WHO BUILT HIS OWN COFFIN

RAILROADS

This county was served by two railroads in 1905. The Pere Marquette, Coleman to Mt. Pleasant Branch: *Coleman*, 0 miles; *Wise*, 4 miles; *Delwin*, 7 miles, *Leaton*, 9 miles; *Jordan*, 10 miles; *Isabella*, 12 miles; *Mt. Pleasant*, 15 miles.

A switch engine and a few cars made this run every other day in 1970. (Now the C. & O.).

Ann Arbor Railroad: *Toledo*, 0 miles; *Shepherd*, 156 miles; *Mt. Pleasant*, 164 miles; *Rosebush*, 171 miles; and *Clare* (Clare County), 179 miles. (Railroad operating 1970).

POST OFFICES

Isabella has had at least 37 post offices during its history. In 1918, six of these remained, and are post offices in 1970.

GHOST TOWNS

ALEMBIC–in 1883, settled in 1859. Post office established in 1874. Chippewa Township, population 100, George Howarth, postmaster. Two sawmills and other business places.

In 1905 population 100, 6½ miles east of *Mt. Pleasant*. Two churches. W. B. Potter, postmaster. Had a blacksmith shop and general store. Probably other businesses.

In 1877 Jonathan Foutch was postmaster. Baptist church still standing in 1953.

———

BUCHTEL–see *Loomis*.

———

BOYDEN–was a post office in 1893. 1905, a farmer's post office in Deerfield Township, 7 miles west of *Mt. Pleasant*. Two general stores, lath factory, cooper shop, etc. Post office closed about 1902. In 1910 population 25. 1918, one store, RFD *Mt. Pleasant*.

————

BRINTON–formerly *"Leston."* Post office in 1890. 1905 population 250. In Coldwater Township, 7 miles south of Lake. S. F. Frye, postmaster. Had general stores, hotel, farm implements, harness maker, and blacksmith shop.

1910 population 125. RFD *Lake*. In 1918, two general stores, hardware, grocery and drug store, meat market, and hotel.

Most of the buildings burned. Ralph Geasler moved one old hotel and converted it into a home, where he is living at this date (1970). Earl St. Johns moved a store building 1 mile south on Brinton Road and operated as a general store until 1968.

John Fitch, the old blacksmith, saw his time coming in the early 1930s. He spent his last years carving a handsome coffin from native oak and hardwood. *"I always have bad dreams when I sleep on my back, and when I die I want to be buried laying on my side,"* he said.

Fitch constructed the coffin oversized and deeper than an ordinary coffin in order to be placed on his side. He also contracted with the village band to play at his funeral and paid them in advance. One song requested, his favorite, was *"Pretty Red Wing."* The requests were stipulated in his will. The casket was used and he was buried on his side. The band was instructed not to play, so his other request went unfulfilled.

The Geasler's are the only remaining "old-timers" who recall the good-old days when the town was booming and people from miles around came to town on Saturday to do their trading, then stayed for the Saturday night dance, while the men folks visited one of several saloons.

————

BROOMFIELD–1877, the post office at *"Corning,"* a village in Sherman Township, 17 miles from *Mt. Pleasant*. *Farwell*, 15 miles northeast on the F. & P. M. Railroad is the shipping station. The Chippewa River affords power for a grist and sawmill. Population 50. Henry Woodin, postmaster. Also flouring and sawmill.

In 1905 a country post office. B. W. Hagerman, postmaster and general store.

In 1910 population 25. RFD *Millbrook*. Now four-corners on M-20.

CALDWELL–was a post office in 1890. Also called *"Two Rivers"* in Deerfield Township, 10 miles west of *Mt. Pleasant.* Has Methodist Episcopal church (1905). C. W. Richardson, postmaster and hotel. Had blacksmith shop, general stores, and a doctor. Sawmills were located on the river a short distance west.

In 1910, population 80. In 1918, RFD *Mt. Pleasant.* S. 0. Smiley, general store.

All that remains of *Caldwell* is the old hotel (1968). Unpainted and weather-beaten, it was used for a residence for many years, finally filled with junk and deserted. The hotel was sold at auction in 1968 for about $1,500. Probably the most valuable items were the many old farm implements, etc. littering the yard. The foundations of a saw or gristmill remain near the site on Coldwater River.

CALKINSVILLE–later changed to *"Rosebush"*–in 1877 a post office and place of 35 population in Isabella Township, 7 miles north of *Mt. Pleasant* and 8 south of *Clare.* Ship's staves, hoops, and lumber. James Graham, postmaster. James Bush, hotel; Burton Calkins, general store.

In January 1889, a plat for the village was recorded and the name changed to *"Rosebush,"* after Elizabeth Rose Bush, wife of James L. Bush.

CRAWFORD–6½ miles south of *Mt. Pleasant,* was settled in 1863. Was a post office in 1877. 1884 population 37. *Riverdale* station on the Saginaw Valley & St. Louis Railroad, 11 miles distant, was its railroad point. Mail stage to *Mt. Pleasant.* J. Darrow, postmaster. Had a steam sawmill, grocery, and shoemaker.

Was a post office until 1902-03. 1910 population 25. RFD *Shepherd.*

Evidence of this town lies on the McMacken farm at 2757 E. Blanchard Road between *Shepherd* and *Winn* (1970).

DUSHVILLE–a post office in Fremont Township in 1890. Listed as the *"Winn"* post office in 1904. Several original buildings remain and the Mor-Bark Company, manufacturer of logging and pulp wood machinery is a large factory at this location today (1970). Many original buildings remain. Population less than 100.

HERRICK–was a village 3 miles east of *Clare* near US-10, Wise Township. Settled about 1875 as *"Lansingville."* Post office granted in 1895 and named *"Herrick."*

Had a sawmill, blacksmith shop, charcoal kilns, and the Herrick Full Cream Cheese Company. Church built in 1890. Still standing. Brick school built in 1903.

In 1905 Henry F. Badgley was postmaster. Had general store, railroad station, etc. 1910 RFD *Clare*, population 30.

ISABELLA CITY–the first county seat until 1860, was first called *"Indian Mills."* In 1877 name changed to *"Longwood,"* in Isabella Township, 2 miles north of *Mt. Pleasant*, on the Chippewa River. G. F. Grinnell, postmaster. Had hotel, general store, etc. Was originally an Indian village and trading post. Several original buildings stand. A bronze plaque mounted on a large rock marks the location at the north *Mt. Pleasant* city limits on Old US-27.

LONGWOOD–see *Isabella City.*

LOOMIS–first named *"Butchel."* In 1877 located in Wise Township, 16 miles north of *Mt. Pleasant* on the F. & P. M. Railroad. Settled in 1870. Has hemlock extract factory, two shingle mills, and a sawmill. Town hall, Methodist church and two hotels. Population 350. Seth Bowdish, postmaster. Several general stores, two saloons, meat market, two hotels, etc.

Phil Worden, aged 87 in 1955, said two men named Wise and Loomis started lumbering in the area shortly after the Civil War. During the building of the railroad in the late 1860s, 700 to 800 people lived there in anything that afforded shelter. The present store in *Loomis* was at one time a hotel built by Patrick Holden nearly 100 years ago, Worden said.

Sam Zeiter owned a combination saw and shingle mill, one of the largest. Zeiter also owned a race track and race horses. The track was about 80 rods west of the present main corners.

The original frame schoolhouse was moved about 1895 and the present brick one built. From about 1960 until 1969 it stood vacant. The building was sold to a private party to be used for a home.

The Methodist church, built about 1875, was sold and moved to *Clare*.

The village was never incorporated but had a justice of the peace, a dog warden, and constable. During the logging days Tom Lommison, a husky saloonkeeper, was turnkey in a makeshift jail attached to the town hall. Town records were kept by the justice of the ceace, but burned with the town hall.

Until about 1960, when passenger train service was ended, four trains a day pulled into the depot. Wesley Delmarter was an early station agent. A hit-and-miss stage line operated to *Gladwin* via a plank road. *"If you could catch it and hop on, then find room, you could ride,"* Mrs. Rodman said.

Until the 1890s lumber was stacked along the streets in every available space, leaving only a narrow aisle for wagons and sleighs to pass. Mills ran full-time until the timber ran out. *"You could stand in the street, if you didn't get knocked down,"* Worden said. *"You could look in any direction and see a fight going on."*

1970 is the centennial of the one-time booming town of *Loomis*, but there are not enough residents to stage a celebration. The village has been crossed and criss-crossed so many times by roads and highways that little remains. Ten years ago the expressway (US-10) bypassed the town and there is little through traffic. One store and a gas station are doing business. Perhaps 15 families live there. A store, gas station, and town hall stand near the main corners.

––––––––

SALT RIVER–in 1877 described as: *"A post office and village of 200 inhabitants in Coe Township, Isabella County, 10 miles southeast of Mt. Pleasant, and 12 miles northwest of St. Louis, the nearest railway station. The village, which takes its name from the stream upon which it is located, was settled in 1865. Contains two sawmills, a gristmill, one planing mill, and a Baptist church. J. J. Struble, postmaster."*
A few years later the name was changed to *"Shepherd"* and in 1889 incorporated as a village with 469 population. Today about 1,500.

––––––––

SHERMAN CITY–in 1877: *"A village of 150 in Coldwater and Sherman Townships, 25 miles northwest of Mt. Pleasant. On the Chippewa River, Farwell, 16 miles north is the nearest railway station, to which it has a weekly stage line. Tri-weekly mail. A. S. Johnson, postmaster and lumber manufacturer."* Had a hotel and livery, saloons, grocery, William Scott (boots and shoes), blacksmith shop, and other places.

In 1884 population 117. 1910 population 200.

In 1918 no population given. Had a hardware and general store. RFD *Lake*.

STRICKLAND–in 1877 population 50, near the southern line of Isabella County, 10 miles south of *Mt. Pleasant* and 8½ miles north of *Riverdale* station, on the Chicago-Saginaw & Canada Railroad. Stage to *Mt. Pleasant* and *Elm Hall* semi-weekly. Samuel W. Titus, postmaster.

Post office discontinued about 1902-3. RFD *Winn*.

––––––––

BURNHAM CROSSING–Vernon Township, 2 miles south of *Clare*. In 1875 had a sawmill, boardinghouse, and banking grounds for logs. Other mills were located nearby. Also two brick kilns and a depot and warehouse. The postal name was *"Russell."*

Fire destroyed the mill in 1896 and the depot was closed. It was purchased by William McKay, moved and used as a home. Post office discontinued and moved to the home of Robert Beaty, ¼ mile east of the crossing. This wrote the finis to *Burnham*, which was never to be reborn.

––––––––

VERNON CITY–although platted in Vernon Township, and settled long before Clare County was organized, it adjoins the city of *Clare* and has not been incorporated or organized as a town.

Today there are at least 75 dwelling and about 150 population, two gasoline stations, a motel, and other business places. To all appearances the cities of *Clare* and *Vernon City* are one today. In 1969 petitions were circulated to annex *Vernon City* to *Clare* so residents would be provided police protection and city services. To date (1970) nothing has come of it.

Vernon City was platted in 1871 by a man named Markley soon after the Pere Marquette Railroad surveyed their right-of-way. The first frame house was built by Fred Fishley in 1872, and it is said the complete job cost $125.

The first sawmill in the area, built in the 1860s, was 3 miles south of *Clare* on present Old US-27. From this mill came the material for the first hotel in *Clare*, the "Alger House."

A famous landmark before the Vernon Township Hall was built, on the same site, was the Holtz Tavern. It was the site of many town meetings, elections, etc. Holtz Tavern was the quarter-house on the stage line from *Mt. Pleasant* to *Clare*. The Holtz Tavern was moved a short distance south and made into a home. In 1955 Elmer Fetters and his wife lived there. Today it appears vacant. A brick schoolhouse, used to store hay and straw, and a brick town hall remain on the corner.

110

COE–was a post office in Coe Township 15 miles southeast of *Mt. Pleasant.* In 1910, RFD *St. Louis*, population 20. Was a post office in 1897.

————

COOMER–8½ miles southwest of *Mt. Pleasant* in Deerfield Township, was a post office in 1897.

————

DELWIN–on the P. M. Railroad, 7 miles south of *Coleman.* Post office in 1890. 1910 RFD *Rosebush*, population 80.

————

JERSEYVILLE–in 1897 a post office 8 miles south of *Mt. Pleasant.* In 1905, daily mail. J. A. Hunt, general store. In 1910, population 20, RFD *Shepherd.*

————

JORDAN–a station on the P. M. Railroad in 1910, 10 miles southwest of *Coleman.* Mail to *Mt. Pleasant.*

————

HORR–10 miles northwest of *Mt. Pleasant* in Sherman Township, was a new post office in 1884. In 1885 William F. Sherman, postmaster and farmer. Had two grocery stores, general store, saw and gristmill. In 1905 RFD *Weidman.* One store.

————

Other place names were:

DREW, MANSFIELD, SUMMERTON, RAND, and *VANDECAR* were other stations or settlements.

WISE–in Denver Township, 11 miles northeast of *Mt. Pleasant* on the P. M. Railroad, 4 miles from *Coleman.* 1905, RFD *Rosebush.* Charles Latimer, general store.

RAND–on the P. M. Railroad, in 1910 mail *Wyman* (over the line in Montcalm County).

————

Nearly ever village had its brick kiln, although not this extensive. This kiln stood near *St. Louis*, Michigan from the 1800s until about 1960, when the last of the crumbling ovens was bulldozed and subdivided. Picture taken about 1910, judging from the horseless carriage parked in front.

Chapter Nineteen

KALKASKA COUNTY GHOST TOWNS, 42 FORMER TOWNS AND STATIONS, AND ONE "REAL LIVE GHOST TOWN"

RAILROADS

Railroads serving the county included the Grand Rapids and Indiana. Beginning at *Richmond*, 0 miles: *Crofton*, 366.4 miles; *Kalkaska*, 371.3 miles; *Leetsville*, 376.1 miles; and *Westwood*, 380.9 miles.

Pere Marquette Railroad - Kalkaska Branch - 1900. *Rapid City*, 0 miles; *Ricker*, 3 miles; *Rugg*, 6 miles; *Leiphart*, 7 miles; *Kalkaska*, 11 miles; *Saunders*, 16 miles; *Spencer*, 18 miles; *Sands* (camp), 22 miles; *Sharon*, 23 miles; *Dempsey* (camp), 30 miles; and *Stratford* (in Missaukee County), 33 miles.

POST OFFICES

The first post office in the county, *Clearwater*, was established May 21, 1869, two years before it became a county. The location is difficult to trace since it moved many times and was located in homes or stores which have long since disappeared. Albert Kellog was the first postmaster. The post office was dicontinued February 28, 1905.

There have been at least 17 post offices during the history of the county. Only three remain.

GHOST TOWNS

AARWOOD–first called *"Littleville,"* in Clearwater Township. Post office established September 7, 1882, and closed January 31, 1901. One time population 200, three saw and shingle mills, school, general store, drug store, and a hotel.

At one time had a newspaper, the *Aarwood Arrows*, published at *Fife Lake*. A news item of May 21, 1896, related that Mrs. J. D. Fry, 86 years old, was fatally burned when their house was destroyed by fire. Mr. Fry was visiting the neighboring village of *Van Buren* at the time of the fire.

In 1918 mail to *Rapid City*.

BARKER CREEK–located on M-72 where the Chesapeake & Ohio railroad crosses the highway. In 1877 a post office in Clearwater Township, in the northwest corner of the county. Ten miles from *Kalkaska*, the county seat. Takes its name from the creek upon which it is situated. W. H. Backes, postmaster.

In 1910 population 100, on the Pere Marquette Railroad.

1918 population 80. Has Catholic and Methodist churches. John Brenneman, postmaster.

A news item of June 16, 1892 read: *"Mr. Mosher has been hauling timber from Stover's Mill to the railroad for the erection of the new depot. It is progressing rapidly, the railroad crossing signs are being put up, and it is thought the road will soon be in running order."*

1905 population 80. Two churches, John Brenneman, postmaster. Two general stores, shoemaker, livery, and other buildings.

Post office discontinued in 1907-08 and re-established for a short time in 1912. 1968 population about 12 people. No stores remain. I was told some people use the old depot for a summer home.

––––––––

CLEARWATER–in 1877 a post office in Clearwater Township, 10 miles from *Kalkaska*. On the Rapid River. One sawmill. Settled in 1868 population 100. Frederick W. Oakes, postmaster.

The first post office was established here in 1869. Discontinued February 28, 1905. In 1910 mail RFD *Alden*. In 1918 RFD *Rapid City.*

––––––––

CROFTON–in 1877 population 75. Settled in 1875. In Boardman Township. A station on the G. R. & I. Railroad. J. F. Hiatt, postmaster. Had two hotels, general store, two sawmills, etc.

1910 population 80. Mail to *South Boardman*. About six people live in the area (1968). No remains of a village.

––––––––

DARRAGH–in Coldsprings Township, 9 miles north of *Kalkaska*, was not a village. James A. Campbell was postmaster from March, 1902, until February 28, 1919. He operated a store there until World War I.

From a news item dated April 21, 1898: *"This new post office in Coldsprings Township is named for Congressman Darragh. The postmaster is Albert Campbell."*

IVAN–in 1905 a settlement in Garfield Township, 10 miles south of *Kalkaska*. Thomas Bates, postmaster. Had a bowl factory.

In 1910, RFD *South Boardman*.

LEETSVILLE–in 1877 a post office and station on the G. R. & I. Railroad, 5 miles north of *Kalkaska*. A new settlement, located in a heavily-timbered region. David Nimmo, postmaster and James Campbell, general store.

A news item of January 8, 1891 stated that the Tiffany Shingle Mill is running again. June 4, 1896: *"S. M. Vinto has disposed of his store and other interests here and is preparing to move to Grand Rapids. He came here 19 years ago (1877) and practically built up the village.*

January, 1904: *"Between 35 and 40 carloads of logs passed through here Sunday headed south."*

1905 population 100. Rapid River Township. W. J. Towers, postmaster. L. M. Tiffany still ran the shingle mill. Had a general store.

1918 population 100. Eugene N. Phelps, postmaster. A few buildings remain (1968) but no population.

LODI–in 1905 a post office in Orange Township, 6 miles south of *Kalkaska*, and 3 from *Spencer*. Laura L. Ayers, postmistress. One general store.

1910 a discontinued post office. RFD *Kalkaska*.

RUGG–first called *"Mossback"* (disdainful reference to a settler by the lumberjacks). Located on the P. M. Railroad in Rapid River Township, 5¼ miles from *Kalkaska*. Business section of the village was destroyed by fire. On February 6, 1902, fire destroyed the store building of J. W. Morey. Only a few of the contents were saved. The rest, probably burned and rusty, lies buried on the site.

In August, 1916 Waldo Yoemans, who owned a large general store went with a search party trying to locate the body of Fred Hill, who drowned in the Rapid

River while fishing. When he returned to town his store was on fire and burned to the ground.

In 1905 John W. Morey, postmaster. Had a saw and shingle mill.

1910 RFD *Rapid City*, population 21.

————

SHARON–was a booming lumbering village on the south line, Section 6, T25N, R6W in Garfield Township. It was at the junction of the Manistee River and Big Cannon Creek, now the western line of the AuSable State Forest.

Many tales of fights and saloon brawls during the logging days are centered around this one-time village. In the 1880s there were 12 lumber camps in the area.

In 1905 a country post office on the P. M. Railroad, 15 miles from *Kalkaska*. George Johnson, general store, hotel and postmaster. Also had several sawmills, express office, and boardinghouse.

Nothing remains today. In 1910 population 40. Post office and store.

In 1917 population 50. Four miles from *O'Neil*. Mrs. Martha J. Tidd, postmistress. General store, hotel, shipped posts and ties.

————

SPENCER–in Orange Township was a logging town served by the P. M. Railroad in the 1880s. Post office from about 1898 to 1912.

A news item of January 10, 1901 read: *"H. Gregory has moved his sawmill to another site, and a man from Leetsville put a mill into the building thus vacated. We now have two mills in our lively town."*

H. Gregory ran a grocery store. L. M. Noble had a bazaar and was postmaster. Allie Gibbs had a shoe shop. A box car was used for a freight house. The train made one trip a day. It started from *Kalkaska* to *Rapid City* then on to *Stratford*. The railroad was built in 1897 and the train ran for the first time in 1898.

A minister came from *South Boardman* and held services. They had an organ that folded up like a suitcase. People brought nail kegs and a plank from Murphy's Lumber Yard and made seats.

Louie Sands had a lumber camp there. Mike O'Brien was a "jobber" in the area. One night he left town, leaving his wife behind, and was never heard from again. The men who worked for him didn't receive any pay for several months work.

In 1918 population 100. Telephone. Edward Ehl, lumber and sawmill; L. M. Noble, millinery and notions; Tice & Carp, general store.

––––––––

SOUTH BOARDMAN–Mrs. E. H. Barber of *South Boardman*, now 76 years old (1970) said her father came there from Maple Rapids in 1878 and lived to be 101 years old. Mrs. Barber was born there in 1894.

"At one time there were five saloons, three lumber mills, two hotels and a company boardinghouse," she said. *"There were also a flour mill, three dams in the Boardman River, one ran the gristmill and another a lumber mill. Two lumber mills burned, at different times, and the whole business section of the main street burned about 1923. So the town kept going down. There were also four churches, now there is one."*

In 1878 *South Boardman* was a post office and flag station on the G. R. & I. Railroad, in South Boardman Township. Settled in 1872, population 25. A. McCoy, postmaster. A. J. Bachelder, hotel; Reverend M. Deitz, Methodist; F. P. Smith, general store; and H. Stone, station agent.

Early settlers walked to *Traverse City*, 25 miles, and carried their groceries home, Mrs. Barber said. A man now living in California wrote a book about the area titled *The World's So Full of Things*, she said.

Mrs. Barber works at the post office, where she started working in 1917. J. J. Neihardt was postmaster at that time. Mrs. Lorna Lisch was postmistress for 35 years, and the present one has been there since 1963.

In 1890 population 231; in 1910, 524; and in 1918 a little over 400. After the fire of 1923 the village was almost deserted. In 1969 a new post office was built and the old building moved across the street and donated to the township for use as a museum. Nothing has been done to set it up at this time (1970).

One huge general store or hotel is converted into an antique shop. A new pavement bypassed the town for about ½ mile. A new restaurant, store, and appliance store has been built on the highway.

A few old store buildings and houses remain empty. The village is a "real live ghost town."

117

SIGMA–located in the north part of Oliver Township, on the M. & N. E. Railroad (1905) and on Sands Creek, 7 miles due south of Manistee Lake was a boom town during the logging days. In 1910 mail to *Spender*.

The village was struck by fire in July, 1912, and most buildings destroyed. A news item of July 11, 1912, said the "Sigma Hotel" and the George Brice general store was destroyed.

In 1918, telephone, W. T. Kirkby, postmaster; George Hollenbeck, hotel; Kirkby Brothers, general store; and Fred Narrin, general store.

––––––––

VAN BUREN–was one of the first settlements, in Rapid City Township until that township was changed to *"Clearwater."* In 1898, upon request of the residents, Congressman Mesick recommended that the name be changed to *"Rapid City."*

News item, December 9, 1897: *"We understand the new railroad is now completed as far as Kalkaska, and that regular trains will soon be running to that point."* February 17, 1898: *"We understand that Wagright Brothers intend to put in a mill and elevator at this place in the spring."*

In the late 1800s the village had a newspaper called *The Rustler*. A news item of October 2, 1902 said: *"Rapid City is to have a newspaper again. J. A. DeLaury will start the Rapid City Record."* In the early 1900s an annual fair was held for several years.

July 6, 1906: *"Rapid City has voted to build a new brick schoolhouse. They will add a third teacher this coming year."*

1918 population 300. Today it has a post office and business section, but the population is less than 100.

––––––––

WESTWOOD–in Rapid River Township, near the north county line, in 1877 described as a small place on the G. R. & I. Railroad (now the Pennsylvania) formerly called *"Havanah."* In a lumbering region, 10 miles from *Kalkaska*. Daily mail. James Campbell, general store and postmaster. (Note: There were either several people by this name in the county, or he moved around frequently, or the same town changed names several times.)

In 1910 population 72. Was a post office and money order station as late as 1912.

118

News item of March 16, 1893: *"Ashton Brothers have taken the job of loading pine logs on flat cars at Madill's Siding."*

A final item, published September 19, 1914, stated: *"Westwood is now without a store for the first time since it was founded."*

————

Other places were:

ANGLING–on the M. & N. E. Railroad, mail to *Spencer.*

BLUE LAKE–on the D. & C. Railroad, mail *Frederic.*

BUTCHER–on the P. M. Railroad, mail *Moorestown.*

CLEMENT–on the P. M. Railroad, mail to *Alden.*

CULVER and *DEIBERT*–on the M. & N. E. Railroad, mail to *South Boardman.*

EASTMAN–on the P. M. Railroad, mail to *Spencer.*

EXCELSIOR–RFD *Kalkaska.*

FAIRBANKS–on the P. M. Railroad, mail to *Kalkaska.*

FLETCHER.

HALSTEAD–on the P. M. Railroad, mail to *Moorestown.*

HAVANAH–name changed to *Westwood.*

KELLEY–on the P. M. Railroad, mail to *Sharon.*

LEIPHART–on P. M. Railroad, mail to *Kalkaska.*

LEWIS BRANCH–on P. M. Railroad, mail to *Kalkaska.*

MCAFEE–on G. R. & I. Railroad, mail to *South Boardman.*

MAHAN–on the P. M. Railroad, mail to *Kalkaska.*

MOEKE–on the P. M. Railroad, mail *Kalkaska.*

NAPLES–on the P. M. Railroad, mail to *Sharon*.

OMEGA–on the G. R. & I. Railroad, mail to *Westwood*.

O'NEIL–on the M. & N. E. Railroad, mail to *Spencer*.

PRESCY–on the P. M. Railroad, mail to *Kalkaska*.

RIVERVIEW–on the M. & N. E. Railroad, mail to *Grayling*.

ROWLEY–on M. & N. E. Railroad, mail to *South Boardman*.

SAUNDERS–on P. M. Railroad, mail to *Kalkaska*.

SOULES–on P. M. Railroad, mail to *Kalkaska*.

SPRINGFIELD–on M. & N. E. Railroad, mail to *Walton*.

WILKINS–on the G. R. & I. Railroad, mail to *Westwood*.

FRANCE–was a sawmill town on the P. M. Railroad, 4 miles southwest of *Rapid City* in Round Lake Swamp. The French Lumber Company of *Battle Creek*, Michigan set up a large steam sawmill there about 1905. It was later called *"French's Landing,"* and was a short-lived settlement.

END OF VOLUME I

MICHIGAN GHOST TOWNS
Of The Lower Peninsula

Volume II

Depot scene back in the days when trains were an important event in the lives of small town people. The coming of railroads brought the outside world to isolated villages in the form of mail, news, and visits by friends and relatives. Photo courtesy of Ruth W. Geister, Roscommon.

Chapter One

EARLY SETTLEMENT OF NORTHERN MICHIGAN

Michigan's logging days and expansion of railroads in the late 1860s and 1870s brought thousands of people to the sparsely populated counties of the northern Lower Peninsula. Most of the newcomers did not consider themselves residents. Their only thought and purpose was to "cut and get out." Very few lumbermen purchased the land upon which the timber grew. They purchased rights to a certain number of acres or entered into a contract with another company to "get out" a specified quantity of pine logs or timber, usually several million feet. Most of the land was owned by railroad companies who sold their timber rights, much the same as landowners today sell oil or mineral rights, but retained the land. As each section, township and county was cleared of its prime timber the railroad companies set up offices to sell the land.

Each company or contractor hired crews (called "swampers") to cut trails through the virgin forests where they set up camps to house workers for the winter. Many of these camps, called "headquarters camps," became permanent settlements, such as *Ketcham* or *Ketchumville* in Midland County and *Moorestown* in Missaukee County.

When the winter's work was completed most of the workers returned to their homes or farms "down below" or took jobs in sawmills of large cities. Very few permanent settlements or villages were established until after the Civil War when returning veterans took up bounty lands awarded them by the government for service to their country. With few exceptions none of northern lower Michigan's towns or cities observed the centennial of their founding until 1970, and many of these jumped the gun by several years.

The first and largest railroad company in this area to offer lands was the Flint & Pere Marquette Railroad (see footnote) who in 1876 ran the following advertisement: *"The entire land grant of this company unsold, consisting of about 250,000 acres, is offered for sale."*

FOOT NOTE: The Pere Marquette Railroad originated in 1862 as an operation from East Saginaw to Mount Morris. Its main function was to keep the mills at Flint supplied with logs. In 1864 arrangements were made which allowed a complete rail service to Detroit. After its Detroit terminals were established the F. & P. M. began extending its operations into the Saginaw Valley timberlands.

For many years the railroad depended on the sale of land granted it by Congress for its financial salvation. Congress had passed a grant which gave six sections of land to the railroads for each mile of track laid. The Pere Marquette's tracks ran though some of the most valuable timber land in the State. The first grant gave the railroad 150,000 acres. In all the F. & P. M. licensed a total of 513,069 acres. Land was sold and bought from $5 to $10 an acre. Their tracks were pushed to Midland in 1867 and in 1874 completed to Ludington. The revenues taken in the early days were almost wholly derived from the lumber and timber products which they carried.

Some of the land still consisted of virgin, pine timberland. Cleared land was described as: *"Farming lands. As good as any in the world are to be found in abundance, and will be sold on the most favorable terms to actual settlers. Some rolling, with Beech, Maple, Rock Elm, etc. In fact, every variety of timber, soil and surface can be found. The railroad is complete to Ludington on Lake Michigan.*

Cheap land and railroad facilities are seldom offered together. And those who wish to secure homes will do well to apply early and take choice selections. TERMS OF SALE: One-fourth down, in all cases, and balance may be paid in three equal annual payments. All contracts and notes are made payable at Merchants National Bank, East Saginaw. Land office at East Saginaw, Mich. William L. Webber, Land Commissioner."

Many inducements were offered prospective settlers, such as free, expense-paid trips to inspect land. Broadsides and handbills were distributed at points of immigration to lure new immigrants to settle. Notices were posted in factories in large cities such as *Detroit, Pittsburgh,* and *Chicago* entreating workers to abandon the sweatshops and enjoy the pure, fresh air, sparkling streams swarming with fish, and "rich farming soil" of northern Michigan. Many of these people invested their life's savings on mere promises and without going to the area prior to purchasing.

The newly arrived settlers were faced with more problems and hardships than their predecessors of half-a-century earlier who had settled "down below." Faced with an ocean of highly inflammable brush and towering pine stumps, most attempts at farming were fruitless. Once the thin layer of mulch and topsoil was exhausted, usually within a few years, all that remained was blowing sand. Each summer the country was swept by forest fires with great loss of life and property. People huddled in sod-covered root cellars, sometimes for days, until the fires burned themselves out or were finally quenched with rain. Thousands gave up the ghost and moved back to the cities and the land eventually reverted to the State for non-payment of taxes.

Some of them, with no other alternative, stayed on. Most of these were Polish, Slovakian, Lithuanian, Hungarian, and newly-arrived immigrants who grubbed out a meager existence and gradually cleared the land of stumps, built their own schools and churches, and became the true natives of northern Michigan.

The Pere Marquette Railroad Company was generous to land promoters and new counties who desired to establish towns and villages along their railroad right-of-way. Many villages were established on sites donated by the company and most towns along their routes gratefully accepted one or more blocks set aside by the company for use as a park, school site, or courthouse square. The Pere Marquette and Grand Rapids & Indiana Railroads are probably responsible for the founding of more northern Michigan towns than any occurrence in its history.

Mainly due to the railroad companies, by 1870 northern Michigan became the melting pot of the nation with settlers moving in from nearly every country in Europe. French and French-Canadians had already arrived. Next came New England Yankees, Swedes, Finns, Polish, Irish, Dutch, Scots, Welsh, and Italians to work on the railroads; Lithuanian, Jewish, Turkish, and immigrants from the Holy Land, most of whom started out as peddlers to follow the rush of northbound settlers. As permanent settlements were made they became the first to set up mercantile and dry goods stores. There are few northern Michigan towns that did not have at least one store founded and operated by a Jew.

There are few records of Negroes in northern Michigan but blacks played an important part in the settlement. Very few communites existed without at least one family of blacks. They came to work as barbers, porters on trains, teamsters, cooks in the lumber camps, and tradesmen, and many took up farmlands. Several northern counties had large black communities such as Mecosta, Lake, Newaygo, Manistee, and Muskegon Counties. Many blacks settled at *Suttons Bay* in Leelanau County and many more settled near fisheries and canning factories, especially along the west Lake Michigan coast.

Although they received no recognition many blacks contributed their share to the advancement and progress of the north. Zachariah Morgan, a former slave, was the founder of *Boyne City* in Charlevoix County, co-owner of the first industry (a brick factory), a leading Republican, county supervisor, and for two terms, treasurer of the village.

Another black, whose name is not recorded, invented an oiler for a steam engine that was considered a great improvement in engineering circles. This man worked in a factory at *Cadillac* and after inventing the oiler was offered a job in a *Detroit* factory, which he accepted, and went on to improve many other methods in the manufacture of engines.

Two Negro brothers, Wallace and William Goodridge, played an important part in recording the history of the Saginaw Valley. Arriving in *Saginaw* in 1862 they set up a photo studio and for the next 50 years took pictures in *Saginaw* and made trips to many lumber camps taking pictures. Many of their photos are preserved in a pictorial history of *Saginaw* published in 1888. Published by a newspaper editor, the Goodridge brothers received no credit and their names were left off the photos used.

There are no Negro families living at *Houghton Lake* in Roscommon County today, but old newspaper accounts relate the activities of an all Negro baseball team from there who trounced all comers.

Most blacks settled on farms or in small communities one family at a time and were so widely scattered that no racial problems existed. Nearly every village had its local Negro barber, handyman, or drayman who did odd jobs of hauling, etc. Many old school pictures, taken during the late 1800s and at the turn-of-the-century taken in northern counties, contain pictures of several Negro children mixed with whites. Pictures of blacks appear in most old pictures of Fourth of July celebrations and on other occasions where crowds gathered. Many of them were dressed in better clothes and had a neater appearance than some of the whites.

Idlewild in Lake County was the only all black settlement in Michigan and probably has the most unique history of any ghost town in the nation.

Many settlers came to Michigan from Europe after receiving letters from relatives already living here. Despite the many hardships, Michigan, as was the rest of America, was looked upon by the immigrants as a haven of refuge with freedoms never before experienced in their homeland.

George P. Graff in his booklet, *The People of Michigan,* quotes from a listing of conditions described by a newly arrived settler. *"Ordinary people are as good as rich folks. He need not take his hat off to anyone. Rich people honor the poor because they work for them. There are good churches here and many of God's people. If one is well he can earn good wages. Women need do nothing more than milk and prepare the food."*

First settlers of the forest covered hills, rippling streams, and vast swamplands of northern Michigan were mainly returned Civil War veterans following blazed trails and surveyor's marks to locate their bounty lands and homesteads. Many veterans sold their land without attempting to locate it, but thousands of Civil War veteran monuments and markers in northern Michigan cemeteries stand in silent memory to those who cleared the land, rooted out stumps, built homes, and raised families.

Others soon followed in their footsteps. Their residences depended upon the source of livelihood. Some worked in the forests as loggers or in the outlying sawmills. Some took up preaching, trapping, peddling, established stores and businesses, or plied their trade.

Chapter Two

GROWTH OF VILLAGES

The unnamed author of the *Lake City Centennial Booklet* (1968) described the growth of a new town very graphically: *"Now came the grocers with their potbellied stoves and cracker barrels; the rough-framed, many cold-bedroomed, steamy-kitchened structures whose sawmill tenants simply termed "The $&!!&!? Boardin' House"; the smoothly finished, warm-lobbied, main street located building sporadically occupied and emptied by the travelling "drummer," land sharks and timber dealers, gamblers and politicos, grandly labeled by its proud owner "THE HOTEL." The rough-and-ready, free lunch-countered, loud and odorous saloon. The whining sawmill with its early morning and short noon whistle commands. The blacksmith shop with its constant companions the glowing forge, skittish horses with their profane owners and ever present acrid stench of scorching hooves, steaming piles of manure in the winter and buzzing hordes of flies in summer."*

Children under the age of 12 were herded off to school with the first snowfall. School was held during the winter because students of any age could be spared only during the cold months for dallying at such fads. The one-room school, made of logs in early days (after 1870 boards were used), contained a wood stove, hard benches, McGuffey readers, and heavily bundled pupils. As late as 1900 most schools were not graded except by readers. Some of the most successful businessmen of the early part of the 20th century progressed only as far as the sixth reader, some even less.

Railroads and luxury items, previously unavailable at any price, arrived simultaneously. Depots were built and the whistle of an arriving train brought village residents rushing to the station. The train became one of the important events in peoples' lives. Rapidly advancing steel ribbons pierced the forests and broke through the wilderness bringing the outside world to the isolated villages in the form of mail, news, and visits by relatives and friends. Tools of industry became available in any quantity. Sawmills, steam engines, plows, sleighs and wagons, big wheels for getting out logs in summer, anvils, shovels, axes, crosscut and circular saws, nails, wire, chains, cook stoves, weighing scales, log tongs, tons of chain, harnesses, and thousands of items necessary to build new towns and mills. Carload after carload bearing household needs and furnishings. Cream separators, pans, coffee and sausage grinders, horsehair sofas, spool beds, pianos and organs, bolts of gingham, chambray and calico, overalls, straw hats that sold for 15 cents each, felt hats, mackinaws, pocket watches, pendulum clocks, shoes, boots, blankets, and bedding.

Empty box cars, intermixed with flat cars carrying the never-ending loads of logs, now furnished a means to ship the products of the wilderness island. Returning cars carried shingles and cedar bolts, barrel staves and hoops, tanbark, ice, potatoes, grain, cream, livestock, ginseng, game, and fish packed in layers of evergreen boughs and ice, journeyed forth into the world. Accompanying telegraph lines constantly clicked out their messages along the miles of railroad tracks; messages of joy, sickness, death, and orders for more goods and merchandise.

Teachers, preachers, doctors, lawyers, and bankers moved into the north country. Scarce money made barter the tool of trade. Stove wood, eggs, butter, and berries were traded for sugar, coffee and salt, boots, hats, and doctoring. Men walked several miles to work, carried round, double-deck tin lunch pails, and worked 12 hours earning from 60 cents to $1 per day with fringe benefits; free air and water. Everyone worked. The 4-year-old toted stove wood and pine chips for kindling. Grandma knitted socks, peeled potatoes, patched pants, made mittens, and transformed flour and feed sacks into shirts for the boys and dresses for the girls. Twelve and 14-year-old boys, depending on their size and strength, were considered adult labor without a man's privileges.

There was no welfare for anyone except the very aged and sickly who had no relatives to look after them. These people were committed to the county poor farm and listed in census records as "paupers," a brand they carried to their unmarked graves. Bums, hoboes, and loiterers were promptly removed to the nearest county line by the sheriff or local constabulary and told to "Get going!"

For half-a-century or more the hardy pioneers of the north lived in an age of home remedies and Indian cures. Hemlock bark for wounds, wormwood and epsom salts, laudanum and carbolic acid, paregoric, castor oil, arnica salve, sassafras tea, calamo, and bread and milk poultices. Skunk oil and a wool sock served for a cold cure. Doctors and hospitals, many miles distant in *Saginaw*, *Bay City,* or *Muskegon* were used only as a last resort for amputation of mangled limbs of severely injured lumberjacks and sawyers who lived to get there.

It was the era of the pack peddler, the itinerant preacher, the brawling, lawless saloons built eight to a block, half-hidden brothels, screeching sawmills, railroad hoboes, salt pork and beans, opera houses, and travelling medicine shows.

These were the days of "quickie justice" administered by the justices of the peace, who averaged nearly 1 to every 5 citizens and laid down the law according to the *Farmer's Almanac*, the *Holy Bible*, or any book he happened to possess. Fines were levied according to ability to pay or dependent on the sobriety of the judge. One case in a dozen reached "His Honor's" court, the others were settled in lumbercamps or saloons where fists, calked boots, and axes opened and closed cases with expeditious and sometimes painful finality, ignoring the rights of appeal or counsel.

A case of so-called "lumberjack justice" was told concerning William (Billy) McCrary who ran the famous Red Keg saloon in the 1870s. McCrary became vexed at the actions or attitude of one of his customers and beat up on the man with no apparent justification. The village constable observed the assault and declared McCrary under arrest. When he started to escort him to the nearest justice, "Swearin" Charlie Axford, owner of a hotel and saloon at *Camp 16* and often called the "Mayor of Edenville," stepped forward. *"What are you taking him to the J.P. for?"* Axford asked. *"Try him before me. I am in the business and can hold court as well as anybody."*

Both parties agreed and adjourned to a nearby hotel. *"Stand up Bill,"* Axford said. *"Are you guilty or not guilty?"*

"Guilty your honor," McCrary said smiling.

"I hereby fine you $3 cash and whiskey for the crowd!" Axford decreed. *"We will now adjourn to Red Keg and collect the fine and costs."*

The boys took a drink and Axford laid the $3 he had collected from McCrary on the counter and said, *"Let's put the fine with the costs. Set 'em up Billy, as long as the money holds out."*

This was the picture of the half-century in the north during the time it took to strip the lands of their white pine forests. The era when booming towns sprouted over night and became deserted as the hungry maws of the sawmills demanded more pine for their ever-whirring iron teeth. With no timber to haul, the Pere Marquette and the Grand Rapids & Indiana (nicknamed "Go Ragged and Independent") abandoned miles and miles of track laid for that purpose. Hundreds of miles of narrow-gauge tracks were removed and shipped north across the Straits or further west to finish the job. Hundreds of ghost towns were left in their wake, surrounded by sawdust and slab piles in an ocean of pine stumps and cedar swamps.

Chapter Three

NORTHERN MICHIGAN IN EARLY 1900S

Shortly after the turn-of-the-century an occasional horseless carriage was seen chugging along the wagon trails and a new era began. Towns that survived the logging days took on a new look. Bandstands and watering troughs for horses were built at the main intersections. Remaining villages had removed all, or at least most, of the stumps from the main streets. Telephones became a common method of communication and mill ponds were converted to generate power for electricity.

Pool rooms replaced many of the roaring saloons under "local option" laws and became the object of fiery sermons exhorting the day's youth of their awful evils. Doctors replaced midwives, lawyers became justices, licensed teachers took over from school "marms" and school masters in the one-room schools, jails were built to save transporting prisoners to *Detroit, Ionia, Grand Rapids* and *Midland*. Resident ministers moved into parsonages, replacing the traveling evangelists and circuit preachers of former days.

In 1895 Rural Free Delivery of mail was established and by the turn-of-the-century most northern residents had shiny, new mailboxes placed in neat rows at wagon road intersections. Children brought the mail home on their return from school or someone walked the mile or two to get the mail. Mail order catalogs demanded cash instead of eggs, trade tokens, or time slips. A half century had passed. A time of hardships, pain, joy, crying, laughter, and love.

By 1918 and the end of the World War I, the Model-T had replaced the mailman's and doctor's horse-and-buggy and the John Deere, Allis Chalmers and Ferguson tractors were on the way to replacing the oxen and teams of horses. Farmers, harness makers, blacksmiths, "stump jumpers," and tradesmen rushed to the cities "down below" to work in automobile factories and war plants, many of them never to return. A large portion of the influx of retirees moving to northern Michigan today (1970) are former natives who moved to *Flint, Lansing, Detroit* and *Grand Rapids* 50 years ago to work in the factories.

Men who had worked for $6 or $8 a month and "keep," discovered they could often earn as much in one day working "piece work" at Buick Motors in *Flint* and the Reo Motor Car Company, Duplex Truck Company, or Oldsmobile in *Lansing*. Beardless boys of 15 were handed a $10 gold piece at the end of a

10-hour 6-day work week in a factory, enough to purchase a "store bought" suit of clothes.

For the next quarter-century the population of the north country declined. More towns were deserted, many more were reduced to one or two general stores at the intersection of two crossroads surrounded by rapidly decaying houses and shacks. With farms rapidly becoming abandoned and villages deserted, and with the coming of the World War I, land promoters and financial experts of the day still held hopes of reviving the barren counties of northern lower Michigan. The *Michigan Gazeteer* of 1917 said: *"Michigan still has an abundance of timber and wood waste which could be used in the wood distillation industry for the manufacture of chemical products which are more valuable than charcoal alone ... Pine stumps can be used for the distillation of turpentine. The chemical possiblities of our innumerable pine stumps have hardly been touched."*

There was, however, no interest by industry or investors in developing the remote possibilities of converting stumps to turpentine, or any other product, when the gasoline engine and automobiles were the coming thing for the 20th century. Chemical factories, such as the mammoth installation at *Jennings* in Missaukee County, closed down their doors and left thousands of workers unemployed. Several abortive attempts at automobile and truck manufacturing were made in northern Michigan towns but failed within a short time-three or four years at the most.

Newly transported workers to lower Michigan cities liked their new mode of living and life in the cities or suburbs that were rapidly expanding in the 1920s to meet the need for new housing. The publications extolling opportunities in northern Michigan could have appropriately added *"How are you going to get them back on the farm?"* - a phrase coined from a popular war song of the day.

Gradually the sea of burned-over pine stumps gave birth to new life in the form of cedar, white birch, and rapidly-growing poplar trees. The barren north country once again turned green with the arrival of spring. After many fires had swept over the land, vast areas of plains sprouted with huckleberry plants and for many years the few remaining natives discovered a new cash crop, free for the picking. During huckleberry season tent cities sprouted up in many areas of both the Lower and Upper Peninsulas. Entire families moved out on the plains away from their homes and spent the summer picking, cleaning, sorting, and packing the lush crop of blueberries into crates and hauling them to the nearest railroad station for shipment. Thousands of bushels of huckleberries were shipped from

9

stations at *Roscommon, West Branch, Lake St. Helen*, and hundreds of depots in the north.

Undisturbed lakes and streams propagated huge populations of fish. By the 1890s deer herds appeared in many counties north of M-46 and by the turn-of-the-century, despite wholesale slaughters by professional hunters, large herds of deer became a common sight.

With the automobile here to stay there was a hue-and-cry for more and better roads. A new breed of sportsmen, travelling by auto, was born. During the heydey of the railroads only the very wealthy and railroad and timber tycoons could afford private pullman cars for excursions to the north in pursuit of grayling, trout, and game. Now the lowest-paid factory worker could afford to take a week or two in summer or during deer hunting season in the fall and make the trip north in his "private pullman," a Model-T, Chevrolet or Overland puddle-jumper piled high with camping equipment, stoves, pots and pans, and hunting and fishing gear stuffed into trunks attached to the back of their autos, and on the running boards and fenders.

A boom in road building during the 1920s gave birth to a new business that was soon christened "tourism." As was the case during the building of railroads every community with more than half-a-dozen inhabitants demanded that the new highways be routed their way. Politicians were wooed and threatened. Some places succeeded in their efforts and the new highways curved, wound and jogged through the northern counties from *Lansing, Grand Rapids, Muskegon*, and *Detroit* to the Straits of Mackinac. If the road failed to reach a village the residents moved to the highway and more ghost towns were created as the natives rushed to meet the demand for gasoline stations with their Indian Gas, White Rose, free air and water, and "flats-fixed" signs. Cabins, motor courts, restaurants, bait shops, hot dog stands, and souvenir shops sprouted up along the highways.

In 1905 the State Highway Department was established and 18 counties had adopted the County Road System to replace former township road commissioners. To build roads money was needed and lots of it. A new golden goose for tax revenue was discovered in 1915 when the legislature enacted the Newel Smith Automobile Tax Law and on January 9, 1917, Secretary of State Coleman C. Vaughan made his report for the first year's operation. During the first two years the law was in effect the amazing total of 1 million dollars was poured into the better roads fund. By 1929, 7,500 miles of State highways were maintained in the State, with 2,723 miles of concrete pavement, and another 400 miles of blacktop or hard surface other than gravel.

Michigan was on wheels. More towns and crossroads settlements grew along the new highways. Many villages that had been nearly deserted revived with the increase of travellers and sightseers, many who had previously rode the trains and seen only the backyards of the north. Now they were free to travel at their own will and leisure, choose their own stopping points, and visit lakes and streams, many of them never seen before except by trappers, surveyors, Indians, and lumberjacks. Cottages and summer homes soon dotted lakeshores in many northern counties. Private clubs were formed and "city slickers" purchased huge tracts of cheap land, built clubhouses, tennis courts, and guest houses and sold lots numbering into the millions to members, many who never bothered to visit the place. High pressure tactics to sell factory workers resort property in these fabulous meccas was almost a revival of the "paper cities" of the early settlement of Michigan.

Banks and real estate agents suddenly discovered that thousands of acres of stump-covered, useless land, that a few years before remained unsold at $10 per acre and was passed up by bidders at tax sales, was worth millions when divided into 30 x 100 foot lots.

During the late 1920s, until the stock market crash of 1929 took effect, the counties north of M-46 extending from *Bay City* to *Muskegon* experienced a rush for land almost equal to the days of logging and railroads. During the depression years of the 1930s most of the land once more reverted to the State for non-payment of taxes. Empty gasoline stations with rotting hoses stood next to vacant motor courts and cabins with doors flapping in the breeze, unpatched roofs, broken windows, and weed-grown service drives. Once more many villages became deserted, or almost so, and more ghost towns were created.

LAKE COUNTY GHOST TOWNS AND THE ONLY NEGRO GHOST TOWN IN THE HISTORY OF MICHIGAN

A historical plaque near the courthouse entrance in *Baldwin,* the county seat, gives most of the recorded history of Lake County. It reads: *"This county was originally set off in 1840 and first named "Aishum" after a well known Potawatomi Indian Chief. In 1843 the name was changed to "Lake" (for no particular reason). For three decades it was attached to neighboring counties until 1871 when settlement was sufficient to warrant organization. Baldwin, the county seat, was settled in 1872. The county's forests helped make Michigan a leading lumbering state. Farming and the tourist industry are the chief activities. Wild life is abundant."*

The first recorded population of Lake County in 1870, was 548. The county reached its peak of population in 1884 with 7,539 inhabitants. In 1960 Lake County ranked fourth of the lowest populated counties in Michigan, with a population of 5,338, a little less than in 1890, averaging 9.3 persons per square mile. A large percentage of the population is Negro.

Baldwin was described in 1875 as: *"A village of some 200 inhabitants and is the new seat of justice for Lake County. (Chase was the first county seat). It is on the line of the Flint & Pere Marquette Railroad about 7 miles southwest of the center of the county and 30 east of Ludington. Excellent water power is derived from the Pere Marquette River, at present not utilized. The place has a steam sawmill and other business interests."* These included a drug store, general store, meat market, boot and shoe store, two hotels, hardware, two saloons, a blacksmith shop, and railroad station.

RAILROADS

Railroads serving the county were:

1890–the Flint & Pere Marquette. Beginning at *Monroe* and entering Lake County at *Chase,* going west: *Monroe,* 0 miles; *Chase,* 211.6 miles; *Nirvana,* 215.6 miles; *Forman,* 220.1 miles; *Baldwin,* 222.6 miles; *Wingleton,* 225.2 miles.

1900–Pere Marquette Railroad entering Lake County at *Olivers,* going west: *Saginaw,* 0 miles; *Olivers,* 93 miles; *Chase,* 96 miles; *Nirvana,* 100 miles; *Ungers,* 102 miles; *Baldwin,* 107 miles; and *Wingleton,* 111 miles.

1900–Pere Marquette Railroad. Grand Rapids to Bay View Branch entering Lake County at *Baldwin*, going north: *Grand Rapids*, 0 miles; *Baldwin*, 74 miles; *Conley*, 81 miles; *Canfield*, 85 miles; *Peters*, 85 miles; and *Irons*, 91 miles.

1900–Manistee Branch of Grand Rapids & Indiana Railroad. Beginning at *Milton Junction*, 0 miles; *Deer Lake*, 5 miles; *Totten*, 9 miles; and *Luther*, 12 miles.

POST OFFICES

There were at least 23 post offices during the history of the county. Only 5 of these remain today.

GHOST TOWNS

BRISTOL–located in Dover Township, described in 1918 as 17 miles northeast of *Baldwin* and 6 from *Tustin*, the nearest railroad station. J. H. Sutton, general store. RFD *Tustin*. The *Bristol* cemetery is in Section 23 on Bristol Road.

———

CANFIELDS–see *Luther*.

———

CAREYS–see *Copley*.

———

CAREYVILLE–see *Copley*.

———

CHASE–located in Chase Township, 13 miles east of *Baldwin* and 7 west of *Reed City* is the oldest village in the county and was the first county seat. During the logging days in the mid 1880s the population was nearly 1,000. By the turn-of-the-century it dropped to about 300 and is much less today.

In 1872 described as an embryo village of about ten families, 8 miles west of *Reed City*. The county seat of Lake County. First settled in 1867. J. J. Tanner, postmaster. Contained one hotel; B. K. Halliday, general store; C. W. Joiner & Son, shingles, lumber and lath; blacksmith and gun smith; and J. J. Tanner, merchant.

In 1877 was the former seat of justice, population 200. Situated on the Marquette River and on the F. & P. M. Railroad. Contains two sawmills, a Congregational church, and good public school. The country comprises fine beech and maple lands. Lumber and some farm products are shipped. Daily mail. N. Clark, postmaster; Harmon Brown & Sons, sawmill and general store;

John Brown, hotel and express agent; Reverend W. L. Camp, Congregational; Reverend Hall, Methodist; William Messenger, blacksmith; and S. F. Mullen, boots and shoes (in addition to 1872 businesses).

Chase was incorporated as a village in 1882 and reincorporated in 1887. In 1885 had a weekly newspaper, *The Eclipse*, and John Knevils, postmaster. After the big fire of 1892 that destroyed most of the buildings the population declined and the village was unincorporated. In 1918 the population had dwindled to less than 300. Residents blame the decline to the fire that was determined as set by an arsonist, apparently for revenge, but the guilty party was never apprehended.

In 1918 Murray E. Nicol, postmaster; Chase Cornet Band; George T. Field, physician; and Alfred Nelson, railroad and express agent.

A few empty store buildings remain in *Chase* today. US-10 highway passes through what remains of the village, about 6 miles west of *Reed City*. One of the only poured concrete wall, two-story buildings standing in northern Michigan remains standing on the main corner facing the highway. Most of the few business buildings are vacant.

———

COPLEY–this is another Michigan town that had several names. Known as *"Careys"* and also *"Careville,"* in 1885 population 300. Daily mail. George A. Cockburn, postmaster and justice. Had two hotels, meat market, saw and planing mill, two general stores, barber shop, a stave and wooden pail factory, and C. J. Meyer (railroad and express agent). By 1890 the population had dropped to 56.

In 1905 listed as a discontinued post office on the Manistee Branch of the G. R. & I. Railroad, 19 miles northwest of *Reed City*.

———

DEER LAKE–in 1885 was a lumbering settlement on the Manistee Branch of the G. R. & I. Railroad in Pinora Township, 5 miles west of *Orno* and 22 northeast of *Baldwin*. *Reed City*, 9 miles southwest furnished daily mail. Population 400. E. P. Hayes, postmaster. J. C. Clark, express and railroad agent; Osterhout-Fox & Company, general store, lumbermen's supplies, and sawmills; E. P. Hayes, mill superintendent. Also had a meat market, shoe shop, constable, and justice of peace.

1890 population 321 (census records), in Pinora Township and on Deer Lake. In 1953 a Deer Lake School, cemetery, and Deer Lake Road remained to show the town ever existed.

EDGETTS–located on the M. E. & W. Railroad in Ellsworth Township, at one time had sawmills and a railroad station. During the logging days reached a population of 300. In 1905 ten miles northeast of *Baldwin* and 6 from *Luther*. Lewis Wenzel, postmaster and general store. One sawmill was operating and owned by Adolph Wenzel.

1917 population 30. Telephone. Fred Lickert, postmaster and general store. Also another general store and Lutz & Schramm, pickle salting station. Nothing remains today.

––––––––

ELMTON–see *Luther*.

––––––––

FORMAN–was one of the first villages settled in the county. Settled in 1873. In 1875 located on the F. & P. M. Railroad. Population 200. Located in Pleasant Plains and Yates Townships, 3 miles east of *Baldwin City*. The middle branch of the Pere Marquette River furnishes water power at *"Forman's Mills,"* 2 miles south of the village, where there are two sawmills and a shingle factory. There is also a population of 100 at the mills.

Lumber, shingles, and farm products are shipped. Daily mail. C. H. Forman, postmaster, general store and lumber. Reverend W. L. Camp, Congregationalist (a circuit preacher). Also contained five other mills. James Forman, hotel and shingles; William Forman, station agent; James Roxburgh, owned a narrow-gauge logging railroad and train extending to *Forman's Mills* (2 miles long). There was also a foundry in the village, and several other stores and buildings in addition to houses for the residents and workers.

Within ten years, 1885, *Forman* seemed destined to become the major village in the county. A new Methodist Episcopal church and district school had been built. The permanent population of *Forman* village on the railroad was 125. In that year Frederic Leavenworth, postmaster. Had two hotels, large supply store, barber shop, blacksmith shop, and Terry & Son (flour mill), 2 miles east of town.

A post office remained at *Forman* until 1913 or 1914. By that time the population had dwindled to only a few people and it was discontinued. Nothing remains today of the two settlements in the approximate location of present day *Idlewild*.

––––––––

FORMAN'S MILLS–see *Forman*.

IDLEWILD–is the only all black ghost town in the history of Michigan. Although the unincorporated village is still inhabited it was at one time large enough to be a city. In fact several unsuccessful attempts were made over the years to incorporate. The *Idlewild* of today is a mere shadow of the town it once was.

Founded as a resort area for Negroes when the Idlewild Resort Company of *Chicago* purchased 2,700 acres of land, including Lake Idlewild in 1915, the spectacular resort all but folded in the 1960s.

The Idlewild Resort Company divided the land into lots 25 x 100 feet. A short time later an advertising campaign was waged by the *Chicago* promoters to sell the lots. Free train excursions to the new development brought as many as 300 Negroes to the area each weekend. Lots were sold for $35 each on terms of $6 down and $1 a week. The company's brochures and ads on billboards and street cars in several states sounded like the latest resort development ads on TV today. *"Beautiful lakes of pure spring water, teeming with fish; high and dry building sites; game of all kinds roaming the green forests; and the promise of tennis courts, golf links, and a ball park"*–a promise that was never redeemed.

A large clubhouse for members was constructed on a small island that later became the center of the entertainment area. By the boom times of 1928-29 grocery stores, eating and drinking places, barbeque stands, hotels and night clubs were flourishing. A dime store, drugstore, and clothing store was soon erected. The clubhouse was converted into a huge roller skating rink and on summer weekends thousands of blacks crowded the island. It was estimated that 25,000 people visited *Idlewild* over the Fourth of July in 1959.

Within a few years after its founding, cottages, cabins, homes, and houses of all descriptions sprang up around the lake. They ranged in size from huge, three-story mansions with cast iron gates and fences, to tiny cottages 12 or 14 feet wide and 30 feet long erected on the narrow, 25-foot lots; rambling two-story buildings advertising "Rooms for Rent" and painted gaudy colors; temporary shacks with "Barbeque" signs tacked out front; and during summer months many people camped in tents. On weekends and holidays auto plates from many states in the Union could be seen. In 1927 a post office was established and remains today. At its peak there were probably 2,000 or more dwellings surrounding the lake and extending to US-10 highway that borders the settlement.

During the depression years of the 1930s, another Chicago real estate firm decided to get on the bandwagon and capitalize on *Idlewild's* prestige and attraction to upper-class Negroes. The company purchased large blocks of burned-over timberland adjacent to the village and in the area north of *Baldwin*, and sold it with the implication that it was part of *Idlewild*. Much of the land was platted into five-acre lots, which were sold as places to retire and to live "off the fat of the land." All that was needed, they said, was a cow, a sow, and a few chickens. The down payment on the lots was so low that it became the "in thing" to buy

16

one. As one man said: *"Five dollars down was nothing, and lots of city people bought just to own land ... a small piece of earth to call his own."*

During the pre-war years of the early 1940s, another element of blacks came to the area as tourists. The famous "Flamingo Club" on the island probably presented more big-time names in the entertainment field than the hot spots in *Las Vegas*, Nevada. Even after the crowds quit coming during the 1960s when color barriers were dropped due to more strict civil rights laws, many big names in show business entertained at the night club, just for old-time's sake, and to help out their "soul brothers." By 1965 big bands were playing to mostly vacant seats. The few residents of *Idlewild* were the sick, poor, and aged.

An article in the *Grand Rapids Press* of 1966 described the downfall of *Idlewild* aptly. *"No more than 15 years ago, Idlewild was America's largest Negro resort, with ten to twelve thousand Negroes jamming in during the summer weeks, more than 20,000 on holiday weekends. Its two big night spots, The Flamingo and Paradise Club, attracted all the big-name Negro showfolk; Al Hibler, Sarah Vaughn, Dinah Washington, Louis Armstrong, etc.*

But that was yesteryear. Now Idlewild, much of Baldwin, all of Lake County plus twelve townships in Newaygo, Mason, and Manistee counties is dirt poor, smacking of (Erskine) Caldwell novels."

The article continues to say that with the lowering of racial bars in the 1950s and 1960s, Negroes began forsaking *Idlewild* for the white spots from which they had always been forbidden. *"And now Idlewild is down at the heels. Streets run through the woods to nowhere. Reeds grow in the muddy waters where thousands of Negroes once swam; the stands where vendors once hawked ribs are boarded up. Gone, all gone, the boardwalks, the lights, the jazz and the noise."*

A local C.A.P. Director (Community Action Project) said: *"It is a community where almost everyone is poor. The tragedy is that this impoverishment has already existed for more than a generation."*

The one-time village is still the object of news articles describing its plight. As late as December, 1970, the *Detroit News* and other papers featured half-page stories on the ghost town of *Idlewild*.

The remains of the village, which at one time hired its own Negro Chief of Police to direct traffic and keep order, is now a ghost town of decaying buildings sprawled over a ten-mile square area. In December of 1970 one of the business places burned and will probably never be rebuilt. The owner of one remaining gasoline station and grocery store across the street said there are many weeks when he takes in only a few dollars and most days only a few cents goes into the till.

17

One run-down hotel on the main corners, across from the once-famous Flamingo Club, has a hand scrawled sign in the window "Rooms For Rent by Day or Week," placed next to a realtor's "For Sale" sign. Most of the other buildings are deserted, with only a few families remaining. Two combination gasoline stations and groceries are open. The one mentioned above near the bridge across the island, and another on US-10 near the entrance to the village from US-10 highway near the railroad tracks. Four churches of various denominations remained open in 1968, and school busses transport area children to a consolidated school.

On a Saturday afternoon in May of 1970 only one man could be seen on the main street of the main business section. The former skating rink and night club was boarded up and in a two-hour period only two autos drove down the main street. The smiling, white-haired Negro said he was 74 years old and retired there 10 years ago from *Detroit*. When asked where all the people were and if he thought *Idlewild* would ever boom again, the old man's eyes brightened and he replied, *"She shore will! She shore will! ... Why when the Fourth of July comes again this year you won't be able to walk down the street it'll be so jammed with folks!"*

Perhaps the old man was right, and some Fourth of July the town will boom again.

———

KENAN–see *Luther.*

———

LUMBERTON–was a short-lived lumbering settlement. In 1882 the Foster & Blackman Company of *Big Rapids* had a steam sawmill on the site, with 100 men working in the woods cutting timber. The company shipped 10 million feet of lumber annually by rail. They owned 3,500 acres of pine timberland where the Morton & Teachout Company had just completed a contract for 4½ million feet of lumber. Foster & Blackman shipped timber and lumber to Indiana, Ohio and eastern markets. On August 20, 1883 fire destroyed 2½ million feet of lumber along with the mill, the company grocery and supply store, and all the buildings.

Named *"Lumbertown"* because of the extensive lumbering operations and shortened to *"Lumberton."*

———

LUTHER–is an incorporated village located in Ellsworth and Newkirk Townships with a population of about 300 today, but at one time had three times the population and was a roaring lumbering town.

John Nelson, Alex Hoover, and Abner Burdicks homesteaded near *Luther* in 1868. All were from Pennslyvania. The village was founded by the Wilson Brothers, David and Robert, and their brother-in-law, William Luther, after who it was named in 1881. They set up a sawmill on the Little Manistee River where it crossed the Old State Road which extended from *Grand Rapids* to *Traverse City*. In that year the Grand Rapids and Indiana Railroad was surveyed. When it was completed in 1882 a spur from the tracks was extended to the site and in a few weeks the population zoomed. In 1883 it reached 1,000 and a few years later, at the peak of the lumbering era, exceeded that.

By 1885 there were four churches, four saloons, several hotels and other business places. The new village boasted a newspaper, photographer, three doctors, and an opera house that seated 1,000.

After 1885 the population began to decline. *"Many of the early business-men and lumbermen had followed the Wilson brothers and Luther from Belding, and when business declined they returned,"* Mrs. Robert Logan said in her history of *Luther* on file at the Luther Library.

The village was incorporated in 1893 with a population of about 300. By 1900 there were about 500 residents, in 1910, 626, and by 1920 was back down to about 300. The population remains about the same today (1970).

In 1903 *Luther* was on the Manistee & Grand Rapids Railroad, an independent railroad company, which extended from Manistee to Keenan, a station 3 miles past *Luther.* It entered the county at *Sable*, 15 miles east of *Manistee* and from there as follows: *Elmton*, 16 miles; *Millerton*, 22 miles; *Canfields*, 31 miles; *Carey*, 39 miles; G. R. & I. Crossing, 41 miles; *Luther*, 42 miles; and *Keenan*, 45 miles. (Canfield Rollway was in Section 12, Newkirk Township near a present-day public fishing site.)

In 1905 *Luther* had four churches, public school, bank, flour mill, shingle mills, two hotels, a weekly newspaper, *The Observer*, and a monthly paper, *The Ideal*. Mrs. Fannie Fairbanks, postmistress.

The first school in *Luther* was built in 1882 and the first high school in 1896. Elight Treadgold was the first doctor in 1883. He also founded the Methodist Church in that year. Dr. Earl Fairbanks followed in 1885.

William T. Burnett was an early blacksmith. His son, Gary, is now nearing 90 years of age and still lives in *Luther* (1969). Samuel Buckner first came to *Luther* as a peddler. He stayed and opened a dry goods store and in 1903 established the first bank in the county.

During the early days the village contained a turpentine factory and charcoal kilns. There was a shingle mill and a hardwood sawmill. The hardwood mill and turpentine factory survived for several years. The saw and shingle mill operated until about the time of World War I.

About 1890 the flour mill was built and for a few years flour was ground from locally-grown grains. Later it served as a gristmill and about 1916 was converted to furnish electric power for the village. The service was limited to certain hours on specified days and served as the only electric service until 1938 when Consumers Power Company extended service to the area.

During the height of the lumbering era there was a cigar factory that made cigars, chewing and pipe tobacco from raw tobacco shipped in. The total output was consumed by the local male population.

The Wilson brothers never lived in *Luther* but Mr. Luther built a home there in 1881 and lived there until his death in 1891. The house is still standing today (1969) and has been altered very little. A Mrs. Douglas operates an antique shop in the old house.

––––––––

MILLERTON–see *Luther*.

––––––––

NORWAY HALL–in 1877 was a post office in Chase Township, 14 miles southeast of *Baldwin City*, and 14 miles northwest of *Big Rapids*. *Paris*, on the G. R. & I. Railroad, is its shipping point. Lumber is the only shipment. It has a stage to Summitville weekly and receives weekly mail. S. Fowler, postmaster.

This was a short-lived settlement and by 1890 no longer had a post office. In 1953 the *Norway* schoolhouse still stood in the southwest corner of Section 32.

––––––––

Other places during the history of the county include:

ELLSWORTH–a former village listed in 1877 as a discontinued post office. Ship to *Ashton* in Newaygo County.

GREENDELL–name changed to *"Chase"* about 1869-70.

HAWKES (also spelled *"Hawks"*)–had a hardwood flooring mill and broom handle factory. In the late 1800s had nearly 300 population. Nothing remains.

IRONS–1918 population 20. On the P. M. Railroad, Eden Township, 18 miles north of *Baldwin*. Ely M. Vorhees, postmaster and hotel. Henry Soldan, general store. Other business places. Shown on conservation and county maps.

20

LITTLE MANISTEE–on the P. M. Railroad below *Irons*.

LINCOLNSMILL–in the late 1800s had a population of 150.

MARLBOROUGH (also spelled *"Marlboro"*)–on the Pere Marquette River, 21° miles south of *Baldwin*. In 1905 mail *Baldwin*.

OLGA–on the railroad between *Hoxeyville* and *Tustin*.

OLIVERS–in 1905 a discontinued post office on the P. M. Railroad, 4 miles west of *Reed City*. The Olivers School was standing in 1953 on US-10 west of *Reed City*. Also an old barn between *Olivers* and *Reed City* with a sign "First Post Office" mounted over the doors in 1970.

PEACOCK–at one time had a population of several hundred. In 1917 population 31. On the P. M. and Manistee & Eastern Railroad, Peacock Township, 12 miles north of *Baldwin* and 12 from *Luther*. Mrs. K. B. Barlett, postmistress. C. B. Cork, station agent. Also a store and livery barn.

PETERS–a short distance from *Baldwin*. 1910 mail *Baldwin*.

PINE RIVER–in 1870 on the old mail route between *Big Rapids* (Old State Road) and *Traverse City*, 22 miles of *Sherman* in Wexford County and 41 miles northwest of *Big Rapids*.

RENOE–in 1877 a post office and station on the F. & P. M. Railroad in Elk Township.

ROBYS JUNCTION–on 1890 railroad maps just below *Forman*.

SAUBLE (also spelled *"Sable"*)–at one time a good-sized village on the Manistee & Eastern Railroad, Elk Township, 17 miles from *Baldwin* and 10 from *Fountain* (across the county line). In 1918 population 40. C. B. Ross, postmaster and general store. Other business places.

STEARNS–shown on 1890 railroad maps on the F. & P. M. Railroad about the same location as *Sauble*. Name could have been changed to *"Sauble"* when the post office was established as there was another *Stearns* in Midland County.

SUMMITVILLE –(also see *Luther*)–in 1877 a village in Chase Township, on the F. & P. M. Railroad, 9 miles west of *Reed City*. *"Has one sawmill and seven other sawmills nearby. S. G. Randall, postmaster and station agent."*

THOMPSON HEIGHTS, UNGER'S CROSSING (the station near *Idlewild*), and *SKOOKUM* on the Pine River between *Luther* and *Bristol* were small settlements.

TOTTEN–a flag stop on the Manistee Branch of the G. R. & I. Railroad 3 miles from *Luther* during the logging days.

TROY–in Troy Township. A Troy Cemetery is located in Section 29 in the southwest corner of the county.

WINGLETON–was an important lumbering village. In 1918 a post office on the P. M. Railroad, Elk Township, 4½ miles west of *Baldwin*. The Wingleton Railroad crossing is shown in Section 36 on present day maps.

WOLF LAKE–shown on 1890 railroad maps near the Manistee County line. In 1910 mail *Peacock*.

———

Chapter 5

LEELANAU COUNTY GHOST TOWNS
AND SLEEPING BEAR DUNES

From her booklet *Our First Families*, Laura Lindley says: *"In the early days Antrim, Leelanau, and Benzie were attached. There were nine townships. Meegezee, Milton, Whitewater, Peninsula, Traverse, Leelanau, Centerville, Glen Arbor, and Crystal Lake Townships."*

George A. Craker, a Presbyterian missionary, moved to *Omena* in 1852. He later retired to a farm. A post office was opened at *Omena* February 9, 1858, and was the first post office in the county.

Leelanau County was organized in 1863 as "Leelanaw." Leelanau was the name of a fictional Indian maiden in one of Henry R. Schoolcraft's stories. He gave its meaning as "delight of life."

The county was formed from land area taken from Grand Traverse County. *Northport* was the original county seat and remained so until 1882, when it was moved to *Leland*.

The history of Leelanau County is intertwined with that of Grand Traverse and the entire region. In May, 1839, Reverend Peter Dougherty, a Presbyterian missionary, established a school at present-day *Elk Rapids*, which at that time included what is now Leelanau County. In 1840 he moved the house across the bay and used it for a schoolhouse, which was set up on the peninsula. In 1841 Dougherty, his wife and infant daughter, along with Deacon Joseph Dame, of *Mackinac*, and Lewis Miller settled at *Old Mission*.

There is an interesting Indian legend regarding Sleeping Bear Point in the county, and the Indians gave it that name. For many years the Federal Government has been trying to set aside a large portion of the county including Sleeping Bear Point, as a national park area. Most of the population of the county consists of wealthy summer resorters and retirees who own large estates in the area, and are opposed to the idea. To this date nothing definite has been accomplished in establishing the area as a National Park.*

Much of the history of the county centers around *Suttons Bay* founded by Harry C. Sutton. It was first called *"Suttonsburg."* George Steimel, a German immigrant, came here in 1864. In 1874 he built a hotel called the "Bay House." It also included a livery and saloon. In 1884 he and Michael Heuss, a German carpenter, built a planing mill here.

NOTE: An act to establish the park was passed by the Legislature in 1970.

In 1861 there were only three houses on the site of the village, one owned by Gershon Porter. The home of H. C. Sutton. And the third house built, was by the Reverend and Mrs. Helms, who built a house 12 feet square. He was the first Protestant minister to come to the village.

The first road between *Suttons Bay* and *Traverse City* was a trail cut through the woods in 1862, called the "State Road." Mail was still delivered by boat from *Traverse City*. The *Suttons Bay* post office was opened August 27, 1861.

Carrier pigeons nested in the Traverse Bay region by the millions during the early days. In 1869 a famous pigeon-catcher from *Chicago*, Thomas Smith, netted thousands of pigeons near the bay. They were packed in barrels of ice and shipped to *Chicago, New York*, and *Boston*. Smith received a receipt from the Fargo Express Company for 16 tons of pigeon meat.

The county is the site of Michigan's first state park. A historical plaque is erected there and reads: *"By the end of World War I, and with the rapid growth of the recreation industry in Michigan, a need for a state-wide parks system had arisen. In 1919 the State Park Commission was established. D. H. Day State Park, honoring the commission's chairman, was the first park set up. When the state parks were transferred to the Conservation Department in 1921, over 20 other sites had been acquired, most of them like the D. H. Day State Park, beautifully located on lake shores."*

RAILROADS

Railroads serving the county were:

1900–Manistee & North Eastern. Beginning at *Manistee*, 0 miles; *Interlochen*, 45 miles; *Filer's Switch*, 47 miles; *Sherman's Mill*, 49 miles; *Lake Ann*, 52 miles; *Cedar Run*, 55 miles; *Solon*, 59 miles; *Fouch*, 62 miles; *Harch's Crossing*, 64 miles; *Greelickville*, 67 miles.

POST OFFICES

There were at least 26 post offices during the history of the county. Of that number 10 remain.

GHOST TOWNS

ALMIRA–see *Omena*.

————

BINGHAM–shown on the 1968 State highway map, located on the shore of Lake Leelanau (formerly Carp Lake). James Lee was one of the first settlers in Bingham Township in 1858. He was one of the first fruit growers in the area, and eventually became a State Legislator in 1875 and was re-elected in 1877. He and his cousin, Robert Lee, built a dock at *Lee's Bay* which was destroyed by a storm a few years later and never rebuilt.

At one time Bingham had a population of 400. The post office was established November 26, 1878. A Mr. Porter was the first postmaster.

The Boone Company, consisting of Boone and Johnson, set up a sawmill owned by S. C. Darrow and sawed the first log in December of that year.

Stores, a blacksmith shop, saloon, sawmills, and a church were soon erected. The first post office was located in the store of Michael Oberlin. There was also a boardinghouse, dance hall, C. Richards (saloon), Simrie Hinshaw (blacksmith.) John Manitou, an Indian, played fiddle for dances.

Al Barnes said the Barker Creek Company took over the mill, they sold out to Herbert Boreghy, who later dismantled it and moved out. There was also a Polish settlement, he said, a log schoolhouse, and in 1899 an Evangelical church.

The Boone families, one of whom started the first sawmill, were descended from Stephen Boone, brother to Daniel Boone of Kentucky fame. Four of the Boone boys served in World War II. They were Arnold, Louis, Robbins, and William Boone.

By the turn-of-the-century very little remained of the one-time village. In 1918 the railroad, now the Manistee and Northeastern, was owned by the G. R. & I. Railroad. There was a shipping point by water 3 miles east on Grand Traverse Bay called *Larkin's Dock*. In 1918 the place had a telephone connection and was RFD *Traverse City*. J. B. Arnold, general store. The post office was discontinued May 31, 1908.

BURDICKVILLE–was named after William Burdick who built a grist and saw-mill on Glen Lake in 1859. Ten years later they burned. In 1867 John Helm ran a store there. The first post office was established in 1868. Mail was delivered twice a week by an Indian mail runner from *Traverse City*. Mr. Helm was the first postmaster.

In 1876 described as located in Empire Township, 7 miles east of *Glen Haven*, its shipping port. *Traverse City* is its railroad center. (Empire Township was organized in 1865). Population in 1876 was 50. Stages to *Glen Arbor* and *Traverse City* four times a week. Mail semi-weekly. Mrs. N. (Nancy) C. Helm, postmistress. She was the first woman postmistress in Michigan and held the office for 35 years. Other places were S. S. Burnett, general store; John Helm, general store; William Agnew, tailor; and Joseph Price, blacksmith.

In 1918 population 150. *Cedar*, 9 miles west was the banking point. M. L. Cook, postmaster and general store; A. M. Atkinson, mill owner; P. Sheffick, railroad and express agent. Shortly after World War I the post office was discontinued.

In 1953 a Burdickville School remained, about ° mile south of the site of the former village. No buildings remain on the site.

CEDAR–shown on 1968 State highway map, no population given. In 1918 population 400. Known as *"Cedar City Station,"* on the Manistee & Northeastern Railroad in Solon Township, 12 miles south of *Leland*. Has a bank. Stage twice a day to *Maple City*. Telegraph and telephone.

G. A. Masson, postmaster and druggist. Elmer Billman, bank cashier; D. A. Clavitt, proprietor of the Cedar-Maple City Stage Lines; Myron A. Culver and son Edward, lumber and cooperage (barrel) stock; G. W. Fralick, physician; Knittel & Company, potatoes; F. W. Lathrop, restaurant; M. S. Rosinski, drayman; J. J. Sbonek, general store; P. A. Shettick, express and telegraph agent; Elmer Billman and G. A. Mason, Cedar State Bank; William Sweet, general store; John Tucker, restaurant; J. C. Slack, meats; J. B. Ward and Myron A. Culver, general store.

EAGLE TOWN–see *Pshawbatown*.

FOX ISLAND–23 miles northwest of *Leland* in Lake Michigan was a village and post office on *South Fox Island*. In 1918 population 60. John O. Plank, postmaster; George Abott, fisherman; John Andrews and Enis Chipaway, fish dealers; Leo Brothers, general store and shingle mill; Paul Thomas, livestock.

GILL'S PIER–on Lake Michigan in Leelanau Township, 6 miles northeast of *Leland* and 5 from *Northport*. In 1905 had 150 population. Daily stage to *Northport*. Telephone. K. A. Nelson, postmaster; general store, hardware, insurance and real estate; Northland Beach Resort, Whitney & Cobaum, proprietors.

William Gill settled there in 1855 and it was named after him. A Gill's Pier Catholic Church is located today on County Road 637, about 1 mile south of M-22 and the former site of *Gill's Pier* on Lake Michigan.

GOOD HARBOR–in 1877 was located 10 miles south of *Leland* and 24 miles southwest of *Northport*, the county seat. Semi-weekly mail. At one time the population was more than 100. By the turn of the century it dwindled and in 1910 population 75. RFD *Maple City.*

In 1918 *Cedar,* 7 miles distant, was the shipping point. J. J. Kilway, general store and implements; Benjamin Minsker, general store; and R. Peterson, fisherman.

———

GREELICKVILLE–see *Norrisville.*

———

ISADORE–in 1918 population 75. Post office discontinued. In Centerville Township, 12 miles south of *Leland,* the county seat, and 3 from *Cedar.* Telephone. RFD *Cedar.* Jacob Rosinski, Jr., farm implements.

———

KASSON–in 1863 Alex Horman homesteaded at *Kasson.* He was a well digger. It is said that some of the wells in the area ranged to depths of 200 feet deep, were dug by hand and curbed with boards or stones as the digging progressed.

In 1877 population nearly 300. Also known as *"Maple City,"* 12 miles south of *Glen Arbor* (formerly *"Sleeping Bear Bay."*) Cordwood, maple sugar, and potatoes are shipped. Stage coach to *Traverse City* and *Glen Arbor.* Semi-weekly mail. William S. Peck, postmaster. L. B. Carr and J. C. Carr, wagonmakers; Reverend D. Cleveland, Methodist; S. S. Clyde, blacksmith; Reverend Prevost, Evangelist; J. Dewing, superintendent of schools; Mrs. A. L. Grandy, millinery; A. L. Grandy, blacksmith; J. S. Stricklin, wagonmaker; Mrs. J. B. Hall, physician; C. W. Williams, Methodist.

In 1953 a West Kasson school remained on County Road 669, about 4 miles south of *Maple City.* The post office was discontinued about 1905. After that send mail to *Maple City.*

———

KESWICK–received its name from the Reverend John A. Lawrence who was born in a village of that name in Canada. Charles Revold settled near the site of *Keswick* in 1872, the same year Reverend Lawrence settled. They were followed by Martin Olson in 1876. The first post office was established September 17, 1889, with Mrs. Lavina (William) Mebert as the first postmistress. She was also the area's midwife.

The first frame house was built by Frederic Allert, who also became the first town preacher. Most of the early settlers were German.

In 1905 a country post office and flag station on the Traverse-City, Ludington & Manistee Railroad, in Bingham Township, 5 miles from *Suttons Bay.* O. M. Olson, postmaster; Joseph Gerard, justice; Laura Lindley, teacher.

In that year (1905) A. W. Mebert, constable; Reverend Benjamin Mohr, Evangelical; Martin Olson, general store; O. M. Olson, carpenter; Fred Revold, Jr., justice; Martha Revold, music teacher; and John G. Weiss, justice.

At one time there was a gristmill on Mebert's Creek, just south of *Keswick*, built by Mebert, Martin Olson, and Levi Lindley. It was torn down about 1905.

By 1910 the population of *Keswick*, at one time totaling nearly 200, had dwindled to 40. The post office was discontinued November 15, 1910 and mail delivered RFD *Suttons Bay*.

———

MAPLE CITY - see *Kasson*.

———

NEW MISSION–see *Omena*.

———

NORRISVILLE–during the 1860s and 1870s a group of Germans settled in the area. Jacob Groesser from *Hamilton, Ontario* was an early settler. Albert Norris had a gristmill there in 1852 and the settlement was named after him. At one time a brick factory here turned out 200,000 bricks a year.

The post office was established about 1890. Walter Greelick was postmaster in 1897 and the town was called *"Greelickville,"* although the post office was listed as *"Norrisville."* In 1902 the post office was discontinued. In 1910 *Greelickville* mail was sent to *Traverse City*.

———

NORTH MANITOU ISLAND–was originally a part of Manitou County (see "The Ghost County" in Volume I). In 1918 population 100. A summer resort off the western shore of Leelanau County, 13 miles west of *Leland*. A U.S. Life Saving Station and lighthouse is located here. Steamers from *Chicago* stop twice a week, H. E. Voice, postmaster; John Newhall, fruit grower; Peter Stormer, logger and timber dealer; Asa Roxberry, general manager.

Captain E. O. Wilbur, who moved to *Northport* in 1856 from the island, said his father was the first white man on the island and cut cordwood for the Piccard Brothers.

———

NORTH UNITY–in 1877 was a small settlement and dock 6 miles north of *Glen Arbor*. Ships cordwood (used for engines on steamboats). Semi-weekly mail.

NOTE: Much of the information used about Leelanau County in this book is taken from the booklet *Our First Families* by Laura Lindley, published in 1954.

ALMIRA–the name was first called *"New Mission."* The first post office was established in 1858, and in 1877 listed as *"Omena,"* also known as *Almira*.

In 1852, the Reverend Dougherty, a Presbyterian missionary, and George A. Craker opened a school there. Another teacher and early settler was John Porter, who came from Pennslyvania with his family in 1854.

In 1877 described as: *"Population 150. In Leelanaw Township, 5 miles south of Northport, the county seat. The country here is high and rolling. Cordwood and potatoes are shipped. Tri-weekly mail. A. B. Page, postmaster. G. A. Craker, farmer and wood dealer. S. H. Doe, general store; A. Miller and V. C. Miller, gardners and distillers of essential oils."*

PASHABATOWN–in 1852 was the location of a Jesuit Mission called *"Eagle Town."* Located on Grand Traverse Bay a few miles south of *Suttons Bay*, the place was never considered a village by the whites and was an Indian village that took its name after Chief Pashaba who lived there when the missionaries arrived. Until shortly after the turn-of-the-century Indians of the village wove baskets and travelled all over the county on foot selling them. Christine Chippewa was a well-known Indian woman who lived there and reached the age of 100 years. The place ceased to be a village in 1895.

An article appeared in the *Detroit News* February 8, 1970, mentions of a new wellhouse constructed there and said: *"It is made up almost entirely of Indian families and only two of them have running water. A new wellhouse next to Immaculate Conception Mission has been completed. Until now other families had to carry water from the two homes with running water. Louis Koon, 'Mayor' of Pashabatown, Reverend Henry Dondzila, former missionary, and Aubery Park built the wellhouse with state assistance."*

PROVEMONT–not shown on 1969 State highway map and not a post office in 1969. Located in Leland Township, 12 miles south of *Northport* on the Carp River, was settled in 1854. In 1877 a shipping point for cordwood, tanbark, cedar posts, etc. Tri-weekly stage and mail. Populaton 100. William Horton, postmaster.

In 1903 a branch of the Manistee & North Eastern Railroad was extended from *Solon* to *Centerville* and into Leland Township and *Provemont*.

By 1918 population had increased to 300. Located 5 miles southeast of *Leland*. Telephone. Paul Plamondon, postmaster and telephone manager. Other business places were Fountain Point Resort, meat market, horse barns, hardware, saw and gristmill, C. K. Lathrop (express and telegraph agent), Northam Hotel, harness shop, shoe shop, livery, three stores, a pickle station, Catholic school, weekly news (*The Provemont Courier*), Julius Prouse, (stage line), Suttons Bay Stage and other places.

————

SCHOMBERG–in Centerville Township, 9 miles from *Leland* and 5½ from *Cedar*. In 1918 population 25. On the M & N. E. Railroad. Telephone. Mrs. John B. Decker, general store, and Peter Swanson, lawyer.

————

SOLON–in 1877 a post office in a farmhouse in Solon Township, 12 miles northwest of *Traverse City*. Semi-weekly mail. M. C. Cate, postmaster, shoemaker, and farmer.

————

SOUTH MANITOU–in 1877 was a village on the island, located in Manitou County (see "The Ghost County" Volume I). *"A general supply store is located here, and wood and fish are shipped."* Captain G. Starkweather operated a general store at this point and sold cordwood to ships. The settlement was formed in 1840.

In 1918 a lighthouse was located here. Daily mail. S. Hutzler, postmaster and dry goods store, and Erwin Beck, grocery.

————

WAKAZOVILLE–Deacon Joseph Dame founded the village and had it platted in 1854. William Voice built the first sawmill in 1855. In that year the first school district and a post office was established. A. B. Paige was the first postmaster and Joseph Dame built the first hotel.

On March 14, 1873, the name was changed to *"Northport"* by an act of the Legislature. By 1876 the population was 300 and contained a gristmill, sawmill, and broom handle factory. Two chuches, Presbyterian and Methodist. Farm produce, cordwood and fish were shipped. Stage to *Traverse City* tri-weekly. Mail tri-weekly. William Gill, postmaster and general store. Had a barber shop, the "Franklin Hotel," bakery, two general stores, boot and shoe store, blacksmith shop, cooperage, millinery store, etc. The first cement block building was built by James Kehl and his brothers, Edward and Christian, in 1902.

————

Other towns or places during the history of the county were:

BODUS–1910 mail *Schomberg*.

EAST EMPIRE–1910 mail *Empire*.

30

ELTON–mail *Provement*.

FOUCH–7 miles north of *Traverse City*, 1910 mail *Traverse City*.

GLENMERE–2 miles from *Glen Arbor*. In 1918 Richard Tobin, general store.
Mail to *Empire*.

HATCH'S CROSSING–1910 mail to *Traverse City*, 6 miles south.

HEIMFORTH.

MANSEAU–1910 mail to *Omena*.

PLEASANT VILLAGE– founded by Father Herbstritt who purchased 6,000 acres
and laid out the town.

PORT ONEIDA–1910 RFD *Maple City*.

SHETLAND–1910 mail RFD *Maple City*.

Chapter 6

MANISTEE COUNTY GHOST TOWNS
AND THE
TOWN THAT DISAPPEARED INTO LAKE MICHIGAN

This county was set off in the original survey of Michigan in 1840. The county government was organized in 1855. The land area was taken from Mackinac, Ottawa, Oceana, and Grand Traverse Counties. The city of *Manistee* is the county seat. It takes its name from the river, first called "Manistee" by the Indians. "Manistee," in their language was the word for red ochre they used for painting their faces. The harbor at the mouth of the river rarely freezes, making it the best winter port on Lake Michigan.

Manistee County played an important part during the logging era. Lake ships from *Chicago*, Wisconsin and other points were lined up in the harbor transporting lumber and lumber products.

Missionaries and fur buyers visited the area in the early 1800s. A Jesuit mission house stood on the northwest shore of Manistee Lake in 1826.

The Campeau brothers of *Detroit* and *Grand Rapids* made fur buying trips to *Manistee* in the early 1800s, and in 1832 a party from Massachusetts explored the river. In an attempt to make a settlement, but were driven off by the Indians. In 1833 a Captain Humphrey came with intentions of setting up a sawmill, but he . too abandoned the project.

In the spring of 1841 John Stronach and his son Adam brought machinery for a sawmill, supplies, horses, cattle, and a crew of men and became the first settlers at the north end of Manistee Lake. In 1845 they sold out to Joseph Humble and erected another mill at what was called *"Stronach."*

Manistee was made famous for its role in the logging industry, producing several wealthy timber barons. It also became noted for its large deposits of salt.

In 1847 *Manistee* consisted of a sawmill and a cluster of shanties. The "Old Mission House" mentioned above, was used as a boardinghouse and another shanty was erected to serve as a store or supply house.

The following winter (1848) Owen Finan and Joseph Harper set up large camps on the river. Roswell Canfield set up a mill in competition with the Stronach's about this same time.

During the first years mail was delivered by a man carrying mail on his back, starting from *Chicago*. He reached *Manistee* about once a month. In the winter there was no mail.

Old-timers speak of *"Stronachtown"* as the county seat.

The Old Mission House was constructed of logs. The house was occupied by Owen Finan and later by John Barrett. It also became the first saloon in *Manistee*.

Joseph Stronach was drowned in Lake Michigan early in the summer of 1850. He was buried in the burying ground near the Humble Mill that he once owned. In 1851 the Humble Mill burned and was never rebuilt.

Other men of reknown during the lumbering days was Louis Sands, who eventually had camps all over northern Michigan. His name became a household word in northern Michigan and is perpetuated in many songs of the lumber camps. *Manistee* was also the home of Silas Overpack, inventor of what the loggers called the "Big Wheels."

The county has an active historical society and much of the history has been preserved.

A historical plaque located 2 miles north of *Manistee* at Orchard Beach State Park tells the story of the great fire that destroyed most of the village in 1871: *"On October 8, 1871, the day the famous Chicago fire began, equally terrible fires broke out on Lake Michigan's east coast in forests parched by a hot, dry summer. The flames were fanned by high winds. In a few hours most of Holland and Manistee lay in smoldering ruins, a fate other coastal towns barely escaped. The fires swept on across the state, clear to Lake Huron, destroying some two million acres of trees. Relief for the thousands of victims came from all over Michigan and the nation."*

POST OFFICES

During the history of the county there have been at least 23 post offices. Eleven post offices remain today.

RAILROADS

1890–Manistee Division, Flint & Pere Marquette. Beginning at *Manistee Junction*, 0 miles; *Batcheller*, 4.51 miles; *Fountain*, 8.10 miles; *Gun Lake Switch*, 10.66 miles; *Freesoil*, 13.35 miles; *Stronach*, 10.89 miles; *Eastlake*, 23.70 miles; and ending at *Manistee*, 26.46 miles.

1890–Cincinnati Saginaw & Mackinaw, Northern Division. Beginning at *Grand Rapids*, 153 miles; to *Baldwin* in Newaygo County, 227 miles; through *Peters* and *Irons* to *High Bridge*, 256 miles; *Manistee Crossing*, 264 miles; *Inland*, 284 miles; then on to *Traverse City*, 301 miles.

1890–Grand Rapids & Indiana, Manistee Branch. *Milton Junction*, 0 miles; *Deer Lake*, 5 miles (Newaygo County), ending at *Carey*, 15 miles.

1890–Michigan Central–Manistee & North Eastern. *Manistee*, 0 miles; *B. & D. Camp No. 1*, 6.15 miles; *B. & D. Camp No. 2*, 8.33 miles; *Onekama Junction*, 9.84 miles; *Chief Lake*, 15.05 miles; *Bear Creek*, 18.25 miles; *Manistee Crossing*, 19.91 miles; *Lemon Lake*, 25.16 miles; *Copemish*, 19.36 miles; *Nessen City*, 32.94 miles; *Green Lake*, 40.99 miles; *Interlochen*, 44.64 miles; and ending at *Lake Ann*, 53 miles.

1890–Onekama Division Manistee & North Eastern. *Manistee*, 0 miles; *Onekama Junction*, 9.84 miles; *Brookfield*, 11.90 miles; *Onekama*, 12.55 miles.

1890–Toledo Ann Arbor & Northern Michigan. Beginning at *Toledo*, 0 miles; *Sherman*, on the Manistee River in Wexford County, 261.2 miles; *Springville*, 264.1 miles; *Gilbert's*, 269.8 miles; *Cleon Centre*, 272 miles; *Copemish*, 274.2 miles; *Onekama*, 295.5 miles; *Manistee*, 303.7 miles; *Bezonia*, 288.8 miles; ending at *Frankfort*, 298.9 miles.

GHOST TOWNS

ARENDAL–1910 population 25. RFD *Manistee*. In 1918, 7½ miles northeast of *Manistee*. No population given. Shown on 1953 conservation maps in Sections 15 and 16 Manistee Township.

———

BUTWELL–in 1910 on the Arcadia & Betsy Railroad mail to *Malcolm*. On the line of Sections 4 and 5 near the north county line in Pleasanton Township at the corner of Butwell and Taylor Roads on the old A. & B. Railroad grade.

———

CHIEF LAKE–1910 population l00. Railroad name *"Chief."* 1917 population 170. E. McCurdy, postmaster; E. L. Reynolds, station agent. Had two blacksmith shops, two general stores, meat market, millinery shop, hotel and livery, creamery, dairy store, pickle station, two sawmills, confectionery, feed and cider mill. Ed Kenny was listed as a "dentist and oculist."

Shown on 1969 Michigan highway maps. No population given.

CLEON–in 1870 described as: *"Population 150. In the northeast corner of the county 8 miles east of Sherman in Wexford County. Settled in 1865, on the Manistee River in a timbered region, but the settlers have turned to farming. Weekly mail. Joseph Seamons, postmaster."*

In 1917 listed as a discontinued post office, 7 miles from *Copemish* RFD.

––––––––––

DUBLIN–was first called *"Wellston."* In 1918 population 100. On the Pere Marquette Railroad, Norman Township, 21 miles east of *Manistee*. Martha V. McDaniel, postmistress, news dealer, gifts and notions. W. H. Cunningham, railroad and express agent. The village also contained a blacksmith shop, general store, auto livery, library, photo shop, insurance and real estate office, post office, railroad station, and three poultry farms. Shown on 1969 road maps.

––––––––––

FLORENCE–was located between *Dublin* and *Irons*, in Lake County, on 1925 road maps. In 1910 at the intersection of the Manistee & Luther Railroad and Pere Marquette Railroad, Norman Township, Section 31. The old M. & L. Railroad grade is evident across the southeast part of the county. Nine Mile Bridge Road follows much of the old grade.

> NOTE: In 1870 another *Florence* listed in St. Joseph County.

––––––––––

GLOVERS LAKE–was a village on the Arcadia & Betsy Railroad. In 1910 mail to Henry. Glover Lake Road on 1969 maps extends from Arcadia to the C. & O. Railroad tracks. Also a lake named Glovers. In 1953 the old Glover School stood in Section 1, Springdale Township on Nuremburger Road. Also a *"Glovers Lake Tower"* in Section 12.

> NOTE: There was also a *"Glover"* in Bay County. See Volume I.

––––––––––

HARLAN–1918 population 75. On the Ann Arbor Railroad, Cleon Township, 6 miles east of *Copemish*. Telephone. E. M. Wagner, postmaster; E. D. Benson, blacksmith; L. Damaska, railroad agent. Also a saw and feed mill, pickle station, wholesale produce, two general stores, and L. Myers, telephone exchange.

Shown on 1969 maps. The Ann Arbor (C. & O.) Railroad is still operating in 1970.

––––––––––

HENRY–1918 population 25. On the Ann Arbor and Pere Marquette Railroad Springdale Township, 4 miles west of *Copemish*. RFD *Thompsonville*, 4 miles distant. P. E. Clugh, station agent.

This village was located in the southeast corner of Section 15. Five old railroad grades intersect at this point near Healy Lake, 1 mile northeast of the "Old Block House," an old landmark.

―――――

HIGHBRIDGE–in 1918 on the Pere Marquette Railroad, 8 miles south of *Kaleva*. Satie B. Lewis, postmistress; Hoffman & Peters, sawmill; and John E. Lewis, grocer. In Dickinson Township shown on the 1969 AAA road map.

―――――

HUMPHREY–was on the Arcadia & Betsy Railroad, Springdale Township, 6 miles from *Copemish*. In 1910 mail to *Henry*. Probably named after a Captain Humphrey who visited the mouth of the Manistee River in 1833 with intentions of setting up a mill, but abandoned the project.

―――――

MARRILLA (also spelled *"Marila"*)–in 1870 a small settlement in Marrilla Township 26 miles north of *Manistee* on the mail route to *Sherman* (in Wexford County). *"The township is new and has yet but little trade. Weekly mail."*

In 1877 on the mail stage route from *Manistee* to *Manton* (in Wexford County). John Brimmer, postmaster.

In 1910 the population was under 100 and in 1918 dropped to 30. Located 7 miles from *Kaleva*. Telephone. George L. Brimmer, postmaster. Had two general stores, R. F. Danville (lumberman and horsedealer), grain elevator, real estate office, and blacksmith shop.

Shown on 1970 AAA map and on the old Manistee & North Eastern Railroad Grade.

―――――

OAK HILL–in 1910 population 150. Mail to *Manistee*. In 1918 in Filer Township. *"Three miles from Manistee by which it is connected by electric railroad."* It had two general stores, a meat market, grocery store, coal yard, and a sawmill.

―――――

PERRY'S PIER–see *Pierport*.

―――――

PIERPORT–was first called *"Turnersport."* In 1872 described as 14 miles north of Manistee on Lake Michigan. *"The area is heavily timbered, mainly with hardwood. Ships bark, cordwood, railroad ties, and potatoes. Semi-weekly mail. Jeremiah James, postmaster. George L. Cole, fisherman; Charles W.*

Perry, general store, shipping and forwarding; and Martin Werle, wood contractor."

Charles W. Perry played an important part in the early history of the county. Born in *Ludlow*, Vermont, January 9, 1845, he moved to *Waukesha*, Wisconsin in 1854. In 1861 his father died and he took a job as store clerk at age 16. In 1862 he enlisted in Company F, 1st Wisconsin Cavalry, in the Civil War. He worked his way up to First Lieutenant and was discharged July 19, 1865.

After the war he spent three years in *New York City* in the stationery and book business. He returned to Michigan, married in 1872, and located at *Pierport*. He was school director, justice of the peace, and Township Supervisor before being elected as State Representative in 1895 and re-elected in 1897.

Apparently the two villages of *"Pierport"* and *"Pierpoint"* were confused by geographers. In 1876, *Pierport* was known locally as *"Perry's Pier,"* after C. W. Perry. Described as: *"A hamlet of about 100 inhabitants on Lake Michigan in Onekama Township, 14 miles north of Manistee. The land is rolling and covered with heavy beech and maple timber. Cordwood, tanbark, lumber and potatoes are shipped. Telegraph. Stage to Manistee and Frankfort tri-weekly. Mail, tri-weekly. Charles W. Perry, postmaster, steamboat and freight agent; George Dwyer, sawmill; Samuel Elliot, carpenter; J. N. Miller, physician; Hiram Pratt, hotel; and Charles Conklin, blacksmith."*

In 1872 a place is described as *"Pierpoint,"* 16 miles north of *Manistee* in Onekama Township. Population 160. Also known as *"Perry's Pier."* Stage daily to *Onekama*. C. A. Ellis, postmaster; William Enos, mason; E. A. Johnson & Sons, carpenters and house movers; Margaret Miller, teacher; C. W. Perry & Company, general store; F. B. Plopper, carpenter; George Shaver, mason; George Shaver, Jr., mason; Eric Soderquist, shoemaker; W. Weller, blacksmith; S. S. Wilson, fruit grower.

Pierport is designated on 1969 State highway maps.

———

PLEASANTON–also known as *"Saile Station"* in 1918. In 1870 a village in Pleasanton Township, 25 miles northeast of *Manistee*. Population 350. Ships timber, potatoes, butter, and maple sugar. Weekly mail. George B. Pierce, postmaster. Samuel Brittan, bucket and basket manufacturer; Rufus Lumley, bucket manufacturer; J. D. Millard, Pastor Congregational Church.

In 1877 eight miles east of *Pierport*. *"Has Methodist and Congregational churches. Stages to Manistee, Benzonia and Traverse City. Mail four times weekly. B. C. Lewis, postmaster; J. W. Allen, school superintendent. Had a general store; furniture maker; blacksmith shop; and D. and R. Lumley, bucket makers."*

In 1917 on the Arcadia & Betsy Railroad. Has telephone. RFD *Bear Lake.* In 1953 there was a Methodist church and a cemetery.

––––––

POMONA–in 1910 population 75. 1918 population 150. On the Ann Arbor Railroad, Cleon Township, 2¾ miles from Copemish. Has Evangelical and Methodist Episcopal churches. Telephone. J. S. L. Griner, general store; W. A. Hupp & Sons, blacksmiths; C. Hysell, grain and potato buyer; Pomona Cornet Band; D. A. Stuart, dry goods.

Shown on some maps today (1970).

––––––

PORTAGE–also known as *"Old Portage."* Settled in 1850. Located in Onekama Township and on the shore of Lake Michigan. In 1870 described as: *"Eleven miles north of Manistee. Situated on a neck of land between Portage Lake and Lake Michigan. Population 150. Ships lumber and fruit. Semi-weekly mail. S. T. Gunderson & Company, lumber; Porter & Company, lumber and general store."*

On May 8, 1871, a post office was established in the Porter & Company store with Augustus Farr as postmaster. Farr was also manager of the store and started working for the company in 1870. When application was made for a post office the postal department requested the name be changed, as there were several *"Portage," "Portage Lake,"* etc. in the state. The name *"Onekema"* was chosen and accepted by postal officials.

Due to a dam built to operate the Porter Mills, farmers in the area were constantly flooded and there was much resentment between the homesteaders and mill owners. On May 14, 1871, less than a week after the village received a post office, some of the farmers held a celebration. In the heat of the excitement one of the celebrants hitched his ox to the "key log" in the dam. As one onlooker graphically described it, *"All hell broke loose!"* People made a mad dash to high ground and from a safe distance watched the amazing results as the water level of Portage Lake dropped almost 15 feet within a few hours. The biggest part of the ground where the village stood was washed out into Lake Michigan: trees, land and all.

After they realized the effects of their "little joke" of pulling out the dam, many of the farmers were concerned about what the law might do if they found the culprit who pulled out the log. It soon became apparent that a better harbor had been made as a result and one which could not have duplicated by paid engineers. It also returned much of the farmer's lands formerly covered with water.

For several weeks after the huge washout, skippers of Great Lakes boats and schooners were going "out of their tree" when they suddenly became grounded in the middle of a forest far out from shore in what they thought to be open seas.

The next day the Porter Campany's bank of logs, totalling several million feet, were stranded about 40 rods from the edge of the lake. The company then built a narrow-gauge railroad and hauled the logs to their mill but soon abandoned the project.

In 1877 the village was described as: *"Population 100. At the mouth of Portage Lake."* Stage to *Manistee* and *Frankfort* tri-weekly. W. (Marvin) Farr, postmaster, saw and shingle mill and store; H. W. James, general store.

NOTE: 1870 description *"on a neck of land"*–in 1877 there was no neck of land.

In 1880 the village was moved to the east end of the lake where it remains today as *"Onekama,"* with a population of 450. A few empty buildings remained on the old site which eventually vere torn down or gave way to the elements. The huge piles of sawdust and even the old cemetery now lie buried beneath the shifting sands of Lake Michigan or beneath summer homes and cottages built on the site.

SAILE STATION–see *Pleasanton*.

STRONACH– is not designated on 1969 Michigan highway maps but is listed as a post office. Named after Joseph Stronach, an early settler (see history of County) and settled in 1868, there is no record that it was incorporated, but the 1873 *Michigan Gazeteer* describes the village as: *"An incorporated village of about 350 population in Stronach Township. It is at the mouth of the Little Manistee River where it joins Manistee Lake, 5 miles southeast of Manistee. It contains two sawmills, Western Union Telegraph and some stores and shops. Shipments consist almost wholly of pine lumber. Semi-weekly mail. Adolphus Magnan, postmaster."*

In that year (1872) the village was the headquarters of the Stronach Lumber Company who had sawmills and a general store in the village. Also Horace Butters, later to become a big name in lumbering; Paul A. D. Cannin, Trans-Atlantic Exchange and ticket office; Magnan & Company, sawmill and general store; Charles Seyfert, telegraph operator; and Frank Whitacker, land looker and surveyor.

John Stronach and his son are credited with being the first settlers of *Manistee* about 1845. Their first mill was set up at what was called *"Old Stronach,"* so must have been at a different location than present *Stronach Village*.

By 1877 the population had increased to 400 and had three shingle mills, a sawmill, and two hotels. Nearest railroad at *Ludington*. Stage to *Manistee* daily, and daily mail. Adolphus Magnan, postmaster. John Bloch ran one hotel and saloon combined and John Mayer ran another. F. X. Magnan, carpenter; G. Smith, physician; William Zanders, butcher; Peter Welbes, justice; and Camine Paul & Company, shingle mill and store, in addition to Stronach Lumber Company.

There is no population given for the village in 1890 but population of the township was 710.

By 1918 and the end of lumbering the population had dropped to less than half that of 1877 and had only one general store and a hotel. Charles Wisner, postmaster in 1917.

————

TANNER–probably an abbreviation for *"Tannerville"* shown on most maps. 1910 population 30. In Bear Lake Township. Send mail to *Chief*.

Shown on 1970 AAA map at the corner of Tannerville Road and McClellan Road and on Big Bear Creek.

————

TANNERVILLE–see *Tanner*.

————

TURNERSPORT–see *Pierport*.

————

WELLSTON–1918 population 150. On the Pere Marquette Railroad, Norman Township, 20 miles east of *Manistee*. Telephone. Raymond Richards, postmaster. Had a hotel called "The Wellston" and the "Wellston Garage." Also two groceries, a hardware, general store, real estate office, meat market, and H. Minnick, physician.

The old *Wellston C. C. Camp* was on a trail at the northeast corner of Round Lake near M-55 in Section 13, Norman Township.

Wellston is designated on 1969 road maps.

NOTE: Another village in the county was named *Wellston* and changed to *Dublin*. (See *Dublin*.)

WILLIAMSPORT–although designated on 1970 AAA road maps, *Williamsport* never got off the ground as a village. After the disaster that washed *Portage* "out to sea," William Shanks and his wife operated a boardinghouse and platted a village that was to be called *"Williamsport."* Shanks was issued a license to operate a ferry at this point in 1871 and a sawmill was erected here but burned a short time later and was never rebuilt.

Other towns and places:

BARK–in 1910 on the P. M. Railroad. Mail to *Kaleva*.

BEARCREEK–1918 a station on the A. A. & N. E. Railroad. Mail to *Kaleva*.
NOTE: *Bear Creek* was originally the post office for *"Tanner."* Both places were in the same location.

BECSCIES–1918 on the Au Becscies River, Springdale Township, 10 miles east of *Pierport*. Mail to *Bear Lake*, 6 miles south.

BLACKSMITH PETERSON'S CORNERS–in Section 18, Brown Township at the corner of Coates and Collins Roads.

BROOKFIELDS–1910 on the M. & N. E. Railroad. Mail to *Onekema*.
NOTE: Also a *"Brookfield"* in Eaton County.

BROWN–in 1870 a newly established post office.

BURNHAM–was a settlement on the north county line and due north of *Arcadia*.

CLEMENT–1910 on the Manistee & Luther Railroad. Mail to *Dublin*.

COATES CORNERS–in Section 13, Dickson Township.
NOTE: Also a *"Coated Grove"* in Barry County.

COLLINS CORNERS–about 1½ miles south of *Norwalk* on Collins Road north of the Norwalk Lutheran Church and cemetery.

41

CONGER–shown on 1899 railroad maps north of *Dublin*.

––––––––

FLARITY'S FLATS–1½ miles north of *Highbridge* and about ½ mile north of Chicago Road in Section 31, Brown Township, on the north side of the Manistee River.

––––––––

GOODRICH–in 1910 mail to *Norwalk*.
> NOTE: Also a *"Goodrich"* in Genessee County in 1870.

––––––––

GUSTAVS or *GUSTAFS*–1910 on the M. & N. E. Railroad. Mail to *Marilla*.

––––––––

HILLIARDS–1910 on the P. M. Railroad. Mail to *Kaleva*.

––––––––

HOPPER–1910 on the P. M. Railroad. Mail to *Stronach*.
> NOTE: Also a *"Hoopertown"* in Allegan County and name changed to *"Pullman."*

––––––––

LEMON LAKE–1910 population 30. On the M. & N. E. Railroad, Marilla Township, between *Kaleva* and *Marilla*. RFD *Copemish*.

1918 Willard Smith, general store.

Shown on 1969 AAA maps on 13 Mile Road as *Lemon*. Also a lake by that name.

––––––––

LITTLE–1910 on the P. M. Railroad, mail *Peacock*. In Section 31, Norman Township near Nine Mile Road, 1 mile northwest of *"Lake of The Woods"* is the old "Little" cemetery.

––––––––

LITTLE RIVER JUNCTION–1910 on the Manistee & Luther Railroad. Mail *Stronach*.

––––––––

MALCOLM–1918 population 25. On the Arcadia & Betsy Railroad, Pleasanton Township, 4½ miles east of *Arcadia*. Shown on 1969 AAA maps on Glover Lake Road.

MANISTEE CROSSING–on 1899 railroad maps northeast of *Chief.*

———

MARSH–1910 on the P. M. Railroad mail to *Filer City. Marsh Siding* is shown on maps in Section 28, Stronach Township, about 1 mile south of *Stronach* and on the P. M. Railroad.

———

NEWLAND–1910 on the P. M. Railroad. Mail to *Manistee.* One-half mile south of *Arendal.*

———

NORMAN–Section 6, Norman township on an old trail about 20 rods north of M-55 and ½ mile east of Huff Road.

———

POLLOCK HILL–is not shown on any map but in 1910 was on the Manistee & Northwestern Railroad, mail to *Manistee.* Some people say it had a population of 500 in 1890 but there is no such town listed for that year in *Michigan Legislative Manuals.*

First known in the late 1870s as the *"Canfield Settlement"* after a man by that name who erected sawmills on the site. The village soon grew to become a good-sized settlement with 25 or 30 houses and buildings. Situated on a bend of the Manistee River, a cemetery was on the side of a hill away from the river.

About five years after the settlement was made (1881) Polish families began to move into the village and most of the early settlers moved away. The Canfield Mills ceased operations about the turn-of-the-century and by 1904-05 only one or two houses remained. Only a few worn-out lilac bushes remain on the site to show a village existed.

———

SAILE–between *Humphrey* and *Malcolm* on 1925 road map. Was on the M. & N. E. Railroad about 1 mile northeast of Mud Lake where the old railroad grade crosses US-31 highway.

———

SANDS–1910 on the M. & N. E. Railroad, mail *Marilla.*
NOTE: Also a *"Sands"* in Marquette County in 1918.

———

SAUNDERS–on 1899 railroad maps a few miles east of *Arcadia.*

43

SORENSON.

———

SPRING DALE.

———

STAR CORNERS–at the intersection of M-55 and Skocelas Road in Stronach Township.

———

STATE ROAD or *STATE CORNERS.*

———

TANNER–see *Bear Creek.*

———

WERLE'S CORNERS.

———

YATES CORNERS.

———

Chapter 7

MASON COUNTY GHOST TOWNS
AND ONE OF ONLY A FEW GHOST TOWNS
IN MICHIGAN DESIGNATED WITH A
STATE HISTORICAL MARKER

Mason County was originally set off as Notpecago County by the Legislature April 1, 1840. The county was organized under a Legislative Act approved February 13, 1843, and named in honor of Stevens T. Mason, the last territorial and first State Governor of Michigan. He was also the youngest governor ever elected. The land area was taken from Ottawa and Oceana Counties.

Probably the first white man, other than Jesuit priests, to settle here was William Quevillon. Quevillon was in the employ of Louis Campeau, the fur trader who founded *Saginaw* and *Grand Rapids*. After visiting the area about 1836 as a fur buyer and trader, Quevillon later settled at *Ludington* and platted a subdivision on the north side of town. In 1872 he operated a drug and grocery store on Loomis Street.

The county lies mainly in the basin of the Pere Marquette River, named after Father Pere Marquette, but also includes the Great and Little Sable, which enter Lake Michigan north of Ludington. The surface varies in height between 50 and 500 feet above the level of the lake.

The mouth of the Pere Marquette River was visited by the Jesuits in their voyage of discovery. The burial of Father Marquette was said to have taken place near the mouth of the river. His burial site has been a matter of controversy among historians since that time. His remains were taken back to *St. Ignace* and reinterred where a monument is erected. A historical plaque dedicated to his death is located at *Frankfort* in Benzie County and reads as follows: *"On May 18, 1675, Father Jaques Marquette, the great Jesuit missionary and explorer, died and was buried by two French companions somewhere along the Lake Michigan shore of the lower peninsula. Marquette had been returning to his mission at St. lgnace which he had left in 1673 to go on an exploring trip to the Mississippi and Illinois country. The exact location of Marquette's death has long been a subject of controversey. Evidence presented in the 1960's indicates that this site, near the natural outlet of the Betsie River, is the Marquette death site and that the Betsie is the Rivere du Pere Marquette of early French accounts and maps. Marquette's bones were buried at St. Ignace in 1677."*

In 1966, a year after this plaque was dedicated, a local historian from *Ludington* presented proof that *Ludington* was the site of Father Marquette's death. On May 18, 1966, a plaque was erected on this site similar to the above.

45

The Legislature located the county seat at *AuSable* by an act approved February 28, 1861. It was later removed to *Ludington*, where it still remains. By 1871, *Ludington* had a population of 2,500. The village plat was recorded September 10, 1867, when there was only one store in the village. Captain E. B. Ward of Detroit bought property there and made most of the improvements within the next two or three years. In 1872 it contained seven sawmills, a shingle mill, planing mill, foundry and machine shop, two banks, three hotels and a weekly newspaper, the *Mason County Record*. The largest lumber company, the Pere Marquette, was owned by Delos B. Filer and Luther H. Foster.

Captain E. B. Ward also had sawmills. Ward was president of the Pere Marquette Railroad and came to *Ludington* in 1869, when the railroad was being extended westward across the State to terminate at that point on Lake Michigan. *Ludington*, as were hundreds of other towns and villages, was founded mainly as a result of the Pere Marquette Railroad and would not have developed as a city without the railroad.

POST OFFICES

During its history, Mason County has had at least 33 post offices. Of these, 6 remain today.

RAILROADS

1893–the Manistee Division of the Flint & Pere Marquette Railroad extended from *Manistee Junction*, 0 miles; *Batcheller*, 5 miles; *Fountain*, 8 miles; *Freesoil*, 13 miles; ending at *Manistee*, 26 miles.

1893–the Mason & Oceana line began at *Buttersville*, 0 miles; *Harleys*, 7 miles; *Wileys*, 11 miles; *Adamsville*, 15 miles; *South Branch Camp*, 23 miles; and ended at *Stetson*, 27 miles.

1893–Flint & Pere Marquette, beginning at *Stearns*, 229 miles; *Branch*, 4 miles; *Manistee Junction*, 3 miles; *Weldon Creek*, 3 miles; *Custer*, 3 miles; *Scottville*, 3 miles; *Amber*, 2 miles; and ending at *Ludington*, 253 miles.

GHOST TOWNS

AMBER–1877 population 50. A village and station on the F. & P. M. Railroad, 7 miles from *Lincoln*, the county seat, and 7 east of *Ludington*. Has two steam sawmills and a wooden bowl factory. Daily mail. W. F. Fairbanks, postmaster. George A. Brown, station agent.

In 1910 population 55. 1918, two miles from *Scotville*. Mrs. Villa Parmaelee, grocer and railroad agent.

No population given for 1960.

AU SABLE–see *Lincoln. Au Sable* was the first county seat.

———

BACHELOR–railroad name *"Batcheller."* 1918 population 30. On the P. M. Railroad, Sheridan Township, 3½ miles from *Fountain.* Telephone. K. F. Schanke, postmaster and general store. Also railroad agent. Had two hotels, livery barn, blacksmith, and J. Brandenburg, stage line.

———

BATCHELLER–see *Bachelor.*

———

BLACK CREEK–see *Ferryville.*

———

BRANCH–in 1877 a post office and station on the F. & P. M. Railroad in Branch Township, 20 miles east of *Ludington.* Settled in 1875, population 10. A shipping point for lumbermen's supplies. Daily mail. B. F. Barnett postmaster, hotel and station agent.

1910 population 100. In 1918 population 75.9 miles from *Custer.* Settled in 1876. Telephone. Bessie M. McLees, postmistress. Had a hardware, three general stores, two sawmills, hotel, livery, and two real estate dealers.

———

CHAPPLE'S CORNERS–in 1870 was the post office for *"Sable Bridge."* Had a sawmill and general store on the Great Sable River, Victory Township. Pardee & Cook Company, sawmill and store.

1877 a post office on the Big Sable river, 14 miles northeast of *Ludington.* Lumbering is the chief pursuit. Settled in 1864. Population 25. Daily stage. In addition to the mills had a doctor, two carpenters, Methodist minister, and other business places.

———

EAST RIVERTOWN–in 1877 a post office and settlement of about 150 within a circuit of 2 miles. Formerly known as *"Indiantown"* in Riverton Township, 11 miles southeast of *Ludington.* Potatoes, cabbages, and sauerkraut are exported. Settled in 1863. Weekly mail. Samuel Hull, postmaster.

———

FAIRVIEW–in 1870 population 250. In Summit Township, on the lake shore, 6 miles south of Ludington. *"Has one steam sawmill, ships cordwood, bark, ties, bolts (short blocks from which shingles were made), and cedar posts."* Daily mail. Charles T. Sawyer, postmaster.

FERRYVILLE–1877 a post office in Eden Township, 12 miles east of *Ludington.* *"A station on the F. & P. M. Railroad known as "Black Creek." Settled in May, 1875. Population 50. Daily mail. E. M. Comstock, postmaster and station agent."*

NOTE: The name was changed to *"Custer"* and is a town today.

———

HAMLIN or *HAMLIN LAKE*–in 1910 on the Ludington & Northern Railroad. Mail *Ludington. Hamlin Lake* is designated on 1969 Michigan highway maps. *Hamlin* is one of the few ghost towns in the State that is honored with a historic plaque. A historic marker is located in Ludington State Park, the site of the onetime logging village and reads as follows:

"Two centuries after Father Marquette's death not far from here in 1675, timber from this area's forests helped build America. Among the lumbering towns of the region was Hamlin, located on the Big Sable River at this site. Lumber from the sawmill was hauled by mule cars on a tramway to long piers on Lake Michigan. In 1888 the mill dam broke. The released waters wiped out the little village."

———

INDIANTOWN–in 1870 was a post office, 11 miles southeast of *Ludington.* Weekly mail. Samuel Hull, postmaster. Name changed to *"East Rivertown."*

———

LINCOLN–the village was located just north of *Epworth Heights* on the Lincoln River. It was founded by Charles Mears, pioneer lumberman, and named after his favorite, Abraham Lincoln, when he became President in 1861. (See picture)

This village was first named *"Au Sable"* and was the first county seat of Mason County. In 1870 the county seat on the shore of Lake Michigan, 17½ miles north of *Pentwater*, and 25 south of *Manistee.* In Lincoln Township, at the mouth of the Lincoln River, 2½ miles north of *Ludington* settled about 1850, now counts about 100 people. One sawmill. Daily mail. Charles Mears, postmaster. David S. Harley, attorney; Charles Mears, lumber manufacturer and general store.

The post office was established in 1861, the same year the name was changed to *Lincoln.*

———

MILLERTON–1910 population 42. 1918 population 100. On the M. & E. W. Railroad and on the Sable river, Sheridan Township, 8 miles from *Fountain.* Telephone. S. E. Bortz & Sons, planing mill; Mrs. Richard Cunningham, general store. Other business places.

———

48

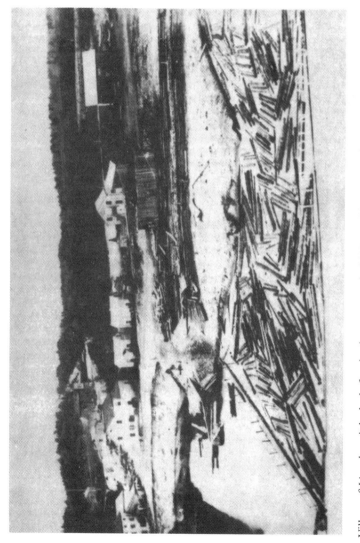

Village of *Lincoln* as it looked after the dam went out in 1910. Nothing remains today. First named *"AuSable,"* this was the first county seat of Mason County. Photo courtesy Michigan Historical Commission. All rights reserved and may not be reprinted without permission.

49

LITTLE SABLE–English version of *"Au Sable."* See *"Au Sable"* and *"Lincoln."*

————

PERE MARQUETTE–name changed to *"Ludington"* in 1867.

————

RIVERTON–in 1870 a post office in Riverton Township, on the Pere Marquette River, 6 miles southeast of *Ludington*. Main shipment pine lumber. Weekly mail. Lucius E. Hawley, postmaster.

The 1877 directory listed two preachers and James M. Wilson postmaster. Was a post office in 1901. Not listed in 1905.

————

SABLE BRIDGE–see *"Chapple's Corners."*

————

SUGARGROVE–was a small settlement and post office in 1877. In 1918 population 18, twelve miles northeast of *Ludington* and 3½ from *Scotville*. RFD No. 2, *Ludington* and RFD *No. 1 Freesoil.*

————

SWEETLAND–in 1890 listed as an unincorporated village in Custer Township. Population 56.

————

WELDON CREEK–1877 population 100. Located in Eden Township, and on the F. & P. M. Railroad, 14 miles east of *Ludington*, on Indian Creek. Settled in 1875 and located on an abandoned Indian reservation. Daily mail. J. J. Gilding, postmaster, general store, and station agent. Had a church, hotel, sawmill, hoop factory, and one other general store in addition to other buildings.

————

WILEY–a post office in 1890. In 1918 a discontinued post office. Population 35. RFD *Scotville*. A general store and creamery was located here.

————

VICTORY–1870 population 100. In Victory Township, 7 miles northeast of *Ludington*, on the Little Sable River. Had a sawmill, hotel, store, etc. Richard Rayne, postmaster. First settled in 1864 by N. L. Bird, postmaster in 1877. Was first called the *"Bird Settlement."* As with many early villages, *"Victory"* was the name chosen during patriotic fervor after the Civil War, similar to *"Liberty,"* *"Liberty Corners,"* etc.

In 1877 had more business places, including a doctor, blacksmith shops, wagon shop, and two churches. Was a post office until 1902.

––––––––

Other towns and places during the history of the county were:

ABBOTT–a settlement that became a post office about 1890 and lasted until 1895. In 1910 another town named *"Abbott"* was in Lenawee County.

––––––––

BASSLAKE–1910 RFD *Pentwater*.

––––––––

BUTTERSVILLE–1910 population 200. Mail *Ludington* (taken from 1912 *Rand McNally Atlas*). Listed as a post office in 1890 and in December, 1906.

1918 mail Ludington. On the P. M. Railroad, Pere Marquette Township. No population given. (See "Other Places")

––––––––

CARRS–Logan Township, 5¾ miles from *Branch*, RFD.

––––––––

CONRAD–on the P. M. Railroad. Mail *Scotville* 1910.

––––––––

ELMTON–on the Manistee & Grand Rapids Railroad. 1910 mail *Freesoil*.

––––––––

EPWORTH–a place on a branch of the Ludington & Northern Railroad. Once famous for its summer excursions and the Epworth "dummy train," similiar to a streetcar coach. Prior to World War I the national guard summer training camp was near here.

––––––––

FERN–1918 in Eden Township, 15 from *Ludington* and 10 from *Scotville*. Population 25. One general store. RFD *Custer*.

––––––––

FERRYVILLE–name changed to *"Custer."*

––––––––

HARDING–on the P. M. Railroad. 1910 mail *Ludington.*

––––––––

HOAGS–on the Manistee & G. R. Railroad. 1910 mail *Stronach*.

MOUNT EPWORTH–see *Epworth*.

––––––––

POULSEN–1918 a discontinued post office, 10 miles northeast of *Ludington*. RFD. Population 22.

––––––––

SHEEPDALE–1910 mail *Millerton*.

––––––––

SIDDONS–1910 RFD *Ludington*. In Grant Township, 14 miles northeast of *Ludington*.

––––––––

SEQUIRESVILLE–a settlement named after Peter Sequire, an early blacksmith. Listed as a post office in 1890. Misspelled *"Squireville."* 1910 RFD *Pentwater*.

––––––––

TALLMAN–a post office in 1890. 1918 population 100. On the P. M. Railroad, Branch Township, 18 miles east of *Ludington* and 5 from *Fountain*. Glenn M. Willis, postmaster. Two general stores and other places.

––––––––

TOMLINS–1910 on the Manistee & G. R. Railroad. Mail *Freesoil*.

––––––––

WEIMER–1918 a discontinued post office. RFD *Ludington*.

––––––––

WESLEY–1918 a discontinued post office, 6½ miles south of *Ludington*. Population 40. RFD *Ludington*.

––––––––

BUTTERSVILLE, TAYLORVILLE, SEATONVILLE, and *FINNTOWN* were one-time villages. About 1900 the total population was 1,900. The four settlements were joined by a long maple plank road originally built by the Butters & Peters Lumber Company.

    Buttersville was named after Mr. Butters of this firm, had a post office (see *"Buttersville,"*) many homes and stores. One street was named "Pig Tail Alley." Also a large boardinghouse.

    The Mason & Oceana Railroad ran from *Butterville* to *Walkerville* in Oceana County. A narrow-gauge railroad ran nearly to *Hesperia* in Newaygo County. In 1888 had a shingle mill, cooper shop, salt block and brine well, coal dock, log dump (banking grounds), depot and warehouse, engine house and turntable. The yearly timber cut was 12 million feet plus another 8 million shingles. The mills employed 300 men.

The summer of 1909 was very dry and there had been no rain for many weeks. On August 25 fire struck the town and burned all the mills. They were never rebuilt. The June census for that year listed 200 people living in *Buttersville*.

The lake freighter *Marshall F. Butters*, used for shipping lumber, was sold to the Stearns Company and sank in a storm on Lake Erie in 1916. A few remaining houses were moved to *Ludington* and a few buildings remain (1955).

Chapter 8

MECOSTA COUNTY GHOST TOWNS
AND THE DAY PARIS BURNED

Mecosta County was named in honor of Chief Mecosta who signed the Washington Treaty of 1836. The name means "bear cub." First settlement was made in 1851, mostly by Canadian immigrants. The county government was organized in 1859 with land taken from Kent and Newaygo Counties. *Leonard (Big Rapids)* was designated as the county seat on February 11, 1859.

Charles Shafer built a general store at *Big Rapids* about 1868. At that time there was no post office north of this point in the Lower Peninsula. In 1855 George B. Warren and Chauncy P. Ives of *Troy*, New York, bought the site from Frederick Hall of *Ionia* and platted it as *Big Rapids*, as it was called by lumbermen.

Until 1863 mail was carried by horseback from *Greenville*, when a weekly stage began making a run from Grand Rapids via *Newaygo*.

In 1860 Leonard consisted of two stores and five dwellings. It was incorporated as *Big Rapids* in 1869 and by 1870 the population had increased to 1,237.

John Parish, first settler in the county, built a trapper's shack on the banks of the Muskegon River just above *Big Rapids* in 1851. In 1867 he started the village of *"Parish."* Later shortened to *"Paris."*

The first railroad reached *Big Rapids* in 1870. It had been extended to *Morley* in 1869. An attempt to raise capital for a railroad was made in 1860, but failed due to the advent of the Civil War. The Grand Rapids & Indiana Railroad was built and operated under the Continental Improvement Company of Pennsylvania. In 1869 a work force of 1,000 men with teams and wheelbarrows were working on the line. By September of that year, G. A. McDonnell & Son contractors, broke ground for the tracks within the city limits of *Big Rapids*. On October 11, 1869, daily trains were run each way between *Grand Rapids* and *Morley*. One passenger train and the other a freight and passenger combined. In July 1870, the G. R. & I. Railroad reached the city, and 1872 had reached the Manistee River, 75 miles north.

In September 1872 the railroad from *Muskegon* to *Big Rapids* under control of the Michigan Central Company was commenced. Called the Muskegon & Big Rapids Railroad, the first train ran in July, 1873. Stations on the line were *Hungerford, Traverse Road, Pingree's Dam, Morgan Station, Alleyton, Worces-*

The old E. J. Bast general store and post office at *Altona* as it appeared about 1890-96. A bakery and restaurant is located today where the small building on the left is shown in this picture and was built on the same foundation from material salvaged from the old general store. Photo by Roy L. Dodge historical collection.

Some of the original houses in *Altona* as they appeared in 1945 when Henry Billings purchased the old hotel in *Altona* and converted it into a general store (still in business, 1970). These houses were condemned and razed about 1950. The man who lived in one of these houses had a traveling show with trained dogs and animals and for many years made *Altona* his winter headquarters. Photos by Roy L. Dodge.

ter, Fremont Center, Fremont Lake, County Line, Holton, Twin Lake, Big Rapids Junction, and Muskegon. A distance of 55 miles. Five years later it was reorganized as the Chicago & West Michigan Railroad.

The Detroit-Lansing & Northern Railroad was the third railroad organized. This road was completed to Big Rapids in the spring of 1880. Regular trains began running on Monday, May 31 of that year.

RAILROADS

1893–Chicago & West Michigan, Big Rapids Division: Muskegon, 0 miles; Woodville, 44 miles; Lumberton, 46 miles; Hungerford, 48 miles; Big Rapids, 55 miles.

1893–Grand Rapids & Indiana, Northern Division: Grand Rapids, 0 miles; Reynolds, 37 miles; Morley, 40 miles; Stanwood, 47 miles; Byers, 53 miles; Big Rapids, 56 miles; Upper Big Rapids, 57 miles; Stimson, 58 miles; and Paris, 61 miles.

1893–Detroit-Lansing & Northern, Stanton Branch: Ionia, 0 miles; Millbrook, 44 miles; Remus, 48 miles; Mecosta, 53 miles; Rodney, 59 miles; Chippewa Lake, 64 miles; and Big Rapids, 67 miles.

POST OFFICES

Mecosta County had a total of at least 17 post offices during its history. Ten of these remain today.

GHOST TOWNS

ALTONA–first settled in 1868. In 1870 had 75 population. Located in Hinton Township, 10 miles northwest of Morley on the Little Muskegon River. Had a general store, saw and shingle mill, flour mill, and blacksmith shop. By 1877, a hotel and about 25 dwellings had been erected and the village had a doctor. Stage to Morley and Millbrook.

By the turn-of-the-century the population was nearly 200. The 1910 census recorded 152 residents. By World War I there were three churches;"Altona House," hotel; E. Bromley & Company, general store; wagonmaker; auto sales; and E. J. Bast, postmaster and general store.

By the 1930s the town was all but deserted, although 28 houses remained standing in a rundown condition. In 1945 Henry Billings, a former resident, moved back there from Lansing, purchased the old hotel and converted it into a general store and gasoline station. A few years later the only other store discontinued business. After operating for nearly 100 years the old flour mill was torn down about 1960. Only part of the old mill dam remains today and a new blacktop road passes near the old iron bridge and mill site.

In 1949-50 many of the empty, original houses were condemned and torn down. The former Bast store was razed and the lumber used to build a rustic restaurant and bakery on the foundation of a former smaller building nearby.

The Henry Billings general store was sold a few years ago and remains as it was nearly a century ago, with a new coat of white paint, green shutters, and standing on a hill overlooking the former village. A church and schoolhouse, now used for a community hall, are still in use. The 15 or 20 residents receive mail RFD *Morley*. A new artificial lake development, Canadian Lakes, owns most of the land within about 1 mile from the 10 square blocks of grass-grown streets that was once the village of *Altona*.

———

BORLAND–was a village on the G. R. & I. Railroad, 12 miles south of *Big Rapids*. At one time it was a busy railroad siding. One or two old buildings remain. One is a former grocery store with silver-grey, unpainted siding and looks like a store on a movie set of old west days. The store was last used by an old Indian Chief called "Chief Elk Horn" for many years until his death about 1955. Dried herbs still line the walls and cabinet drawers and are the remaining stock of the old Chief's herbs that hundreds of people swore cured their ills.

As late as 1950 a bakery operated on the site, furnishing bread for nearby stores. In 1968 an old rusty bus with faded lettering still visible remained on the site. The bus was used by Chief Elk Horn for his 20th century traveling medicine show. Residents of the vicinity say he lived to be more than 100 years old.

———

BIG CREEK–in Deerfield Township was a post office about 1865. The first store was opened by George Magill in 1863. A few years later the name was changed to *"Stanwood,"* a good-sized village today.

———

CRAPO–in 1877 a post office and station on the G. R. & I. Railroad in Greene Township, on the Osceola County line, 8 miles north of *Big Rapids* and 5 south of *Reed City*. Daily mail. James Dixon, postmaster. 1910 population 25. Mail to *Paris*.

———

EMERALD–name changed to *"Chippewa Lake"* about 1875.

———

FORK–in 1877 in Fork Township, 12 miles south of *Chippewa Station*. On the Chippewa River. William Creery, postmaster. Was a post office in 1870. Post office established in 1860. Lewis E. Wolcott opened the first store in 1875. 1910 RFD *Barryton*.

———

MILLBROOK–now the location of a large furniture store and also a nursing home but is far from the village of 500 population it once was.

Settled in 1862 the first store was opened by W. S. Howd in 1865. In 1870, weekly stage to *Morley* and semi-weekly to *Stanton*. Population 300. On the Pine River and also on the line of the projected Ionia-Stanton & Northern Railroad. C. H. Clement, postmaster. Wagon shop, two hotels, restaurants, flour mill (part of building still standing 1970), sawmills, doctor and dentist, four general stores, drugstore, and two blacksmith shops.

In 1877 a furniture shop and four churches were added. Stage line to *Morley, Stanton* and *Sherman City*.

By 1918 the population was down to about 200 but an opera house and bus line had been added. The Adventist Church was closed but three other churches remained. About the turn-of-the-century, and for many years, half the population was Negro and a separate church service was conducted for them.

One old mill and foundations of another remain on the high banks of the river near the remaining business section. Most of the buildings are run down and vacant.

———

MARTINI (also spelled *"Martinez"*)–this was the first post office in Martini Township a few miles southeast of *Barryton*. Post office established in November, 1875. Weekly mail. George Shields, postmaster. John Martiny was the first settler in 1868, after whom the township was named.

———

PARIS–settled and platted by John Parish in 1867. In that year he and Andrew McFarlane built the first sawmill and the first house on the site. The name became mistaken for *"Paris"* and has remained that since.

Once a village of more than 400, today only a few buildings remain along the railroad tracks. A tavern, grocery store, and the Paris Fish Hatcheries are about all that remain.

In 1870 E. M. Stickney, postmaster and general store on Main Street. John Shier ran a saloon next door and welcomed hundreds of loggers and rivermen during the spring drives on the Muskegon River. Mrs. A. G. Davis also ran a saloon on Main Street and during the busy season cared for the overflow from Shier's. J. F. Wykes, station agent. The depot went many years ago. E. Stout,

Every village had one or more livery stables similar to the once pictures above. This picture is believed to have been taken about 1890 at *Paris* in Mecosta County.

shoe and harness maker, Main Street. Andrew McFarlane ran the once famed "Muskegon House Hotel." E. S. Shaler & Company, sawmill on the west side of the tracks. S. A. Silsba blacksmith, and Dr. C. H. White.

By 1877 another hotel, the "Paris House" was added. E. M. Stickney joined with John M. Harman and expanded his general store and also built a lumber and shingle mill and flouring mill on Paris Creek. Another doctor moved in, and things were booming.

On May 26, 1879 disaster hit the town and it was destroyed by fire. Fire started in the rear of Stickney's store early in the morning. People in the nearby hotel barely escaped in their night clothes. The building next door was a crockery store operated by a Mr. Elwood, and owned by Mrs. Annie Hall of *Detroit*. This was soon reduced to a pile of ashes. The large, two-story building, converted from a store to a hotel by Elliot Cheney, also burned. Occupants of this hotel had enough advance warning to save their clothes and baggage. The building was owned by Mrs. Roxy Compton.

A two-family house was next to catch fire. Mr. Judkins, the station agent and one of the occupants saved most of his furniture. A large barn belonging to E. M. Stickney burned and some cow stables. A warehouse at the rear of Stickney's building, owned by Fox & Shields Company of *Grand Rapids* burned.

The post office, located in Elwood's store, saved their letter case and stamp drawer, but the mail pouch which had arrived that morning burned with all the mail. The books and records of the Township of Green, which were in Elwood's store, also burned.

Most of the town was rebuilt and in 1917 D. W. Lydell was postmaster. Had two hotels, a feed mill, three general stores, livery stable, blacksmith shop, and several other business places. About 350 people lived in the village. Jesse P. Marks was in charge of the State Fish Hatchery, which still remains.

––––––

RIENZA–was a post office and settlement in Sheridan Township, 13 miles south of *Lake Station* (Clare County) on the F. & P. M. Railroad. Edward P. Strong opened the first store in 1867. The post office was founded in the spring of 1870. John A. Markle listed as a carpenter in 1870. Not listed in 1890 and never became a village.

––––––

RODNEY–in 1883 was a new village on the Detroit, Lansing & Northern Railroad where the Chippewa Branch joined the main line. William and Almeda Dosenberry were early settlers.

The few residents of the area will probably resent the one-time village (designated on State highway maps) as a ghost town. There is a store and tavern located near a rapidly expanding resort area. Located on M-20 between *Big Rapids* and *Mecosta*. The railroad and business places disappeared many years ago.

1918 population 200. Two churches, general store, livestock yards, the "Rodney House Hotel," livery stable, billiard hall, railroad station, and other industry.

––––––––

RUST–was a village in 1870. Name changed to *"Mecosta."*

––––––––

RUSTFORD–founded about 1862 when Ethan Satterlee erected a small power grist and sawmill on the Little Muskegon River in Deerfield Township, 5° miles northeast of *Morley*. Until 1877 was called *"Satterlee's Mills."* A log schoolhouse was built in 1862. Margaret Quigley, first teacher. George Magill opened the first store in 1863. Post office established about 1865.

In 1877 Charles Ostrander was postmaster and ran the grist and sawmill. Stage to *Millbrook* and *Morley* every other day. Mail three times weekly. Had a general store, blacksmith, and a constable. On October 6, 1876, fire swept the area and one child was burned to death.

A few people still live near the narrow, iron-railed bridge on Monroe Road where it crosses the Muskegon River near the site.

The remains of the old dam still forms a pond at the mill site and one house is visible from the road (1969). A Michigan Conservation Department sign reads "Public Access - Rustford Pond."

One-half mile west of the former village, near the corner of 130th Avenue and Three Mile Road stands a white church. It was once the Rustford School and was moved to its present location about 1959 to be used for a church. This settlement was at one time called *"Sandy Town."*

––––––––

SYLVESTER–one of two villages settled in Hinton Township. The township was named after John Hinton, a native of Wales, who moved there in 1855. By 1870 Sylvester, named after Silver Creek upon which it was located, had a population of 70, two general stores, three saw mills, one steam mill, blacksmith shop, wagon shop, and a boot and shoe store. Travis Kelly was postmaster and wagonmaker. Andrew Farrar, a country doctor who moved to *Millbrook* about 1855, ran a store in *Sylvester* and also owned a 40-acre farm about ° mile north of the village. Farrar served the entire area of *Millbrook, Mecosta,* and *Sylvester* as a family doctor for more than half-a-century, until his death about 1918 in *Big Rapids*.

The village had a peak population of about 100. In 1877 a hotel was built and there were two doctors and a Seventh Day Adventist pastor.

Probably the biggest event in the history of *Sylvester* was the day the steam sawmill blew up and killed two men. It was never rebuilt. By the turn-of-the-century the sawmills were gone and only one store remained. With the advent of the automobile a gasoline station was built in front of one of the stores. Today all that remains to show *Sylvester* was once a town are half a dozen decrepit houses, one-time streets overgrown with weeds and grass, a few dying, giant Lombardy poplar trees, and the Sylvester Adventist Church.

––––––––

SANDY TOWN–see *Rustford.*

––––––––

SATTERLEE'S MILLS–see *Rustford.*

––––––––

TITUS–in Sheridan Township, 7 miles south of *Barryton* and 7½ north of *Remus*. 1910 population 20. 1918 population 16. Nothing remains. RFD *Remus*.

––––––––

Other settlements and places during the history of the county were:

CHATTERTON–1910 on the P. M. Railroad. Mail *Barryton.*

EMERALD LAKE–1910 population 22. RFD *Evart.*

HIGBEE–1910 RFD *Morley.*

HILL–1910 RFD *Barryton.*

HUGHES–was the site of the Hughes Shingle Mills about the turn-of-the-century. Located 3 miles north of *Mecosta*.

LOWER BIG RAPIDS–a station on the east side of the river at *Big Rapids*. The abandoned depot, in a sad state of disrepair, still stands (1970). The business area is now a part of *Big Rapids*.

MARSHFIELD–in the northeast part of the county. Shown on 1890-99 railroad maps.

MCKAY–1910 on the P. M. Railroad. Mail *Mecosta*.

MEC–1910 on the P. M. Railroad. Mail *Mecosta*.

MILLER–1910 on the P. M. Railroad. Mail *Remus*.

MOILES–1910 on the P. M. Railroad. Mail *Mecosta*.

NEWTON–1918 a discontinued post office. Mail to *Blanchard*.

POGY–1910 RFD *Hersey*.

RUST–1877 a station on the G. R. & I. Railroad. Seven miles south of *Big Rapids*.

STIMSON–1910 population 20. Seven miles from *Big Rapids*, RFD.

STIRLING–1910 on the P. M. Railroad. Mail *Remus*.

WEAVER–RFD *Paris*.

WEST MILLBROOK–1910 population 62. RFD *Millbrook*. Two or three houses stand between *Millbrook* and *West Millbrook*. A nursing home is located at what was known as *West Millbrook* and a furniture store is in *Millbrook* (see *"Millbrook."*) Both places are ghost towns. *Millbrook* was on the P. M. Railroad and was the station for *West Millbrook*.

———

Chapter 9

MIDLAND COUNTY GHOST TOWNS
AND THE VILLAGE THAT WAS LAID OUT
IN PIE-SHAPED LOTS AROUND A CIRCLE

Midland County was one of twelve counties laid out at the same time in 1831. The county government was organized in 1850 and the land area taken from Saginaw County. It is one of the few northern counties unnamed by Henry Schoolcraft and was always called "Midland."

Harold W. Moll, *Midland* historian, says the first record of a white person in the territory is a letter written January 1, 1676, by a Jesuit priest to his superiors at Quebec. The letter concerns Father Henry Nouvel's missionary journey from *St. Ignace* on November 8, 1674, down Lake Huron into the Saginaw River and up the Tittabawassee to a winter mission located at *"Bamosey,"* as the Indians called the area.

Robert Clark, Jr., whose father was a member of the famous team of Lewis and Clark, stayed where *Christ Camp* had been located when surveying in this area in 1831, Moll said.

In 1819 a village known as *"The Forks"* was located where the two rivers, Tittabawassee and Chippewa, join. At the treaty of 1819 the Blackbird Reservation was set aside south of *Smith's Crossing* for 6,000 Indians and was called *"Upper Forks."*

In 1822 Joseph Wampler surveyed the reserved lands of the Saginaw Treaty, which were completed in late 1832 under the direction of Major Robert Rogers.

In 1845 Stephen Smith settled in Homer Township. Charles and Lydia Cronkright were the first settlers in Jasper Township in 1859. The De Pues, William T. Nicholas, and Marshall S. and Alanson Bailey founded *Pleasant Valley*.

Some other early settlers included several Negroes. John H. Johnson and Oliver Highgate were Negro barbers in *Midland*.

Duck Ley, of Chinese descent, came in 1882 and set up *Midland's* first laundry.

Probably the largest chemical deposits in the State underlie the county, and although the Dow Chemical Company started utilizing the chemicals at an early date, lumbering became the first large industry of the county. In 1880 Wright and Ketchum Company moved in. They had interests in lumber, banking, real estate, and private railroad organizing. The first year they hired 325 men and had a $200,000 payroll. They told glowing plans of shipping crops out by rail, and sold thousands of acres of stump lands to settlers. After the land was sold they picked up their rails and moved out, leaving several ghost towns in their wake.

Lincoln Township was established March 20, 1861, and Mills, the last one formed, is in the northeast corner of the county. The county is divided into 16 townships, but four (Hope, Lincoln, Homer and Mount Haley) embrace only 33 sections.

Col. William L. Stearns led a group of settlers from *Berea, Ohio* in 1882, and on April 3 of that year Greendale Township was formed.

On March 16, 1871, Midland County was ordered to pay damages to Clare County of $7,134 and ceded the land area now consisting of Grant and Sheridan Townships to that county.

In 1874 Midland relinquished Roscommon County, which also included the west half of present Gladwin County. No agreement could be reached with *Roscommon* for a settlement and several lawsuits followed. Finally, in 1883, it was agreed that Midland County pay them $6,000.

The history of Midland County is well documented. The Grace Dow Memorial Library in *Midland* has many past records and contains one of the largest museums and artifact displays of any county in the State. There are also active historical societies.

The Dow Chemical Company is now one of the largest firms of its type in the world, and has expanded its interests to nearly every corner of the world.

RAILROADS

1899–Flint & Pere Marquette Railroad. Beginning at *Saginaw*, 0 miles, entering Midland County at *Smith's Crossing*, 15 miles; *Averill*, 26 miles; *Sanford*, 28 miles; *North Bradley*, 34 miles; *Dorr*, 37 miles; and *Coleman*, 40 miles.

POST OFFICES

Midland County has had a total of about 35 post offices in its history. Today 6 post offices and one sub-station, the *"Circle,"* in Midland remain.

66

GHOST TOWNS

AVERILL–the former village of *Averill*, famous during the early logging days of Michigan and the Saginaw Valley, lays in a built-up business section bordering Old US-10 highway between *Sanford* and *Midland*. Present-day signs advertising a lumber yard, cocktail lounge, and other business places named "Red Keg" are the only reminders of the notorious saloon with a whiskey keg mounted on a pole and painted red that inspired lumberjacks to call the place "Red Keg."

Located on the Tittabawassee River, and later the terminus of the Flint & Pere Marquette Railroad, *Averill* was the gateway to the vast expanses of white pine timber in the world's most famous lumbering center, the Saginaw Valley.

First settled in 1860, *Red Keg* or *Averill* was a quiet frontier settlement until logging the white pine began in earnest at the end of the Civil War. By the time the F. & P. M. Railroad reached the village in 1869 the two combination hotels and saloons were overtaxed during the rush of lumbermen to the Saginaw Valley.

The village of *Averill* was platted in 1874 and consisted of 16 city blocks with eight 66-foot lots to a block. One block was set aside for a village square or park. Streets bore such impressive names as "Grand Avenue," "Park Avenue," and "Maple Avenue," also a "Berry Street" plus the usual "Main Street" and "Moores Street," named after the man who platted the village.

Red Keg was made famous in legends and songs of the lumberjacks. The Valley's most notorious fight between Silver Jack Driscoll and Big Joe Fournier occurred in this saloon, first operated by Billy McCrary, who was no slouch as a riverman and rough-and-tumble fighter. Later the "Red Keg" was run by Edward Francis, who moved to Michigan from Canada. After the big fire that destroyed most of the village in 1875-76 Francis moved to Sanford where he opened another hotel.

Located in Lincoln Township the village first consisted of two hotels, a general store, two company stores and about 50 log and board houses. In 1872 described as population 150. Harrison Averill, hotel; L. W. Averill, lumber; H. Brink, hotel; Annie Draper, schoolteacher; A. M. Hawley, lumber; F. Largius Smith, lawyer; and three shingle mills operated by Cornelius Steele; William Tinker, Sr., and William Tinker, Jr.

In 1877 the population dropped to about 100, due to the fire. Harrison Averill rebuilt his hotel, as did N. T. Stratton & Son who ran a hotel and general store combined. Patrick McCann owned the one remaining sawmill.

In 1918 the post office had been discontinued and only two stores, one the C. W. Siechert general store, was in business.

Today the one-time village is part of a commercialized district bordering US-10. One former general store is converted into an antique shop and a former school building and the old frame Methodist church remain standing between the pavement and the river. One original century-old log cabin remained occupied until the fall of 1970 when it was purchased by the Sanford Area Historical Society and moved to that village to be preserved as part of a museum.

The former Red Keg Saloon and hotel is still standing, only slightly altered, and was moved to another site.

Eugene Thwing, a Michigan author, immortalized the village in his two novels *The Red Keggers* and *The Man From Red Keg*. Published about the turn-of-the-century the books are long since out of print and are now collector's items.

———

BOMBAY–located in Section 32, Mills Township, never got off the ground as a village but was located near lumber camps. It became a favorite hangout for logging camp drifters and drunks returning to camps after a "blow out" at *Red Keg*. The place was first called *"Bums Bay"* but when permanent settlers moved into the area they used the more refined *"Bombay."* Located in Mills Township, it was also known as *"Bombay Mills."*

———

BRADFORD–see *Gordonville.*

———

BUTTONVILLE–see *North Bradley.*

———

EDENVILLE–located near the Gladwin County line on the Tittabawassee River is not a complete ghost town but the quiet village with its few business places, churches, and a cemetery overlooking the river bears little resemblance to *"Camp 16,"* the roaring village of the logging days that stood on the site.

The site was settled possibly as early as 1851. Timothy Jerome, after whom the township was named, arrived before the Civil War and built the first sawmill about 1 mile up-river from the village.

For the next decade *Camp 16* and *Red Keg* became the most notorious and well-known lumber camps in Michigan. Stories of the rivermen and saloon keepers and other characters during the 40-year history of river drives on the Tobacco and Tittabawassee Rivers would fill several volumes.

From 1860 until 1897, 27 billion feet of white pine had been cut in the area and in the quarter century preceding 1884 nearly 50 million feet of logs were floated annually down the river.

During the logging days three hotels, a blacksmith shop, two grocery stores, and lumbermen's supply stores lined the river bank, in addition to sawmills and lumbercamp buildings.

Edenville was part of Jerome Township until 1873 when Edenville Township was established. In 1878 Henry Church platted the village and built the first hotel which was operating in 1863. Daniel Boman built the first house, made of logs, and Kingsley Babcock ran the first general store.

When the post office was established in 1869, Burt Church the first postmaster, looked out over the peaceful rivers on a bright spring day and thought the primeval, hardwood forests and flower-lined riverbanks must be as luxuriant as any in the original "Garden of Eden." He submitted the name *"Edenville"* for the name and it remains as such today.

Of the many characters of and during the logging days hotel and saloon owners were the most notable. Thousands of Saginaw Valley jacks boasted of stopping at Swearin' Charlie Axford's hotel on their journeys to and from lumber camps and during the river drives. *Camp 16* was the only settlement between *Red Keg* and the headwaters of the Tittabawassee many miles north.

Thomas Moore opened his first hotel there in 1866 and within a decade his name became a household word in Michigan lumber camps. Moore studied for the priesthood, it is said, but gave it up before his final ordination and became one of the most popular saloonkeepers of the logging days.

Moore's hotel burned in 1875 and he took his savings of several thousand dollars and purchased the Franklin House in Saginaw. Six months later he returned to his old stomping grounds at *Edenville* saying, *"I would rather be a big toad in a little pond than a little toad in a big pond."*

Herb Nolan, reportedly the hardest, toughest man of *Camp 16* remained after the logging days and related much of its early history. Nolan lived out his remaining days there and his grave on the hill is marked with a large tombstone.

Charles Harper who came from Ohio in the 1870s said he was advised by doctors to move to the pine forests as a last resort to alleviate his fatal affliction of tuberculosis. He ended up in *Edenville* and purchased the general store from Ralph Dunton which he operated until 1944 when he died at the age of 93. The old Harper store is one of the few original buildings standing and the post office is located in the old building.

By the close of the 19th century, *Edenville* had become a near ghost town compared to the days when as many as 200 lumberjacks from rival camps whooped it up along the main street.

In 1918 C. A. Harper was postmaster and general store. The only other business places were Mrs. Alice Wall, hotel; E. L. Marsh, general store; and Lemuel Brown, blacksmith.

The village made a slight comeback in the 1920s when a former citizen, Frank I. Wixom, returned and built power dams at *Edenville* and *Sanford*. *Sanford* and *Wixom Lakes* were created around which hundreds of summer homes and cottages have been built and the tiny village has benefited some from the resulting tourist trade.

During the 1930s *Wixom* staged annual Lumberjack Picnics and treated as many as 60,000 people to a festival of the lumberjack era. Log birlers from as far away as the State of Washington held contests and treats were on *Wixom*. Beset by ill health, *Wixom* was forced to give up the annual celebration in 1941 and died March, 5, 1943. There isn't much left to celebrate in the one-time boom town.

————

EGBERT–Abraham Egbert came to the area in 1851 and settled on the Tittabawassee River banks below the present site of *Edenville* in Section 2, Jerome Township. A sawmill was erected and the place soon became known as *"Egbert."* This was in the days when the only transportation was by water or foot and the few settlers or trappers travelled by flatboat or raft to *Midland* to get supplies.

With the coming of the lumbermen at the end of the Civil War *Camp 16* became the chief settlement. A steamboat, the *Belle Seymour*, then made regular weekly trips up the river carrying supplies and passengers. A few years later a steam barge, the *Aura,* was used to carry lumber from *Camp 16* to *Sanford*.

In 1905 *Egbert* was a country post office 5 miles north of *Sanford*. Daily mail. Charles Geingrich, general store.

————

GORDONVILLE–1918 on the Pine River, Mt. Haley Township, 8 miles from *Midland*. Formerly called *"Bradford."* Telephone. RFD *Midland*. In the northwest corner of Section 4, on the Pine River. 1910, RFD *Midland*, population 22.

————

GREENDALE–located in Section 24, Greendale Township, 14 miles west of *Midland* and on the Chippewa River. 1910 population 100. Mail to *Stearns*. 1917 Mrs. W. W. Betts, general store; George Bigelow, sawmill; W. D. Hewitt, grocer; and H. Remenschneider, general store.

————

HUBBARD–this fabulous village with pie-shaped lots extending from a huge circle drive, enclosing an area for a village park, existed mainly on paper. All that remains today are the circle road where the park was to be established in the center of a 640-acre tract of land.

The village was platted November 5, 1892, when a *Detroit* real estate firm, headed by John E. King, Collins E. Hubbard and George Dingwell, signed documents calling for its establishment.

A story in the *Saginaw Courier-Herald* late in 1893 said Hubbard had designed the village so there would be a social center (the circle park) and thus eliminate the dreary isolation of country life.

"Houses are located around the center (10 acres) so that families will have the benefit of society and cooperation," the article said.

I. M. Barr, a *Saginaw* minister, became the agent for the Hubbard & Dingwell Company and the Michigan Land & Timber Company. Standing timber estimated at about 50 million feet was sold to a *Grand Rapids* company which was supposed to remove about 6 million feet each year, to be used as barrel staves.

Larkin Township Supervisor, Robert A. Kapanka, 60, of 4142 Hubbard Road in 1968 said there was a blacksmith shop, grocery store, saloon, post office, an office building for the company, a school, and a hotel.

Larkin said his grandfather, Henry Kapanka, was among the first German families who moved to *Hubbard* from *Detroit*. *"There was no work in Detroit and they were promised so much in the newly-formed lumbering camp in the forests of Midland County that they moved there."*

"The village was planned well," he said. *"But it never had a chance to grow. If you look northeast from the intersection of Waldo Road and Parrish Road you can still see the line where Bismark Road ran. It led to the center of Hubbard Village in Hubbard Park."*

Newspaper articles of the day boasted an influx of settlers to the village. Barr was quoted as saying that 50 settlers had been taken to *Hubbard* and predicted 500 more would settle there in the summer of 1894.

The *Grand Rapids* lumbering firm allegedly fulfilled their contract the first year by cutting 6 million feet of lumber. Soon after they abandoned the project.

An article in the *Saginaw Courier-Herald* dated October 15, 1899, told of the tearing up of the 12-mile F. & P. M. Railroad spur between *Midland* and *Hubbard* in an overnight operation that took about 300 men to accomplish.

HUBBARD

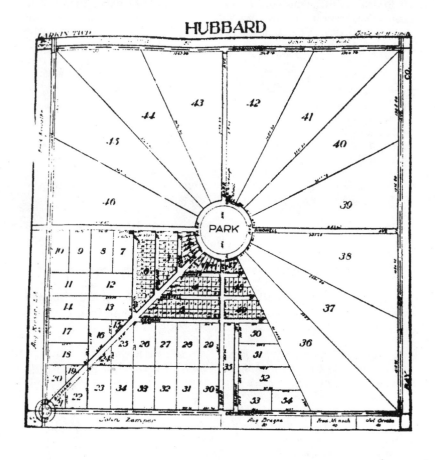

This is probably the only 'pie-shaped' village in the state. Platted in 1892 and named after Collins E. Hubbard of *Detroit*, one of the founders, it became a ghost town in 1899. All that remains is the 10-acre circle surrounded by farm land.

The article also stated that the railroad had served any usefulness it ever had. It was constructed for the purpose of hauling the timber. The wood was not suitable for that purpose, it said, and the road didn't do the business if was intended to do. *"For this reason the Hubbard branch will cease to exist after today"* (October 15, 1899), the article said.

The site of the village is in Section 12, Larkin Township, 5 miles north of the US-10 expressway, just east of Waldo Road. After the village was abandoned the section was divided into eight pieces and sold. Four of them were pie-shaped 80-acre plats owned by J. Kissen, H. Renus, Ed Leisus, and Fred Steinka in the early 1900s. The other four 'eighties' were owned by H. Krantz, E. Mattis, Ted Briebe, and Mrs. H. Draxis. The 10-acre circle in the center is apparently public property.

In 1918 a discontinued post office. Send mail to *Auburn*.

––––––––––

INGERSOLL–in the southeast corner of Ingersoll Township. Also called *Lee's Corners* and about 1898 name changed again to *"Laporte."*

A Winslow family from *Barnard, Vermont,* moved to the site in 1866, taking up government land on which Indian wigwams were then standing. Joseph J. Winslow, born at *Barnard, Vermont*, May 17, 1844, moved there in March, 1866 and later became Supervisor and justice of the peace. He died in *Midland* in 1914. Most settlers came from New England.

1877 population 50. Curtis J. Winslow, postmaster. Mail weekly. Several carpenters; Reverend O. B. Hale, doctor; and the Winslow & Chamberlin general store were listed.

1918 name changed to *"Laporte."* Population 102. Located on Swan Creek, 5 miles west of *Freeland* (formerly *"Jay."*) H. Garrett, general store and Reifenberg & Company, general store.

> NOTE: In 1877 there was also an *"Ingersoll"* 8 miles west of *Lansing,* Watertown Township, Clinton County. Seven families lived there. Settled in 1870. Stave and sawmills and a railroad station. James DeMoss, postmaster.

––––––––––

KETCHAM or *KETCHAMVILLE*–located between *Averill* and *Hope* was the headquarters camp for Wright and Ketchum Lumber Company who purchased large tracts of timber rights in the county about 1878. They soon became the biggest pine timber operators in the Saginaw Valley and had a payroll of 1,000 men.

This was the first lumber company to build their own private railroad for hauling lumber and had their 20 miles of narrow-gauge track operating from Averill north about the same time Scott Gerrish of Clare County built his first logging railroad in the world.

The company became the subject of some of the best known poems and songs of the lumbercamps including the famous song *Wright & Ketchum Line.* Their motto was "cut and get out" with little regard for bettering the territory in which they operated.

Ketchamville, later called *"Ketcham,"* was named after the junior partner Phillip H. Ketcham. Today only a few scars on the earth's surface mark the final resting place of this once important and thriving headquarters town.

————

NORTH BRADLEY–first settled as *"Buttonville"* after an early settler whose last name was Button. 1918 population 140. On the P. M. Railroad and the Salt River, Geneva Township, midway between *Coleman* and *Sanford*. Methodist church; E. M. Beamish, postmaster. Had two large general stores, a meat market, real estate office, blacksmith shop, etc. A. J. McMullen, railroad and express office.

Settled in 1873, with the extension of the P. M. Railroad west from *Averill*. Button set up the first sawmill and by 1877 the population grew to 250. William Babcock, postmaster (1877) and general store; William Button, lumber and shingles; H. Johnson, lumber and shingles; H. Stratton, express agent.

During the logging peak in the 1880s the population swelled to more than 500 and passenger trains made several stops daily at the thriving village.

After the logging days residents moved away and for many years only two stores, a hardware and a gasoline station were in business. In 1960 the village was bypassed by the new US-10 expressway and only a few residents remain, although it still has a post office.

Buttonville has long since been forgotten and only a few buildings remain strung along each side of Old US-10 and the present Chesapeake & Ohio Railroad. *North Bradley* is almost a "ghost of a ghost town."

————

PORTER–shown on 1968 Michigan highway maps. Located in Section 17, Porter Township and on the Pine River. During the 1880s was an important lumbering center and had a population of more than 500.

1870, Lewis R. Brewer, postmaster. Had two cooperages (barrel factory), and other business places.

1877 population 200. Eleven miles north of St. Louis. *"Merchandise is sent via St. Louis on the S. V. & St. Louis Railroad. Weekly mail delivery by stage from Midland."*

1910 population 27, eight miles (west) of *Breckenridge*. Mrs. A. J. Van Epps, general store.

———

WRIGHT'S BRIDGE–in 1870 a post office in Jerome Township, 5 miles north of *Sanford's* on the P. M. Railroad. On the Tittabawassee River. The first settler moved here in 1852. Has occasional mail. L. S. Thomas, postmaster; William Grunsden, lumber; L. S. Holmes, lumber; and Charles Wood, hotel.

In 1877 most of the pine had been removed and farmers moved to the area. In that year L. S. Holmes, postmaster; Charles Woods, sawmill; J. H. Person, general store. Some of the farmers listed were A. M. Hadley, Dennis Hadley, William Holmes, J. Lynch, John and William Magee, Dann Malone, John Springer, and H. Thornton.

———

Other towns and places during the history of the county were:

ALAMANDO–in Section 34, Warren Township, 3½ miles from *Coleman*. 1905 population 25. Mrs. Alma Robinson, postmistress; Clara Burns, teacher; Reverend Parks, Methodist; Miss Wilson, schoolteacher; and Robinson General Store.

1910 a discontinued post office on the P. M. Railroad. RFD *Coleman*.

———

BARNES–1910 a discontinued post office 5½ miles west of *Midland*.

———

BRIER–1918 a post office in Mills Township, near the Bay County line, 9 miles from *Crump*, Section 10. Mail tri-weekly.

———

CAMP 16–see *Edenville*.

———

CRANE–1910 a discontinued post office 4 miles southwest of *Midland*. Population 30.

———

CURTICE–in Section 7, Edenville Township. Roy Crosby, 80, who was born near here, said a main tote-road (still visible) called the "Nickel Road," ran the 5 miles from the high banks below *Edenville* on the Tittabawassee River to *Curtice* where sleigh loads of logs were loaded on the P. M. Railroad there and shipped to the mills. Curtice Lumber Company had a large logging operation in the area for many years, he said (1970).

DORR–shown on 1899 railroad maps.

FLOYD–Section 23, Lee Township, 8½ miles west of *Midland*. 1905 daily mail. John A. Mallory, postmaster; Kinzy Hunt, grocery and drugs.

1910 population 87. In 1918 G. L. Hitsman, general store, and Kinzy Hunt, general store.

GRAY–1910 a discontinued post office, 10 miles north of *Midland*, in Mills Township. Population 30. Frank Kelly, general store.

JAM–Section 26, Mt. Haley Township. 1910 population 35. RFD *Merrill*.

LEE'S CORNERS–see *Laporte*.

LARKIN–in Section 9, Larkin Township, 7½ miles from *Midland*. 1910 RFD *Midland*.

LUMAN–1918 a discontinued post office. RFD *Coleman*.

OLSON– Section 4, Lee Township, 5½ miles from *Sanford*. A log school was built here in 1870 and burned in 1895. In that year the first post office was put in the town store. John Moore was first postmaster. Each name he suggested for the post office was refused because they were already in use. At a meeting one evening, Mrs. Jake Larsen said, *"Name it Olson after my father."* Mr. Moore submitted the name and it was accepted.

Carl Tohm was the first mail carrier.

The "Olson Store" is a historic landmark. In 1904 it was purchased by L. P. Larsen who built the present store in 1924 and has been in the Larsen family for 66 years. *Olson* never became a town.

PANSY–1910 a discontinued post office 10 miles north of *Averill* in Hope Township at the intersection of Sections 10, 11, 14 and 15.

———

PLEASANT VALLEY–an early settlement on the Little Salt River, 8 miles north of *St. Louis*, Jasper Township, Section 17. The place was founded by the DePues, William T. Nicholas, Marshall S. and Alanson Bailey. Charles and Lydia Cronkright were the first settlers in the township in 18S9.

1910 population 75. RFD *St. Louis*. R. E. Hitchcok, general store.

———

RED KEG–see *Averill*.

———

REDSTONE–in Section 29, Porter Township, 5½ miles west of *Breckenridge*.

1910 a discontinued post office. Population 15.

———

SMITH'S CROSSING–in Sections 35 and 36, Midland Township, on the P. M. Railroad.

1910 population 35. RFD *Freeland*.

———

SMITHVILLE–listed in 1870 as a newly-established post office.

———

ST. ELMO–1910 mail to *Stearns*.

———

STEARNS–founded in 1882 when Col. William L. Stearns led a group of settlers from *Berea, Ohio*. On April 3 of that year Greendale Township was formed and soon after the village.

1917 a discontinued post office 17 miles west of *Midland*. Send mail to *Midland*. Located in Greendale Township.

———

Chapter 10

MISSAUKEE COUNTY GHOST TOWNS AND MICHIGAN'S BIGGEST GHOST TOWN

Missaukee County was once a part of Antrim and Grand Traverse Counties and was set off in 1840. The first survey was made by W. L. Coffinberry in 1853-56. The county government was formed in 1871. It derives its name from an Ottawa Indian chief who signed the treaties of 1831 and 1833. The name means "mouth of a large river."

As were most northern counties, Missaukee was settled primarily by timber interests. The first road was built near *Falmouth* in 1867 by a Mr. McDonald.

W. Windson established the first logging camp in 1865 on the bank of the Clam River, two miles below *Vogel Center*. Many of the early settlers were Dutch immigrants who came from near *Holland,* Michigan.

Short stretches of logging railroads, running on improvised wood and strap iron rails, were built in 1876-77. In the spring of 1890 the Missaukee Branch of the Grand Rapids and Indiana Railroad was extended from *Cadillac* to *Lake City*. This was later extended to *Falmouth* and *Merritt* but the Merritt branch was removed many years ago. About 1953 the abandoned railroad branch was purchased by a private corporation and features old-fashioned steam train rides under the direction of Howard Noble. Some of the former stations along the line, such as *Sandstown* and *Veneer Junction*, have been revived. The railroad also transports pulpwood, Christmas trees, and other shipments by rail between *Cadillac, Lake City*, and *Falmouth*.

Much of the county's cutover land has been planted to tree plantations and is undergoing a planned reforestation, although tourism and resorts around the many lakes constitute the main industry today. Oil wells are also an important part of the economy.

As most northern counties, Missaukee has no published history. A typed history of the county is on file at the Lake City Library and during the centennial of 1968 a *Lake City* centennial booklet was published. Population of the county declined nearly 10 percent in the decade between 1950 and 1960.

RAILROADS

1890–Toledo, Ann Arbor & North Michigan. Entering at *McBain* from *Park Lake* (Osceola County), 0 miles; *McBain*, 7.1 miles; *Lucas*, 4.1 miles; and on to *Cadillac*.

1890–Grand Rapids & Indiana Railroad, Missaukee Branch. Beginning at *Missaukee Junction*, 0 miles; *Round Lake*, 4 miles; *Lake City*, l4 miles.

1890–Cadillac & North Eastern Railroad (now Lake City & Cadillac Railroad privately-owned). Beginning at *Cadillac*, 0 miles; *G. R. & I. Crossing*, 1 mile; *Beckett's Crossing*, 8 miles. Entered Missaukee County at *Mitchell's Crossing*, 10 miles; *Komoko*, 11 miles; and *Lake City*, 14 miles.

1899–the county was served by the Kalkaska Branch of the Chicago & West Michigan Railroad at *Stratford* near the north county line. This line began at *Van Buren* in Kalkaska County and ran for a distance of 33 miles, with *Stratford* at the southern terminus.

POST OFFICES

There have been at least 26 post offices during the history of the county. Today only 4 remain (1970).

The first post office was in the home of Daniel Reeder at *Reeder,* now *Lake City*, established in the spring of 1872. Mail was also brought to settlers by those who made trips for provisions, either to *Hersey, Farwell*, or *Traverse City*, the nearest settlements. Mail delivery averaged once in two months.

GHOST TOWNS

ARDIS and *ARDIS JUNCTION*–listed in the 1910 *Rand McNally Railroad Guide* on the G. R. & I. Railroad. Mail to *Missaukee*. The former lumbering center was probably named after Samuel Boyd Ardis, wealthy mill owner and merchant, who came here in 1883. Ardis was also a partner in the Ardis and Keelan Land & Lumber Company which was located here in 1906. William Keelan, Superintendent.

———

ARLENE–shown on 1969 Michigan maps between *Lake City* and *Manton*. 1905 a country post office in Caldwell Township, 7 miles northwest of *Lake City*. Daily mail. Martin Duffy, postmaster and proprietor of the Arlene Merchantile Company owned by himself and four sons, Martin, Stafford, Carl, and Joseph. Benjamin Hartger, general store; William Berger, blacksmith; Janette Chick, teacher; Duffy & Stratton, general store; Samuel Rock, sawmill; and Reverend E. Van Korlaar.

1917 Alfred D. Whipple, general store. Daily mail.

Was a post office as late as 1927.

———

79

BUTTERFIELD–in Butterfield Township, 4 miles south of *Merritt* and on Butterfield Creek was at one time a good-sized village. Some of the original log cabins remain in the area. A grocery and gasoline station remains, two nice churches, and one empty store building in good repair.

In 1906 George E. Bowman, blacksmith; C. M. Gibson, postmaster and general store; M. B. Steffy, deputy sheriff; Charles B. Marsh, landlooker; George C. Miller, lumberman; J. Scott, lumberman; and E. Shrauger, sawmill. 1910 population 45.

1917 daily stage to *Lake City*. Richard A. Williams, postmaster, general store and real estate. Had blacksmith shop, grain and bean warehouse, and other buildings.

––––––––

CALDWELL–listed in 1878 as a village. A Caldwell Free Methodist Church is in use today (1970).

––––––––

CRANMER–in 1910 on the G. R. & I. Railroad, mail to *Lake City*. Probably on the shore of Muskrat (Missaukee) Lake.

Fred Hirzel said Jacob Cummer & Sons started lumbering white pine in 1876 and this was one of their many lumber camps. This company later became Cummer & Cummer and finally changed to Cummer & Diggins (Fred A. Diggins), lasted the longest of any lumber company in Michigan, starting in 1876 and lasting until 1936, Hirzel said.

––––––––

CUTCHEON–a post office in 1890, and had a population of more than 100. Located in Section 2, Forest Township, at present-day Cutcheon and Edwards Roads.

1917 located 10 miles north of *Lake City*. Dennis Nowlin, postmaster, real estate and loans; C. Barkman, station agent; Nowlin & Company, general store; J. D. Phillips, real estate. In 1906 S. A. Phillips, highway commissioner. Post office last listed in 1927.

––––––––

DINCA–1917 in Aetna Township, 12 miles southeast of *Lake City* and 4½ from *Falmouth*, RFD. School standing in Section 29 (1953).

––––––––

DOLPH–was a post office in 1899. In 1906 William Jones (who settled there in 1880), hotel; R. W. Rayan, shingle mill; and M. G. Stevens, lumberman.

NOTE: "Lumberman" was the name used for a "lumberjack."

80

This old house with moss-covered roof, shreds of curtains and remains of a picket gate on the front lawn, is typical of those standing in hundreds of Michigan ghost towns until the 1930s. Now only hollows in the ground remain. This house still stands in *Jennings* (1970), one of the few ghost town with buildings.

1917 a country post office 8 miles north of *Leota* in Clare County. Daily mail and telephone.

Section 2, Clam Union Township, on east bank of Muskegon River. The site of *Dolph* now lies on the edge of the Houghton Lake State Forest at the end of an old trail about 7 miles south of M-55. Old Dolph School stood about ° miles northwest of the site in 1953.

———

EDSON CORNERS–a post office in 1890. 1910 mail to *Dolph*. Last listed as a post office in April, 1899.

———

FORWARD–1910 RFD *Marion*. 1917, Riverside Township, 7 miles from McBain. Joseph Neiderhood, general store.

———

FREY–1910 mail to *Lake City*. 1917 on the G. R. & I. Railroad, 6 miles east of *Lake City*.

———

GALT–one of the first settlements in the county and one of three post offices listed in 1877. Described as: *"A post office in Riverside Township, 14 miles east of Clam Lake (Cadillac) and 9 south of Lake City. Grain, hay, and potatoes are raised, all for use in neighboring lumber camps. Weekly stage from Clam Lake and Falmouth. William McBain, postmaster."*

Listed as a post office until 1907, Andrew Young, who settled there in 1878, postmaster. 1910, mail to *McBain*. Nothing remains.

———

HAYMARSH (also spelled *"Haymarch"*)–was a post office from about 1903 (listed October 1904) until 1921, 22 miles northeast of *Lake City*. Daily mail. Shown on 1920 road maps between *Star City* and *Michelson* near the Missaukee-Roscommon County line.

———

HOOP–1910 mail to *Moorestown*. Not on 1920 road maps.

———

JENNINGS–postal name *"Round Lake"*–one of few Michigan ghost towns with original buildings still standing. With the exception of *AuSable* in Oscoda County (see Volume I). *Jennings* was probably the largest town in the State to become a ghost town. First called *"Mitchell,"* after the lumbering firm of that name with headquarters in *Cadillac* who set up huge mills on the shores of Crooked Lake, the rapidly-growing village became a post office named *"Jennings"* about 1890.

Factory of the Cummer-Diggins Company chemical plant at *Jennings*, Michigan. One of several large sawmills and factories in the town of more than 2,000 residents. Called an "extracting factory" it produced charcoal and by-products of wood alcohol, acetate of lime, etc. Only the weed-grown basements remain. Photo from Fred Hirzel Collection.

Another post office by the name *"Mitchell"* was already located in Antrim County, so the name had to be changed.

During the late 1800s the lumber mills employed 600 or more men. At one time the population contained 2,000 residents who awakened each day at dawn to the shriek of whistles from the whirring mills that operated 24-hours-a-day to meet the demands for Michigan pine lumber to build the cities of the rapidly-growing western frontier.

Manes Dewing erected the first sawmill on the site in 1878. A settlement soon grew around the mill atop the high hills overlooking the lake. Jobbers (individual lumbermen) set up camps in the area to harvest the virgin pine. During the next few years farmers came to the area to clear the stumps and make their homes. Some of the new settlers were the Jorgenson brothers, Fred P. and Valdemar, and John R. Hill. Then followed Adolph Gunnerson, and in 1889 Frank Anderson moved to *Jennings*, established a store, and the following year was elected township treasurer and appointed postmaster of the new village.

In 1882 the Mitchell brothers, William and Austin, bought the Dewing Mill and erected a much larger mill. They were the first in northern Michigan to use a double-cut band saw, which doubled the speed of sawing lumber from logs. The Mitchells extended logging railroads as far north as Kalkaska County to keep their mills supplied with logs. They often shipped 22 carloads of lumber per day on the Grand Rapids & Indiana Railroad.

Factories of the Cadillac Chemical Company employed several hundred men and consumed cordwood by the thousands of tons from which wood alcohol, acetate of lime, and other chemicals were obtained before it was reduced to charcoal and shipped to smelting plants at *East Jordan* and the Upper Peninsula. The steel ovens, in which a flatcar loaded with wood could be processed, were the invention of a Mr. Saunders of *Cadillac*. Before that time, crude brick kilns were hand-fed and the new ovens increased production a hundredfold.

With the coming of the railroad the village was booming (1889). Goods previously brought in by oxen and teams now came by the carloads.

When the logging boom ended about the turn-of-the-century, the huge Cadillac Chemical Company moved out and the population of the village began to dwindle. As late as 1905 the village retained 800 residents. There were two churches, Methodist Swedish and Lutheran. Fred R. Anderson, postmaster, bazaar, notions and newsstand; three doctors, Arthur Barnum, U. S. C. Bush, and A. F. Burnham; Henry Curtis, hotel and barber; C. J. Comly, barber shop; Robert Jones, dry goods; Frank J. LaChance, livery; J. F. Nelson, general store; and C. P. Nordenberg, dray line.

In 1910 the population dropped to 450, but a few years later, 1917, jumped to 1,200 and experienced a brief boom during a cleanup of hardwood, cedar, and other small timber and the demand for ice from the lake. In 1918 described as: *"On the G. R. & I. Railroad, Lake Township. Settled in 1881. Has Catholic, Methodist, Swedish, Baptist, and Swedish Lutheran Churches. Telephone. William W. Atchinson, postmaster and news dealer; M. B. Curtis, hotel; Frank J. LaChance, livery; James McConnell, ice; Mitchell Brothers Company, general store and sawmill; J. F. Nelson, general store; C. P. Nordenberg, ice; F. R. Servis, band leader; and A. W. Steimel, station agent."*

During the summer of 1922, with the forests leveled for miles around, the village found itself without an industry. Mitchell Brothers moved out, closing their huge general store and lumberman's supply. The now defunct Acme Motor Truck Company of *Cadillac* was hired to move the long row of company houses to *Cadillac*. Special trailers were made to haul the houses on the 14-mile journey through sand trails and over high hills to their destination. Several old-timers living today remember the strange procession as half-a-dozen trucks and trailers pulled into *Cadillac* with their unusual cargo. Only the concrete foundations of the houses remain today along the main road leading north to *Jennings* from M-55. The land where they once stood has been planted to evergreen trees, now nearly 15 feet high.

The sawmill was torn down and the population continued to diminish until by the 1930s only a few people remained. The post office remained to serve the few residents who stayed on until 1958, when nobody could be found in the village to assume the office.

Grass-covered trails that were once busy streets, weed-filled basements and vine-covered foundations, perhaps a dozen empty houses in various stages of decay, and one grocery store open part-time, stand in sharp contrast among newly-built summer homes and a few modernized older buildings in *Jennings* today. Rapidly-growing up to oak, white birch, and poplar trees, the surrounding countryside is dotted with huge stumps for miles around.

One of the original buildings, at one-time a large school housing more than 200 students, is now the "Jennings Mission," the only church remaining. The village is one of few ghost towns in Michigan with stretches of concrete sidewalk, mostly overgrown with weeds, weathered, unpainted picket fences surrounding many empty houses and buildings, and with most of the old basements and foundations plainly evident.

Two cemeteries remain in the area. The "Old Jennings Cemetery" is located on County Road 597 (main street) in Section 17, and the "New Jennings Cemetery" is on the same road about ½ mile south of *Jennings*.

KOOPMAN–the first store in the county was erected here by John Koopman in October, 1869, and was a log home and store combined. 1912, on the G. R. & I. Railroad, population 63. Mail to *Lake City*.

Henry John Koopman, sawmill operator, came from the Netherlands to America in 1865 and settled here in 1879.

LIBERTY CORNERS–in Section 30, Butterfield Township. Was a post office in 1906. Although not a village, a hotel and saloon was located at the intersection and did a thriving business during the lumbering days.

Named by Seth St. Johns, a Civil War veteran who thought the name appropriate. St. Johns was born in 1836 and settled here in 1888 and built the hotel.

LUCAS–shown on 1969 State highway map. Now a farming community of nice homes near the site of the former village of nearly 300 population bordering the Ann Arbor Railroad in Richland Township, 4 miles northwest of *McBain*.

Was a post office on December, 1890 and in 1956.

1905 population 250. William M. Taylor, postmaster; R. Maxwell, hotel; Curtis Sunday, boardinghouse; and F. E. Simmons, sawmill.

1910 population 100. As late as 1918 Lucas was a busy village with five general stores, broom handle factory, gristmill, potato warehouses along the tracks, lumber and coal yard, pickle station, and the Lucas Creamery Company (Richard Lucas secretary.) In that year John L. Kieldsen was postmaster.

A coal yard still operates on one siding. A tile block building, part of the lumber yard buildings, and a general store building (no longer a store) remain on the site today.

MISSAUKEE–a former village 8 miles north of *Lake City*. In 1905 a country post office. Robert Olson, millwright and train engineer.

1910–on the G. R. & I. Railroad, population 60.

1918 no population given. Daily mail. Bert M. Forquer, postmaster and Forquer Brothers, general store. (See picture)

Fred Hirzel of *Moorestown* said *Missaukee* was a good-sized village. Located just south of *Stittsville* it contained a depot and roundhouse built for the

General store and post office at the former village of *Missaukee* about 1890. This village contained a depot and train roundhouse on a branch of the G. R. & I. Railroad and had a population of more than 100. All that remains are one to two huge oak trees in the center of an open field. Photo from Fred Hirzel Collection.

Porter Cedar Company and was on a branch of the G. R. & I. Railroad, which ran from *Ardis*. *"The last time I visited there (about 1910) I rode into town with Charlie Barret, the mail carrier. One of the Forquer brothers was postmaster at Missaukee and the other was postmaster at Moorestown,"* Hirzel said.

Nothing remains on the site today. The former railroad grade runs west in a straight line and is visible for more than ½ mile. The site of both *Missaukee* and *Stittsville* are located near County Road 571. *Missaukee* on the west side of the road and *Stittsville* on the east.

NOTE: *Missaukee Junction* and *Missaukee Village* have no connection. (See Wexford County.)

MISSAUKEE PARK–was a station and flag stop on the G. R. & I. Railroad. 1910 mail to *Lake City*. Hirzel said it was located on the south side of Missaukee Lake. A Mr. Winans was section boss from this point on the railroad to *Falmouth* and *Michelson* on the Missaukee-Roscommon County line.

MITCHELL–name changed to *Jennings*.

MODDERSVILLE–this one-time village of 250 or more population is located on Thirteen Mile Road, about 2 miles north of the Clare County line, northwest of *Leota*. Was a post office in 1890 and in 1933.

In Clam Union Township. 1917 John W. Modders, postmaster. Daily mail. Chris Ebels, general store. Also a blacksmith shop, feed mill, and two sawmills. The last big two-story general store closed its doors about 1967 and is still standing. A few families live on the site, including the Normans, a pioneer family of the area. Archie Norman, now nearing 90, is one of only two persons living who remembers the day *Dodge City* burned. (See Clare County, Volume 1).

Another two-story house, vacant for many years, stands on a high hill overlooking the one-time village. An old cemetery and what appears to be a sawmill site are located at the end of a trail and cowpath about 1 mile east of the four-corners where the old store building stands.

Named after a Modders family. Dick Modders, born in Holland in 1855 moved here in 1874 and was a timber estimator. In 1906 John W. Modders, postmaster, general store, hardware, drugs, clothing, etc. Telephone. James E. Durkee, Henry W. Modders, and Evertt Vanderwal, school directors; Thomas White, sawmill.

MOORESTOWN–first called *"Perry's Camp"* after J. Henry Moores' lumber camp foreman. Fred Hirzel said Joel Perry set up a headquarters camp on the site in 1881. *"He chose this site due to the rich soil needed to raise vegetables for lumberjacks in Moores' camps and hay to feed the 20 or more teams of horses,"* Hirzel said.

Perry was replaced by Samuel H. Hemphile of *Big Rapids*, who took charge of railroad construction and logging operations for Moores. *"One day in June of 1882 a procession of 100 teams pulled into Moorestown with 100 loads of railroad track, which were unloaded from the G. R. & I. Railroad cars at Fife Lake,"* Hirzel said.

This railroad, known as the West Branch and Moorestown, had articles of association filed with the Secretary of State, according to an article in the *Lake City Journal* of March, 1882, and capital stock of the company was listed at $100,000.

More than 8 million feet of logs had been cut in the area and Moores was anxious to get them to the Muskegon River to be floated to the mills.

Mr. Moores of *Lansing*, for whom the town was named, logged until May of 1887 when his timber had all been cut. He sold his interests to Edwin P. Stone of *Saginaw*, who moved into what is now the oil headquarters district east of *Moorestown*. Stone connected his railroad with that of Blodgett & Byrne, who were lumbering in Crawford and Roscommon Counties and the two firms joined forces in placing their timber in the Muskegon River, Hirzel said.

After the timber was gone the population of the once-booming village declined. Hirzel gives Moores credit for founding the village and doing a good job of logging. *"He is probably the only timber baron in the history of Michigan who took the pains to buy seed and sent men out to plant grass seed on all the stumped over land,"* Hirzel said.

Over the years fire destroyed many buildings in the village. At one time there was a hotel and saloon called the "Arlington Hotel," T. J. Beugnot, proprietor, several stores, one run by L. M. Courter called the "New Store."

1905 population 125. Godfrey Hirzel, postmaster. Three general stores, blacksmith shop, and a sawmill. M. B. Steffy, deputy sheriff.

1918 population 100. In Norwich Township, 20 miles northeast of *Lake City*. Telephone. W. M. Nichols, postmaster and general store. Blacksmith shop and hotel.

Several original buildings remain, one a vacant general store. Part of the Godfrey Hirzel store building is now used as a residence and stands near the former "main street." Since the 1940s the village has made a partial revival as a tourist and deer hunting center. A new supermarket has been built and the main street is paved.

Was a post office in 1890 and in 1956. Now RFD *Lake City*.

MOREY–probably named after William J. Morey who homesteaded here in 1867. One large, two-story vacant store building remains on the site. Located in Pioneer Township about 6 miles north of *Lake City* on M-66. Was a post office in 1890 but never reached village status. F. S. Bardwell, who moved to the county in 1875, was postmaster in 1906. The post office was located in the Bardwell General Store.

In Section 31, Pioneer Township, Mitchell Brothers Logging Company had extensive banking grounds and log rollways near her in the 1890s.

1918, John R. Eubank, general store. Send mail to *Pioneer*.

MYNNINGS–a former village in Section 5, Aetna Township. School standing in 1953. During the 1890s had considerable population due to lumbering. 1910 on the G. R. & I. Railroad, population 15. Mail to *Lake City*, 9 miles distant.

1906 C. J. Parks, postmaster, sawmill and lumber dealer. Wellington Armstead, a lumberman, lived here in 1897. A. H. Hunt, Township Clerk in 1906.

NIXON–listed as a post office in 1877. James Nixon, who worked for the Thayer Lumber Company, lived there in 1892.

NORWICH–founded in 1878. Name changed to *"Stittsville."*

PINHOOK–name changed to *"Falmouth"* when post office was established. Probably the first settlement of any size in the county. *Falmouth* (not a ghost town) was described in 1872 as: *"The county seat of Missaukee County ... There are but two post offices in the county, Falmouth and Reeder, and no regular mail service in either place. Falmouth is on Clam River, 18 miles east of Clam Lake (Cadillac), and 30 miles north of Farwell (Clare County) from whence it receives its mail."*

Business listings were John Cavanaugh, proprietor of "Falmouth House Hotel"; Perley-Palmer & Company, blacksmith shop; grist, saw and shingle mills; E. W. Watson, postmaster, county clerk, register of deeds, and tax agent. A courthouse was built here in 1871.

OWENS–name changed to *"McBain"* which became a village and is now a city.

PIONEER–located on M-66, twelve miles northeast of *Lake City*. The old general store, now vacant and in good repair, stands on the corner of M-66 and the road leading to *Moorestown*. Fred Hirzel said this is all there ever was on the site and it was never a town.

1877 in Pioneer Township, 15 miles southeast of *Fife Lake*, its nearest railroad point. Also known as *"Moreys."* Mail once a week. W. J. Morey, postmaster.

From 1898 until 1904 a narrow-gauge railroad connected with *Stittsville*, a few miles southeast. A Pioneer School and cemetery remains in Section 14 near the old railroad grade, about 1 mile east of the store.

1906 Martin Iverson, timekeeper for Mitchell Brothers Lumber Company, lived here. Also Reverend H. S. Lamb and Mrs. Etta Goff, second white child born in the county in 1870.

1910 population 18, RFD *Lake City*. H. A. Ingersoll & Son, general store.

———

PROSPER–shown on 1969 State highway map. In Clam Union Township, 3 miles from *Falmouth*. In 1906 T. Veldman, deputy postmaster. Prosper Grocery Company, owned by Thomas Veldman and Albert Brunigh, dealers in produce, provisions, hardware, and general merchandise. Gerrit Vis, Township Clerk.

1918 R. Dykhause, general store. RFD *Falmouth*.

A church serves the area today (1970).

———

PUTNAM–name changed to *"Star City."* See *Star City.*

———

REEDER–in 1872 one of two post offices in Missaukee County, 12 miles northwest of *Falmouth*, the county seat. *"It is on the edge of a large lake known as Muskrat Lake. This has been a settlement since 1868 and now numbers about 500 souls. It has an occasional mail. Daniel Reeder, postmaster."*

Five years later (1877) *Reeder* was also called *"Lake City,"* but the lake was still "Muskrat Lake."

Clam Lake (now *Cadillac*), 14 miles southwest, on the G. R. & I. Railroad, was the shipping point. William Reeder, postmaster. Two grocery stores; Charles Pillen, hotel; and Daniel & William Reeder, sawmill.

In 1874 Daniel Reeder had the growing village platted into 129 lots. In 1873 a courthouse was built here and the county seat moved from Falmouth. The name of "Muskrat Lake" was changed to "Lake Missaukee." Most of the buildings in the village burned in 1911 and were rebuilt, many made of brick. In 1944 the courthouse burned and the old, wood-frame jail was sold and removed from the property. *Lake City* is a thriving village and resort center today.

––––––––

REEDSBURG–was a station on the G. R. & I. Railroad. 1910 mail to *Michelson*.

––––––––

RIVERSIDE–mentioned in 1878 newspapers.

––––––––

ROUND LAKE–on the G. R. & I. Railroad. 1910 postal name for *Jennings*.

––––––––

ROUND LAKE JUNCTION–on the G. R. & I. Railroad. Mail to *Jennings*.

––––––––

ROY–see *"Star City."*

––––––––

SANDSTOWN–1 mile south of *Lake City*. Hirzel said the station was named after Charlie Sands, son of Louis Sands of logging day fame, and was the location of the Sands Salt & Lumber Company and on Mosquitoe Creek, which furnished power for the sawmill. The place only lasted two or three years, he said.

Listed in 1912 *Rand McNally Atlas*, mail to *Lake City*.

––––––––

STAR CITY–formerly called *"Putnam"* and also known as *"Roy."* Name changed when post office was founded because there was another *"Putnam"* in Lenawee County.

Located in West Branch Township, 4 miles west of *Merritt*. Nothing remains today, unless perhaps a few foundations. At one time population 500, and at the corner of present day Wagner and Star City Roads in Sections 24, about 1 mile north of M-55.

Was a post office in 1890 until 1923-24. 1905 population 175. Daily mail stage to *Lake City*. Telephone. Sarah J. May, postmistress; A. D. Bell, sawmill; Jacob E. Gray, general store; Frances May, hotel and livery; Sunderland & Stevens, hardware; Gertrude Wolfe, teacher.

Mrs. Laura Bell, who came to the county in 1877, taught school here in 1895.

1910 population 24. 1917 Uretta J. Stevens, postmaster; J. Gaukel, dairy; R. Hoover, farm implements; Mrs. D. M. Loveless, milliner; Arthur Merrill, hotel and livery; C. C. Miller, general store; Eland C. Miller, grocer; Mrs. Glenn Robinson, bakery; and E. M. Snyder, physician.

———

STITTSVILLE–1905 population 100. Formerly called *"Norwich"* after the township, 15 miles northeast of *Lake City* and 9 from *Stratford*, nearest railroad. Daily stage to *Lake City*. Frank Coffey, teacher; Nate (Nathan) Dougherty, hotel and saloon; J. B. Fish, barber; George Freeman, restaurant, hardware and blacksmith; W. W. Gorthy, justice of the peace; Mitchell Brothers, general store; F. E. North, manager; and John Sulter, livery.

1906 T. A. Barthlomew, postmaster and barber; George Freeman, blacksmith; A. W. Hall, carpenter and builder.

Was a post office in 1893 until 1933-34.

Fred Hirzel, 86, now living in *Moorestown*, said Mitchell's store and Than Dougherty's Hotel were on the east side of the road, which was platted as a village. Other buildings were across the street but not officially in *Stittsville*.

The first store was built by Gustavus V. Meyers in 1883, he said. Meyers was a doctor and at one time was Health Commissioner of the county. After Meyers left William Becker owned the store, then J. V. Moran.

Mitchell Brothers Lumber Company purchased the store and built a big warehouse and lean-tos on the north and west sides of the original building. In 1898, the Mitchells put in a narrow-gauge railroad that ran through *Morey* on present M-66 and northeast through *Stittsville* to their *Camp 29*, ½ mile from there. The railroad was removed in 1904, Hirzel said. The old grade is clearly defined today extending across open fields.

Hirzel said James Stitts built the first store in the village in 1878, built of logs. G. V. Meyers sold the store to Mitchells who operated it until the tracks were removed.

Last persons to operate the store were the Forquer Brothers. Bert operated the *Stittsville* store and Arthur the *Missaukee* store. The building then stood vacant for some time. The last occupant was Leonard "Len" Watson and his wife and several children who attended the *Stittsville* school. The store was razed in 1917.

General store at *Stittsville*, Missaukee County, about 1900. Mitchell Brothers Lumber Company purchased the original store (center) and built wings on each side about 1898. Note people waiting for their mail brought by team and wagon who also delivered merchandise. Photo from Fred Hirzel Collection.

Typical hotel, saloon and pool room of logging days. Note livery barns in background. This hotel at *Stittsville* was owned by Nathan (Thane) Dougherty and his wife "Mate" formerly of *Harrison*. Built in 1896 and torn down in 1916 and the lumber shipped to *Lansing* where it was re-used to build houses. Photo from Fred Hirzel Collection.

Hirzel said the village at one time had a barbershop; another hotel without a bar; a hardware; I.O.O.F. Hall, also used for dances, travelling shows, etc; a bicycle agency and repair shop for "Rambler" bicycles, operated by Joe McGee, agent; blacksmith shop with three employees; a jail; and post office.

1910 population 175. 1917 down to 40. In that year had telephone; J. S. Eshelby, postmaster, grocer and dry goods; and L. Richards, sawmill.

The big Mitchells store was torn down in 1918, Hirzel said. The large livery barn, east of the hotel, was originally on the Old State Road and was razed in 1912. Than Dougherty's hotel and saloon was torn down in 1916 and the lumber shipped to *Lansing* where the material was used for constructing houses.

All that remains of the former village is two 80-feet-high Lombardy poplar trees that died from old age. Across the road is a two-story house covered with insulbrick. Windows are broken and the roof is sagging. Hirzel said the house started deteriorating in the last two years. Before that time it was sound and in good condition.

A barn and a small wood building, neither painted, also are on the site. This is the former home of Miles E. Stitts, the youngest of several brothers and a descendant of the original settler after whom the village was named.

The house faces a half-mile section of the remaining stretch of the Old State Road that once intersected the county. The Stittsville Methodist Church is about ½ mile south near the corner of Phelps Road and Seven Mile Road north of M-55.

————

STRATFORD–former railroad station and logging village was founded in 1898 and deserted in 1910 after the timber was logged off. (See picture.) A post office here was listed in 1899 until September 1906. In 1897 a railroad was built connecting *Stratford* with *Rapid City* in Kalkaska County. (See Kalkaska County Railroads, Volume I.) The first train ran in 1898.

Through the efforts of Fred Hirzel the site was recently marked by the Michigan Department of Natural Resources. A large plaque tells the history of the short-lived village. This town originated in 1897 with the purchase of 13,400 acres of virgin red and white pine by the Thayer Lumber Company. A railroad came the same year and hauled logs six days a week for twelve years. In 1908, the last of the pine logs were hauled and *Stratford* became deserted. The site was purchased by the State in 1937. Sites of former buildings are marked with individual plaques, showing their locations.

In 1905 described as population 100. On the P. M. Railroad in Norwich Township, 22 miles from *Kalkaska*. Charles A. Rader, postmaster; Thayer Lumber

This village was established by the Thayer Lumber Company at the terminus of the Kalkaska Branch of the Chicago & West Michigan Railroad for the purpose of removing 13,400 feet of pine timber. The village lasted about 10 years, from 1898 to 1908.

97

Company; George Washburn, boardinghouse and station agent. James Post, saloon, liquor and cigars.

The Thayer tract of pine was one of the last two remaining in Michigan, Hirzel said. During the 12 years the village existed, the Thayer Company harvested 450 million feet of timber, and other logging companies along the 32-mile stretch of railroad probably harvested that many more feet, Hirzel said. *"I have seen nine steamed-up locomotives here at one time waiting to haul out cars of lumber,"* he said.

The town was named after a town named *"Stratford"* in Canada.

Nothing remains on the site of *Stratford*. Through the efforts of Fred Hirzel of *Moorestown* (standing looking at plaque) this plaque was erected on the site in 1967 and tells the history of the ghost town. Other plaques mark the site of each building in the former village. Photo from Fred Hirzel Collection.

Other towns and places were:

VENEER–in 1910 mail *Lake City*.

VENEER JUNCTION–1910 on the G. R. & I. Railroad. Mail to *Lake City*.

WAGNER–a flag stop in the G. R. & I. Railroad near LaChance Road. Had a stage to *Jennings* and a tiny, clapboard house for a station. 1910 mail to *Jennings*. Located in Section 14, Reeder Township, on present day Lake City & Cadillac Railroad.

WARDVILLE–1910 mail to *Michelson* (in Roscommon County).

––––––––

Chapter 11

MONTMORENCY COUNTY GHOST TOWNS AND THE GHOST TOWN THAT CAME BACK

First named "Cheonoquet" after a well-known Chippewa chief, whose name meant "Big Cloud," when it was set off in the survey of 1840. The present name, adopted in 1843 by the State Legislature, was taken in honor of Count Morency, who aided the United Colonies in the war with England.

The county was formed in 1881 and the land area taken from Cheboygan and Alpena County. The 1884 census recorded 845 population. By 1920 population had reached 4,089 and has remained about the same since that time. 1960 population 4,424. One-third of the county, about 120,000 acres, is state-owned land and contains 126 lakes.

Hillman was the first county seat and a few years later (about 1891), was moved to *Atlanta*. *Hillman* and *Atlanta* are the only villages ever incorporated during the history of the county. Both were incorporated in 1891: *Atlanta* with a population of 113, and *Hillman* with 233. *Hillman* reached a population of more than 250 and remains about the same today. Both villages were unincorporated about 1950-51.

RAILROADS

1906–Michigan Central Railroad, Twin Lakes & Clear Lake Branches. Beginning at *Grayling*, 0 miles; *Clear Lake Junction,* 19 miles; *Pratts*, 6 miles; *C. B. Junction*, 11 miles; *Johannesburg*, 13 miles; *Dana*, 25, miles; *Vienna Junction*, 27 miles; and *Lewiston*, 28 miles.

Most of this railroad grade, long since removed, is visible today. "Twin Lakes" is the name of the two large lakes at *Lewiston*. *Vienna Junction* was located between the two lakes.

Another railroad ran across what is now Fletcher's Pond. The grade can be followed extending east to west across the center of the county, with several spurs and branches. Some of the places along the line were *Connor, Rust, Stoddards, Dobbins, Hemlock, Watson, Kingsland, Atlanta, Briley, Green, Boston Camp, Fitzpatrick, Stevens, Camp 21, Huffs, Brush*, and *Gibbs*, near the Otsego County line.

POST OFFICES

There have been at least 13 post offices in the history of the county. Of these only 3 remain today.

GHOST TOWNS

BIG ROCK, formerly called *"Remington."* 1917 population 100. Montmorency Township, 4½ miles west of *Atlanta* on M-32. *"Has Congregational Church. Daily mail. William H. Remington, postmaster and general store. Also a meat market, sawmill, and some houses."*

Named for a huge granite boulder that still remains. The stone has an impression that appears to be a human footprint, perhaps that of an Indian wearing a moccasin. The big rock and the church are all that remain.

———

BONARD–listed in 1912 Railroad Atlas on the Au Sable and Northwestern Railroad. Mail *Comins*.

———

BRILEY–shown on 1899 railroad maps. See railroads.

———

DANA–1917 on the Twin Lakes Branch M. C. Railroad, 24 miles northeast of *Grayling*. Mail *Lewiston*.

———

GODFREY–a post office in 1906, 4½ miles north of *Hillman*. 1910 population 24. Mail *Hillman*.

———

HEATHERTON–Vienna Township, 12 miles west of *Atlanta*, on present day Meridian Road. A one-time lumbering center. 1905 population 75. *Lewiston*, nearest railroad, connected by daily mail stage. Lemuel Plumley, postmaster. W. S. Coy, railroad express agent; two sawmills, Peter Beckett and Roby & Marrow; "Heatherton House Hotel," N. Willard, proprietor; general store; grocery; Reverend E. Elsey, Presbyterian; and Reverend Tiffney, Congregational.

1917 population 30 and only one general store, run by Robert Campbell. By the 1920s last of the hardwood had been cut and *Heatherton* died. Shown on today's maps.

———

HERRICK–1910 mail *Comins*.

———

IDLEWILD–on 1893 maps in southern part of the county.

———

KISSIPIE–a post office in 1927.

———

KLEIN–1905 a country post office, 11 miles southeast of *Atlanta*. Mail semi-weekly. 1910 RFD *Hillman*.

———

LOUIE'S TOWN–a lumber camp on East Twin Lake in Albert Township during the late 1870s. Named after Louis Anderson, walking boss for Mr. Hansen, who owned a lumber mill at *Gaylord*. Anderson pushed the men to get more work and so was called "Hungry Louie." Jensen established the first mill on the site when it became a village and the name shortened to *"Lewiston."*

1905 Charles Drake, postmaster. 1918 Samuel S. Fuller, postmaster.

Lewiston reached a peak population of about 1,000 during the logging days, and in 1905 dropped to 800. From 1918 on the population dwindled and by the 1920s was a ghost town. Many original buildings were standing but the M. C. Railroad pulled out and the area was a sea of stumps and blowing sand.

The village slowly revived after World War II, with the increase in tourism, and during the past decade has again became a principal town in the county. One business block has been rebuilt with new store fronts, other buildings renovated, and a large factory is located near the village. *Lewiston* is one of few ghost towns in Michigan to make a comeback.

———

REMINGTON–name changed to *"Big Rock."* See *Big Rock*.

———

ROYSTON–1918 in Montmorency Township, 7 miles north of *Hillman*. Mail to *Hillman*. Alexander, sawmill; Robert McQueen, general store; and Albert Steinke, sawmill.

The town hall stood ½ mile east, on County Road 452, in 1953.

RUST–1910 a discontinued post office. RFD *Comins*. Was a post office again in 1926. On the old railroad grade, just south of M-32. Town hall standing, Section 21, in 1953.

————

VALENTINE–1905 population 16. Briley Township, 9 miles north of *Atlanta*. Mail tri-weekly. E. Ewing, postmaster. Macomber & Bale, shingle mill. Nothing remains. 1912 mail *Atlanta*.

————

VIENNA–on the west county line, Vienna Township, founded in 1887. Most of the property and business places were owned by the Furloughs. Was a post office from 1893 until about 1913 when the hotel and most business places were destroyed by fire.

Camp Number 26, owned by Hansen's of *Gaylord*, was located on Swede Lake, just over the line in Otsego County. Herman Loundeen was superintendent for Neil & Biglow Company of *Bay City* who owned the mills at *Vienna*.

Vienna was never rebuilt after the fire and only a store stands today. The school and cemetery are on the west county line in Otsego County and the village was almost on the line.

Old-timers recall the days when sawdust piles and steam whistles of mills and trains echoed through the woods. A resident of *Vienna* wrote the words to a song about Herman Loundeen and the Neil & Biglow Lumber Company paid $25 for a copy. It was sung in lumber camps for many years in northern Michigan.

"Michigan Slim" was a famous character of the camps who came from *Vienna*. He was also called "Piano Kickin' Slim." Slim detested honky-tonk piano music and one time, after a few drinks in a Cheboygan saloon, Slim kicked a piano apart with his calked boots when another jack started playing the piano.

In 1910 the population was 47.

————

VIENNA JUNCTION - 1910 mail *Lewiston*. See railroads.

————

Chapter 12

NEWAYGO COUNTY GHOST TOWNS AND HOW "PINCHTOWN" GOT ITS NAME

Newaygo is an Indian word meaning "great water" or "much water" and was the name of a Chippewa Indian chief. Newaygo County was formed in 1851 from parts of Kent, Muskegon and Oceana Counties.

Croton and *Big Prairie* played an important part in the early settlement of northern Michigan. For many years *Croton* was the only post office north of *Grand Rapids*. Between that point and *Traverse City* mail was carried through the wilderness by Indian runners.

Newaygo was the first major village and first county seat. It was incorporated in 1867 with more than 1,000 population. After the lumbering era population declined and it lost its importance as a village. In 1912 the county seat was moved to *White Cloud* (formerly *"Morgan Station."*)

Population in 1870 was 766 for the entire county and by 1874 had nearly doubled. By 1890 it had risen to 5,418. Since 1900 there has been a steady increase and in 1960 was 24,160.

In recent years the Muskegon River has been planted with the new strain of Coho salmon and *Newaygo* is rapidly becoming a hot-spot for sportsmen and anglers.

RAILROADS

1899–Chicago & West Michigan Railroad. Beginning at *Grand Rapids*, 0 miles; *Ashland (Center)*, 28 miles; *Grant*, 30 miles; *Newaygo*, 36 miles; *White Cloud*, 47 miles; *Diamond Loch*, 52 miles; *Otia*, 58 miles; *Brookings*, 61 miles; *Bitely*, 63 miles; *Lilley*, 65 miles.

1899–Chicago & West Michigan Railroad, Big Rapids Branch. Beginning at *Railroad Junction*, 4 miles; *Fremont*, 24 miles; *Worcester Hill*, 29 miles; *Ryerson*, 30 miles; *White Cloud*, 35 miles; *Field*, 44 miles; *Woodville*, 45 miles; *Lumberton*, 46 miles; *Hungerford*, 48 miles; and *Big Rapids*, 50 miles.

1907–Pere Marquette Railroad, Grand Rapids to Bay View. Beginning at *Grand Rapids*, 0 miles; *Bailey*, 26 miles; *Grant*, 30 miles; *Newaygo*, 36 miles; *White Cloud*, 47 miles; *Diamond Loch*, 52 miles; *Otia*, 58 miles; *Bitely*, 63 miles.

1907–Pere Marquette Railroad, Big Rapids Branch. *Muskegon*, 0 miles; *Reeman*, 22 miles; *Fremont*, 25 miles; *Wooster*, 30 miles; *White Cloud*, 36 miles; *Field*, 41 miles; *Woodville*, 45 miles; *Hungerford*, 49 miles; and *Big Rapids*, 56 miles.

POST OFFICES

There were at least 53 post offices during the history of the county. Of these 7 remain.

GHOST TOWNS

AETNA (also called *"Pinchtown")*–1877 a small village in Denver Township, 16 miles north of *Newaygo* and 9 northwest of *Morgan Station (White Cloud)*, on the White River. Saw, shingle and gristmill. Stages to *Morgan* and *Hesperia*. Tri-weekly mail. Settled in 1860, organized in 1871. Population 75. C. A. Stone, postmaster.

Thomas Stanley built the first mill. In 1867 Sours & Simon had a general store. Mr. Simon was noted for his precise methods of conducting his business. He never shorted a customer, and at the same time made certain he didn't cheat himself. One time while weighing a pound of crackers for a customer he pinched some off one cracker to balance the scales. The story soon became told around and from that time forward the town was known as *"Pinchtown"* by the residents.

1905 a discontinued post office. RFD *Hesperia*. Had a creamery, feed mill, liquor store, blacksmith, and grocery. Miss M. Roost, teacher, and John Stender, general store.

1917 G. W. Doud & Son, general store; and L. Stout, general store. In 1953 a Pinchtown Bridge remained across the river.

———

ALDERSON–a post office in 1908 and 1915. 1910 population 40. On the P. M. Railroad, Lilley Township, 5 miles from *Bitely*, RFD. J. J. Alderson, general store.

———

ALLEYTON–1877 a thriving place of 500, on the Big Rapids Branch of the C. & M. L. S. Railroad, on the White River in Everett Township. Ships lumber and shingles. Tri-weekly stage to *Hesperia*. Daily mail. S. A. Fleming, station agent; J. W. Hay, express agent. Had hotels, saloons, general stores, restaurants, hotel, etc. The place was named after J. Alley who owned the lumber company and was an important lumberman.

1884, an unincorporated village. Population 340.

Alleyton became a part of *White Cloud* after that village was incorporated in 1879. *Alleyton* was on the opposite side of the river near the site of White Cloud State Park. An Alleyton Bridge was standing in 1953 across the White River, after which *White Cloud* was named. (See *Morgan Station*).

———

ASHLAND–1877 the post office at *Grant*, a station on the Grand Rapids, Newaygo & Lakeshore Railroad, Ashland Township, 6½ miles south of *Newaygo*. Population 50. Daily mail. Frank Gardner, postmaster. There is also a village of this name in the same township, the post office of which is *Lake*.

1910 population 75. RFD *White Cloud*. 1917 C. L. Jones, general store.

———

BARTON–listed in 1855. See *"Beaver."*

———

BEAVER–1870 a new post office. Formerly called *"Barton."* Has one store ran by Alonzo Yates. Other residents are lumbermen: W. Barton; W. W. Dickinson; A. J. McDonald; and S. N. Wilcox.

———

BIG PRAIRIE–1870 a post office 8 miles north of *Croton*. 1877 in Big Prairie Township, 6 miles from *Morgan Station*. Weekly mail. William S. Utely, postmaster, notary, and land agent. Had a hotel, wagonmaker, two doctors, and several lumbermen.

Many residents took up farms in Mecosta County after 1850 and some businessmen moved to the new town of *Big Rapids*.

———

BITELY–residents of this one-time village don't consider it a ghost town. It now has a tavern, two or three stores, and a gasoline station, and is located on Old M-37 in a tourist and resort area. Was a post office in 1890 and remains today.

During the logging days the population was at times more than 500. On the Pere Marquette Railroad, 1917 population 150, about four times that of today. Had a bank; Bitely Lumber & Supply Company; Wallace Giddings, blacksmith; several general stores; hotel and livery; and produce warehouses.

Remains of old sawmills can be seen along the east side of the tracks. Several old, vacant store buildings line the one-time main street. Other former streets are mere trails, with grass and weeds growing between the tracks. *Bitely* is a ghost town.

———

BRIDGETON–1872 population 200, in the southwest corner of the county. *"Bridgeton Township, on the Muskegon River and on the line of the G. R. & N. Railroad now being built."* Settled in 1849. George H. Brown, postmaster. Blacksmith, general store, shingle mill, clapboard factory, and sawmills.

1877 population 75. Mail stage to *Newaygo* tri-weekly. Reverend H. S. Mellon, postmaster and Baptist minister. Joseph Truckey, general store.

1910 population 75. 6½ miles from *Grant*. Telephone. RFD *Newaygo*. 1917, Wallace F. Scott, general store.

———

COOK'S STATION–1870 a post office on the mail route from *Big Rapids* to *Traverse City*, 17 miles from *Big Rapids*. Daily mail. Myron Stone, postmaster. Name changed to *"Woodville."*

———

CROTON–a picturesque village above the Croton Dam on the Muskegon River. Not a ghost town but far from the bustling, frontier village of 500 population it was during the rush of settlers to northern Michigan.

1872 population 400, settled about 1840, platted in 1854 and incorporated in 1870. By 1894 the population was down to 91. By 1902 there were only 59 residents, and about five years later became unincorporated.

1872, daily mail. P. L. R. Fisk, postmaster, general store and drugs. Had a flour mill, shoe store, two general stores, wagon maker, sawmill, the "Union Hotel," and other places.

1877 population 250, at the junction of the Big and Little Muskegon Rivers, in Croton Township. Daily stage to *Newaygo* and *Howard City*. Congregational church and district school.

1917 RFD *Newaygo*. No business places listed. The original church stands here today with a pointed spire, overlooking the huge Croton Pond and looks like a picture postcard. The place is a resort center.

––––––––

DENVER–1870 Lewis Martin, postmaster. Weekly mail. 1877 population 60, Denver Township, 8 miles north of *Fremont Station* and on the White River. *"Has a sawmill, gristmill, and carding machine. Daily stage to Hesperia and Morgan Station, three times a week. L. E. Paige, postmaster, drugs and groceries. Restaurant; Mansfield Sawmill and general store; planing mill; John Rooke, flour mill; and J. A. Tinney, blacksmith."*

Was a post office in 1890, not in 1893. A *Denver* school and bridge standing in 1953.

––––––––

DIAMOND LOCH–1884 population 215. See *Ramona*.

––––––––

ENSLEY–1870 a post office 9 miles southeast of *Croton*. Semi-weekly mail. A post office in 1893. 1899 maps shown in Montcalm County. 1953 an *"Ensley Center"* shown on maps.

––––––––

FIELDS CROSSING–one of several towns and flag stops along the C. & M. L. S. Railroad. The sawmill, owned by a Mr. Williams, burned. 1910 mail *Woodville*. Nothing remains.

––––––––

GRANT–see *"Ashland."* *Grant* is not a ghost town.

––––––––

FREMONT CENTER–not a ghost town. Name shortened to *Fremont*. Settled in 1858. J. H. Darling, postmaster in 1872. Population 200.

––––––––

HOME–1872 a post office in Barton Township, 13 miles west of *Big Rapids*, and 4½ miles south of *Cook's Station* where it gets weekly mail. J. T. Chapman, postmaster; B. L. Ewing, lumber; T. R. Inman, hotel.

1877–Traverse Road, 5 miles distant, nearest railroad. Justice Chapman, postmaster. Benjamin Ewing, general store and sawmill. Not a post office in 1890.

HUNGERFORD–1877 a post office on the C. & M. L. S. Railroad, Norwich Township, 8 miles east of *Big Rapids*. Settled 1872. Population 100. Daily mail. George French, postmaster. Charles R. Barstow of *Big Rapids* owns the mill. Miss Mary Bullman, acting postmistress. Captain Ives of *St. Louis*, Michigan, owned another mill; and Tibbals & Cannon, another mill.

1905 Abel Lant, postmaster. Two justices; Thomas Mills, grocery; Flora Hond, teacher; and Fausta Storm, teacher.

1910 population 102. On the P. M. Railroad. Mail *Woodville*.

––––––––

LAKE–1872 a settlement of five families and a steam sawmill in Grant Township, 9 miles south of *Newaygo* on the mail route to *Grand Rapids*. Nearest railroad station *Casnovia*, 5 miles distant. Renselaer Brace, postmaster.

Locally known as *"Shantyville."* "Buckhorn Hotel", R. Brace, proprietor; J. T. Knight, sawmill. 1877 was the post office for *Ashland*. Population 50. Daily mail. Christian Pfeifle, postmaster and general store; S. Armstrong and S. Peterson, general stores; J. Jones and R. Baker, sawmills.

1912 send mail to *Grant*.

––––––––

LILLEY–shown on 1970 State maps, 9 miles south of *Baldwin*. Post office established 1884. 1910 population 65. On the P. M. Railroad. 1917 population 70. Alfred Ellis, postmaster and general store. Elijah Payne ran a feed mill and several summer resorts in the area were listed.

––––––––

MCLEAN–1905 a country post office in Bridgeton Township, 12 miles southwest of *Newaygo*. Daily stage to *Newaygo*. John W. McLean, postmaster and for whom the place was named. McLean was also a Baptist minister, breeder of Blue Hummer doves, a photographer, and a very accomplished man.

Other talent in the village was Henry Smith, township clerk; Grace Smith, music teacher; Sadie Smith, music teacher; M. Shuefelt and J. M. Stone, physicians; and W. O. Whitman, justice of the peace. 1918 population 30. RFD *Grant*.

––––––––

MINERAL SPRINGS–in 1877 a discontinued post office in the southeast corner of the county. Mail to *Sand Lake*, 8 miles east.

––––––––

MORGAN STATION–1877 at the junction of the G. R. N. & L. S. Railroad and the Big Rapids Branch of the C. & M. L., population 300. In Everett Township, 11 miles north of *Newaygo*. J. L. Morgan, postmaster. J. W. Bragg, hotel; J. W. Burson, hotel; William Ferguson, saloon; James McLeod, hotel; David Smith, hotel; two saloons; lumberman's supply store; two general stores; two meat markets; blacksmith shops; railroad station; etc.

1879 incorporated as a village and name changed to *White Cloud*, which became the county seat in 1912-13.

––––––––

OTIA–1917 population 100. On the P. M. Railroad, Merrill Township, 11 miles north of *White Cloud* and 6 from *Bitely*. W. C. Cantrell, postmaster and general store. M. Tourcourt, hotel.

––––––––

PINCHTOWN–see *"Aetna."*

––––––––

RAMONA–formerly *Diamond Loch*. 1917 population 100. On the P. M. Railroad, Lincoln Township, 5 miles fron *White Cloud*. Andrew Foss, postmaster. Had a resort, hotel and livery, general store express agent, etc. Shown on 1969 highway maps.

––––––––

SITKA–1872 a post office in Sheridan Township, 15 miles west of *Newaygo*. Weekly mail. H. W. Crawford, postmaster. 1877, five miles from *Holton*. H. W. Crawford, general store. 1910 population 30. RFD *Fremont*.

––––––––

TRAVERSE ROADS–see *Woodville*.

––––––––

VOLNEY–1910 population 40. Beaver Township, 10 miles northwest of *Newaygo*, and 6 from *Walkerville*. 1917 RFD *Bitely*. Had a general store and creamery. Catholic church and a school standing in 1953. Shown on 1969 maps.

––––––––

WOODVILLE–formerly *"Cook's Station"* and *"Traverse Roads,"* on railroad timetables. 1877 a flag stop on the Big Rapids Branch of the C. & M. L. S. Railroad in Everett Township, 11 miles west of *Big Rapids*. Has shingle mill and two sawmills. A. W. Ensley, postmaster, A. D. Hoag, station agent.

1917 population 90. On the P. M. Railroad. Settled 1872. Marion L. Carpenter, postmaster. N. Carpenter, station agent. Had two general stores, hotel, livery stable, elevator and feed mill, pickle station, blacksmith, milk station, produce warehouse, etc.

––––––––

WOOSTER–1917 population 35. On the P. M. Railroad in Sherman Township, 7 miles from *White Cloud*. Telephone. H. J. Redder, postmaster and general store, creamery, pickle station, and produce warehouse.

––––––––

Several lumbering settlements were located along the Big Rapids Railroad that extended from *Big Rapids* through *Hungerford, Woodville* and *White Cloud*. *Field* or *Fields Crossing* was the first town. *Swains Crossing* was the second stop. T. B. Gray built a mill there. D. T. Swain, after whom the crossing was named, lived there and loaded logs at the siding.

Number 3 was *Hayes Siding*. A saw and shingle mill was located there.

Number 4 was *Woodville*, or Traverse Roads.

Number 5 was *Lumberton*.

Number 6 was *Norwich*. This was a banking grounds and loading station, no settlement.

Number 7 was *Trumbull's Siding*.

Of all these towns and stations *Woodville* is the only one remaining. In 1926 there was a store and an auto repair garage plus a few buildings.

Woodville is shown on 1969 highway maps on M-20 between *White Cloud* and *Big Rapids*. What appears to have been a store remains but is now used as a residence (1970).

––––––––

Other towns and places were:

BISHOP–1917 a creamery and Haveman Brothers, general store. RFD *Newaygo*.

BROOKS–1910 mail *Newaygo*.

BROOKSIDE–1910 population 20. Mail *Fremont*.

COLE CREEK–1910 RFD *Hesperia*.

DEVILS LAKE CORNERS–about 3 miles north of *Fremont*.

DIAMOND LOCH–see *Ramona*.

DICKINSON–1910 RFD *Grant*.

DREW–1910 on P. M. Railroad. Mail *Newaygo*.

ERWIN–1910 on P. M. Railroad. Mail *Newaygo*.

GILBERT–1910 on P. M. Railroad. Mail *White Cloud*.

GOODWELL–Goodwell Township, 20 miles north of *Newaygo*. 1910 RFD *Stanwood*.

GROVE–1910 population 100. RFD *Sand Lake*. 1917 population 75. Ensley Township. George F. Cook, general store, and Mrs. H. B. Hardman, general store.

HAWKINS–1910 population 75. RFD *Reed City*. 1917 a discontinued post office, 8° miles from *Reed City*.

HOMEDALE–1917 a discontinued post office. Mail to *Big Prairie*.

HUBER–1910 RFD *Hesperia*. 1917 a discontinued post office, Denver Township, 24 miles northwest of *Newago*.

KENO–1917 a discontinued post office on P. M. Railroad, 20 miles north of *Newaygo*. Mail to *Woodville*.

KIRK–1910 population 36. RFD *Walkerville*.

KOPJE–1910 on P. M. Railroad, mail *Otia*.

MARL LAKE–1910 mail *Newaygo*.

NEWAYGO LAKES–1910 on P. M. Railroad. Mail to *Newaygo*.

OAK GROVE–just north of M-46 in the southeast part of the county. A church, school and cemetery bordered M-46 in 1953.

PANAMA–1918, five miles northwest of *Fremont*. Mail there.

PARKS or *PARK CITY*–1884 population 158. 1910 population 22. 1917 a discontinued post office in Barton Township. RFD *Paris*.

PINGREE'S DAM–1877 on the C. & M. L. S. Railroad. Listed as a station.

PLUMBVILLE–1910 population 25. RFD *Sand Lake*. 1917 a discontinued post office, Ensley Township, 14 miles southwest of *Newaygo*.

REEMAN–on 1925 road maps.

REYNOLD–on 1925 road maps.

RYERSON–1912 mail *White Cloud*.

SHANTYVILLE–see *Lake*.

SHAW–1910 RFD *Bitely*.

SUN–on 1899 railroad maps. 1912 RFD *Newaygo*.

STUMPY CORNERS–about 5 miles north of *Fremont*.

WILCOX–1917 a discontinued post office. Mail *Fremont*.

————

Chapter 13

OCEANA COUNTY AND THE GHOST TOWNS
OF TIGRIS, COB-MOO-SA, AND PAPA ME

Oceana County was set off in 1840 and was a part of Ottawa County until organized in 1851. Formal organization of the government did not take place until 1855.

Named by early settlers reminded of the ocean by Lake Michigan, upon which it borders, the county was settled primarily for its pine timber. In 1840 there were 496 inhabitants. During the next decade it fell to 300. Peak population of 18,739 was reached in 1910. In 1930 was down to only 13,805 and in 1960 a little over 16,000.

RAILROADS

1870–served by the Chicago-Michigan & Lake Shore Railroad.

1899–Chicago & West Michigan Railroad. Beginning at *Allegan*, 0 miles; *Rothbury*, 82 miles; *New Era*, 86 miles; *Shelby*, 90 miles; *Mears*, 96 miles; *Hart*, 99 miles; then back to *Mears* and *Pentwater*, 103 miles.

1899–Mason & Oceana Railroad. Beginning at *Buttersville*, 0 miles (Mason County); *Riverton*, 7 miles; *Wileys*, 11 miles; *Fern*, 15 miles; *South Branch Camp*, 23 miles; *Stetson*, 27 miles.

1906–Mason & Oceana Branch of the Marquette & Southeastern Railroad Company. Beginning at *Buttersville*, 0 miles; *Riverton*, 7 miles; *Wileys*, 11 miles; *Fern*, 15 miles; *Peachville*, 23 miles; *Walkerville*, 27 miles; ending at *Goodrich*, 32 miles.

POST OFFICES

In 1872 there were 24 post offices in the county. During its history there were at least 45. Of these 8 remain.

GHOST TOWNS

ALICE–1872 a post office on the main lakeshore stage route, 19 miles south of *Pentwater*.

———

ALLEN CREEK–1872 population 72. Colfax Township, 20 miles east of *Pentwater*. Settled 1863. *"There are as yet no business houses, although a steam sawmill is projected."* Calvin Woodworth, postmaster. 1877 same, except John Bean, sawmill.

Post office discontinued 1903-04 and RFD *Walkerville*.

———

BENONA–1872 on shore of Lake Michigan at the mouth of Stony Creek. Benona Township, 7 miles southwest of *Hart*, the county seat. Settled 1853. Population 200. Ships lumber products.

William Banks, miller; "Brown Hotel"; Ira Minierd, store and lumber mill; A. Oldsen, boots and shoes; H. W. Reid, wagons, buggies and sleighs; Ransom Sabin, physician and drugs; S. J. Sundell, blacksmith.

1877 stages to *Montague, Pentwater* and *Shelby*. Daily mail. Henry G. Hoffman, postmaster. Other additions were general store, flour mill, and Methodist minister.

1910 RFD *Shelby*. No population given. Shown on 1969 maps.

———

BIRD–first called the *"Bird Settlement."* 1872 a post office in Leavitt Township, 13 miles east of *Hart*. Settled 1866. Rufus J. Carpenter, postmaster; manufacturer of threshing machines; sawmill; blacksmith; B. W. Hipp, sawmill; M. E. Church; and David Scott, physician.

1877 one sawmill, hotel, etc. Population 30. Rufus Carpenter, postmaster. Weekly mail.

1890 listed on railroad maps as *"Stetson"* and post office by this name. Sometime between 1894 and 1896 name changed to *"Walkerville."* 1960 population 260. Is a post office.

———

BLACKBERRY RIDGE–1872 a post office in Benona Township. On the lakeshore mail route, 12½ miles south of *Pentwater*. James Gibbs, postmaster. General stores; Kerswell & Remick Company, manufacturers of clapboards; J. H. Sammons, general store, staves and lumber.

1877–daily stages, James Gibbs, postmaster; Charles Dodge, station agent; Alonzo Hyde, lecturer; C. Meers, express agent and sawmill. Not listed in 1890.

———

115

BLOOMING VALLEY–not a post office but in 1877 the center of a large fruit-raising district near *Shelby*. Schoolhouse standing in 1958. Section 14, Shelby Township.

––––––––

CLAY BANK–1870 a village in Clay Bank Township on the lakeshore and on Flower Creek. *"Has a bowl factory and sawmill."* Tri-weekly mail from *Montague*. Settled 1849. Alex S. Anderson, postmaster; Thomas Phillips, doctor.

1877 a post office 9 miles west of *New Era*. Tri-weekly stage to *Montague*. Same postmaster. Was a post office until about 1902. After that RFD *Montague*.

––––––––

COB-MOO-SA–1872 a post office in the eastern part of the county. Weekly mail. Dwight M. Croff, postmaster.

1877 in Elbridge Township, 12 miles east of *Hart*, the county seat. Semi-weekly stage to *Pentwater* and semi-weekly mail. David E. Lattin, postmaster. Reverend James Braysin, M.E.; D. M. Croff, physician.

Post office discontinued about 1915. 1917 mail *Walkerville*. Had general stores, wooden bowl factory; Charles Daingo, livery; real estate office; and William Twinning, hotel.

Cob-Moo-Sa Lake is in Section 26, Elbridge Township, and a monument in Section 28 on Taylor Road (1953).

––––––––

COLLINSVILLE–1872 a newly-established post office 8 miles south of *Pentwater*, not on a stage route. *"Three miles west of Hart but the exact location of the prospective village is in dispute."*

Petitions had been circulated, as required, and application submitted to the postal department for a post office and there was a controversy over what place in the township would have the honor. Many battles were waged in those days to obtain a post office and the successful applicant usually won the appointment as postmaster and had the town named in his honor.

The application was finally approved but K. R. Collins, who made the application and was appointed temporary postmaster lost the battle. The name was changed to *"East Golden,"* after the name of the township, and located 5 miles south of *Hart* in a different location than originally planned.

116

In 1877 the name was changed to *"East Golden,"* as there was a town named *"Collins"* in Ionia County. Population 75. A station on the C. & M. L. S. Railroad, also known as *"Collins."* Lumber and staves are shipped. *"East Golden is the mail and shipping point for Crystal Lake and Homer Lake. (Also called "Homer Lake"). Daily mail. E. Remick, acting postmaster; assignees of Davis & Hoffman, sawmill, 4 miles distant; Betts & Kelly sawmills; Dewey & Son, sawmills, 1½ miles; E. Remick, lumber dealer.*

The post office lasted only a few years. Not listed in 1890. Apparently the mills moved out or burned and nothing remained. Today East Golden Pond lays near the Chesapeake & Ohio Railroad, Section 36, Golden Township, near a trail called Log Road.

———

EAST GOLDEN–see *Collinsville.*

———

FERRY–founded in 1872 by William M. Ferry, a Presbyterian minister and former missionary who left Mackinac Island in 1833 and became a land speculator and timber baron. In 1834 he founded the city of *Grand Haven* and from that time forward his landholdings and investments spread far and wide. In 1850 he built a mill at *Pentwater* and this soon became a booming city and supply center for most of the county.

Ferry, in 1872 a post office in Ferry Township (see *Reed*).

1877 population 150. North branch of White River, near present Landin Lake, 6 miles east of *New Era.* Settled 1872. Stage to *Shelby* tri-weekly. Daily mail. William H. Hubbard, postmaster. Two general stores; two blacksmith shops; three sawmills; two furniture factories; Levi Powers & Son, hotel and flour mills; Reverend W. L. Snyder, Methodist minister.

At one time population was over 500. 1910 down to 165. 1917 E. L. Benton, postmaster and general store; two general stores; two groceries; gristmill; saw, shingle and lath mill; Charles E. Wood, drugs.

Shown on today's maps and is a rural branch of the Shelby post office. No population given.

———

FLOWER CREEK–named after the creek it was on. 1872 a post office 10 miles northwest of *Montague* from whence tri-weekly mail. Adam Huston, postmaster.

1877 a post office and village in Clay Banks Township, 6 miles east of *Greenwood Station*. Population 160. Adam Huston, postmaster. Saw and grist-mill, general store, saloon, and Reverend James Draper, Methodist. Was a post office until 1901-02. 1910 population 42.

All that remains is a *Flower Creek* school (1953) and cemetery.

————

FOREST CITY–1872 a post office in Greenwood Township, 4½ miles west of *Fremont*. On the *Newaygo* to *Whitehall* mail route. Settled 1855. Weekly mail. Henry D. Clark, postmaster. *"There is no business other than farming."*

1877 on the C. & M. L. S. Railroad. Not a post office in 1890.

————

GOLDING–1877 a post office in Golden Township, 6 miles west of *Hart* and 4 from *Mears*. *"Two sawmills that were located here were recently destroyed by fire and have not been rebuilt."* Contains 15 families. Tri-weekly mail Henry Howarth, postmaster. Not listed in 1890.

————

GREENWOOD STATION–1877. See *Malta*.

————

HANSEN or *"Hanson"*–1872 a post office in Ferry Township, on Rathbone Creek, a branch of White River. Weekly mail. A. W. Sparks, postmaster.

1877, 8 miles east of *Shelby*. Settled 1870. Population 120. Stage to *Shelby* and tri-weekly mail. H. M. Foster, postmaster. Two general stores; blacksmith; A. Z. Moore, express agent; gunsmith; Powers, sawmill; Powers, gristmill; and S. Powers, hotel; Powers, sash, door and blind manufacturer; and two doctors. Also other businesses.

————

HAZEL GROVE–1872 a new post office on the *Whitehall* to *Newaygo* mail route. Settled 1868. One sawmill. Weekly mail. Leland H. Shaw, general store.

1877 population 50. Greenwood Township, *Holton*, 5½ miles south is the nearest railroad. *Hazel Creek*, after which it is named, is a branch of the White River. Has extensive saw and shingle mills.

————

HOMER LAKE–see *East Golden*.

————

118

KLONDIKE–1905 a post office in Leavitt Township, 7½ miles from *Walkerville*. Daily stage there. Telephone. John Wilder, postmaster. Had telephone; general store; Alva E. Walker, school principal; and other business places.

Post office from about 1898 to 1906-07. 1910 population 24. 1917 RFD *Hesperia*. William Nixon, general store.

———

LATTIN–1905 population 260. Daily mail stage to *Hart*. Free Methodist and M. E. churches. Telephone. H. R. Lattin, postmaster and general store. Had sawmill; machine shop; L. Slocum & Son, orchestra; Edward Studer, teacher.

1910 population 70. Mail *Cob-Moo-Sa*. 1917 population 50. Elbridge Township, 11 miles southeast of *Hart*. The Smith Company, general store. Telephone. Mail to *Hart*.

———

MALTA–1877 the post office at *"Greenwood,"* a flag station on the C. & M. L. S. Railroad, Grant Township. Settled in 1856 and has 90 voters (township). Daily mail. Clark L. Parks, postmaster. Reverend Horace Keyes, Baptist; two lumbermen listed.

———

MAPLE RANGE–1877 population 50. Ferry Township. Daily stage to *Shelby* and *Hesperia*. Daily mail. Mrs. S. J. Mallison, postmistress.

———

MEARS–in 1877 was predicted to become *the* city in Oceana County but for some reason never materialized, probably because Charles Mears, after whom it was named, centered most of his attention to Mason County. Mears was the proprietor of several villages in west Michigan, including *Whitehall* in Muskegon County, first named *"Mears."*

In 1877 *Mears* was a new village in Golden Township. *"It is a station on the C. & M. L. S. Railroad, 7 miles south of Pentwater. A large lumber interest centers here, and considerable trade of all kinds. The population is now 100 and increasing rapidly. The village was platted in 1872 but not much attention was given to its development by the proprietor, Honorable Charles Mears, until the fall of 1874 when he made the village his headquarters and commenced a series of improvements, which, if carried out, will make Mears "The Village" of Oceana County.*

There are already located here three sawmills, a shingle mill, bowl factory, a broom handle factory and clapboard mill. Peaches, lumber, shingles, bowls, wheat and potatoes are shipped."

119

1877 A. G. Avery, postmaster. Had a sawmill; shingle mill; Charles Mears, general store and lumber; another general store; etc.

Although Mears centered his attention in Mason County, the village experienced a boom for sometime and in 1884 reached a population of about 500. However, by the turn-of-the-century the population dwindled as the timber disappeared.

1917 on the P. M. Railroad, 4 miles west of *Hart*. Baptist and Methodist churches, a newspaper and a bank. Telephone. O. S. James, postmaster. Two groceries, general stores, wagon sales, two blacksmiths, hotel, dry goods, lumber yard, bakery, C. B. Tucker (railroad and express agent), a feed mill, and livery stable. Population about 190.

Mears is shown on today's maps, no population given, and has a post office, but it is doubtful if it ever makes a comeback as the booming village it once was during the logging days.

———

REED–1872 a small place in Shelby Township, 14 miles southeast of *Hart*. Population 100. *"Has a sawmill, gristmill and some stores and mechanics shops. E. W. Powers & Company, saw and gristmill; L. Powers, blacksmith; E. J. & T. F. Reed (after whom the town was named), general store and land agency. Also a doctor, architect, and contractor."* (See also *Ferry*.)

1877–name changed to *"Ferry."*

———

Other towns and places during the history of the county:

BARNETT–1884 an unincorporated village in Shelby Township.

BRADYVILLE–1910 RFD *Shelby*.

ELBRIDGE–1910 population 50. RFD *Hart*. 1917, six miles east of *Hart*. H. N. Beatty, general store. Now on Taylor Road. Town hall standing (1953) and cemetery.

GALE–1910 a discontinued post office in Newfield Township. RFD *Hesperia*.

GOODRICH–shown on 1915 railroad maps, southeast corner of the county.

HOGGMAN–1910 RFD *Shelby*.

HOLSTEIN–1910 RFD *Montague*.

HOMER LAKE–see *East Golden*.

HOUSEMAN–1910 discontinued post office. Mail to *Cob-Moo-Sa*. 1917 mail to *Lattin*.

LITTLE POINT SABLE–on Lake Michigan 10 miles west of *Shelby* in 1917.

PAPA-ME–five miles from *Cob-Moo-Sa*, its post office (1917).

PEACHVILLE–1917 post office discontinued. Mail to *Walkerville*.

PEACH RIDGE–1910 RFD *Shelby*.

SMITH'S CORNERS–1917 discontinued post office. RFD *Pentwater*.

STEBENSVILLE–listed in 1872.

STETSON–see *"Bird."*

TIGRIS–1917 a discontinued post office, Hart Township, 5 miles from *Hart*, RFD.

WAGAR–1910 a discontinued post office. RFD *Hesperia*.

WEARE–1872 a post office, 9 miles east of *Pentwater*. Not a post office in 1890. 1910 RFD *Pentwater*.

WOODBURN–a post office in 1890 and in 1899. 1910 mail to *Crystal Valley*.

———

Chapter 14

OGEMAW COUNTY GHOST TOWNS AND THE "LOST CITY OF DAMON"

Ogemaw County was named after "Ki-Keto," Chief of the Ogemaw tribe of Ottawa Indians and means Chief or Head Speaker. The land area was taken from Cheboygan, Midland, and Iosco counties, organized April 15, 1873, and reorganized in 1875.

A settlement called *"Logan's Mills"* was made at the forks of Ogemaw Creek and the West Branch of the Rifle River in 1863. By 1875 there were about 125 people in the area and the village was incorporated under the name *"West Branch,"* as it was called by area lumberjacks.

April 15, 1876, a special meeting was held by the Board of Supervisors to establish a county seat. Before that date persons arrested for crimes were transported to *Tawas City* and held for trial.

In November, 1875, two men were arrested and accused of arson in the burning of the Weidman & Wright Hotel. Sheriff William H. Hosier and Supervisor Phinney made a resolution requesting that the trial be held in Ogemaw County. Thus began a battle between *Ogemaw Springs* and *West Branch* vying for the location of the county seat.

During the following year a courthouse, jail, and several frame houses were built in *West Branch*.

In 1872 the Jackson, Lansing & Saginaw Railroad had tracks laid to *Wells*, 14 miles south of *West Branch* in Arenac County. By 1890 the Michigan Central Railroad Company had completed the line from *Bay City* through *West Branch, Ogemaw Springs, Beaver Lake, St. Helen's* and on to *Mackinaw City*.

W. H. Edwards of *Saginaw*, one of the first settlers, came to Edwards Township in 1867. The township is named for him. Cork Blakely was another settler who had a store and was postmaster at *Walkers Corners* in Edwards Township.

George Decker ran a large saw and shingle mill on *Indian Lake*, just over the line in Gladwin County. After the mill closed down, Decker set up a restaurant and livery stable in *West Branch*.

As late as the early 1900s many Indians lived in Edward Township, around Elk Lake, Indian Lake and Frost Lake near the south county line.

Henry Craner moved his family to Richland Township in 1869.

Thomas Nester of *East Saginaw* owned large tracts of timberland in Logan and Richland Townships in the 1870s and 1880s. Nester put in a 20-mile long, narrow-gauge railroad for hauling logs.

John Klacking, of Klacking Township, Christopher Keetz, and Horace Sherman homesteaded in 1872.

Captain S. V. Thomas and Dr. C. L. Nauman were the first permanent residents of *West Branch*, coming there April 15, 1873. They were associated with lumber companies in the *Beaver Lake* and *Ogemaw Springs* area. *West Branch* was incorporated as a village in 1885 and as a city in 1905. County population in 1870 was 12; 1880, 1,914; and in 1920, 7,786. 1960 population was 9,680.

RAILROADS

1890–Michigan Central-Beaver Lake Branch. *Beaver Lake*, 0 miles; *Piper*, 6 miles; *Ambrose's*, 7 miles; and *Sages Lake*, 8 miles.

1890–Detroit-Bay City & Alpena Railroad. *Alger*, 0 miles; *Moffat*, 4 miles; *Shearer*, 7 miles; *Prescott*, 11 miles; *Mills*, 16 miles; ending at *Alpena*, 105 miles. (See Volume I - Arenac County for picture.)

1890–Michigan Central-Mackinaw Division. *Bay City*, 0 miles; *Alger*, 40 miles; *Summitt*, 44 miles; *Welch*, 48 miles; *West Branch*, 53 miles; *Ogemaw*, 56 miles; *Beaver Lake*, 61 miles.

1906–Detroit & Mackinac Railroad, Prescott Division. *Emery Junction*, 0 miles; *Mills*, 7 miles; *Prescott*, 12 miles.

1906–Rose City Division D. & M. Railroad. *Emery Junction*, 0 miles; *Smith Junction*, 19 miles; *South Branch*, 20 miles; *Maltby's*, 22 miles; *Lupton*, 27 miles; *Rose City*, 32 miles.

POST OFFICES

There were at least 23 post offices during the history of the county. Of these 5 remain.

GHOST TOWNS

BEAVER LAKE–was the largest ghost town in the county. Settled as a lumber site August, 1872, it became a station on the railroad and was a booming town. Located in Ogemaw Township, 8 miles north of *West Branch*, on the present New York Central Railroad, it had three hotels, the "American," "Beaver Lake

Hotel," and "Sherman House"; several general stores; a drug store; seven saloons; blacksmith shops; church; and schoolhouse. Stage daily to Ogemaw Springs and Piper, 7 miles northeast. In 1888 it was estimated that 50 million feet of timber had been cut in the area. By 1905 there were only 25 residents and it became a flag stop on the railroad. Robert Aikman, grocery.

1877 George F. Damon, postmaster; Cutting & Damon, general store, lumber, shingles, and a hotel.

Old-timers say that during the logging days there was a crossing each 4 miles along the track and a train passed through every 14 minutes with loads of logs and lumber products.

All that remain are some sunken holes in the ground and a cemetery. Ralph Beemis of *West Branch* said there was a boot hill cemetery just south of Beaver Lake with a few headstones. A few years ago (1960s) one of the tombstones turned up miles from there. State Police returned it to the cemetery.

Two miles east is a high hill near an old logging trail known as "Preacher Brown's Hill." A Negro preacher and his family lived on top of the hill during the logging days. As members of his family died they were buried on the side of the hill and their graves marked with large rocks. It is said the preacher is also buried there.

At the foot of the hill, near the site of the former Frank Crawford homestead, is a large tract of Michigan cactus. This is one of the few places in the State where these plants grow, and possibly the only place in the interior. Many residents of *St. Helen* have transplanted plants in their lawns and they spread rapidly and bloom each spring.

———

CAMPBELL'S CORNERS–was a post office in 1890. 1905 population 145, West Branch Township, 5½ miles north of *West Branch*. *"Has Catholic and Methodist churches. Daily mail stage from Sage to West Branch. Charles C. Hacht, postmaster. James Campbell, saw and feed mill; Roesser & Company, grocers. 1910 population 50. 1917 RFD West Branch. V. Kilbur, grocery; and Roesser Company."* *Campbell* school standing, 1953.

———

CANFIELD–Hill Township, on Laird Lake, 8 miles west of *Hale*. 1905 a farmer's post office. Mail three times weekly. George L. Miller, postmaster. 1910 population 60. Had blacksmith shop; Tom Early, grocery; J. Love, railroad agent; G. W. Spooner, express agent; Joe Wilson, sawmill. 1917, T. Early and Joe Ranger, stores.

———

CHURCHILL–1877 a recently established post office. *"The settlement was formed in 1872 in a timber section. Population eight people. Weekly mail. A. S. Rares, postmaster."*

Was *Churchill* in 1890. A short time later name changed to *"Rose City."* Incorporated as a city in 1905 with 540 population, and remains about the same today.

———————

DAMON–was settled by and named after George F. Damon of Damon & Cutting logging company. Located 15 miles north of *West Branch* at the corner of Old State Road (now Fairview) and McGregor Road, Foster Township. Most of the timber was owned by the H. M. Loud Company and Potts Company of *AuSable* and *Oscoda*. After they cut the virgin pine in the late 1880s, the Davison Company moved in and timbered second growths of cedar, tamarack, etc. All their supplies were brought in by wagon from *Beaver Lake*, the nearest railroad station.

The village was laid out into four business blocks. In 1900 the Davison Brothers warehouse was 50 x 80 feet. Their general store, facing McGregor Street, was 100 feet long. McGregor Street, now road, was named after Robert McGregor, a riverman who worked on log drives out of Rose City in the 1870s. A tote-road for hauling logs ran from *Luzerne* south on State Road to *Damon*, then east to *Rose City* and the banking grounds. The logs were floated down the creek to Rifle River, then to the booming grounds in Saginaw Bay.

McGregor settled in Oscoda County, just over the county line, north of *Damon* in 1884. A few years later he purchased 240 acres, which became part of *Damon*.

The Davison Company owned all the business interests including a large, two-story hotel, which in later years was run by Jack and Laura Warner. The lower floor of the hotel was divided into four rooms. The large room, called the "Men's Room" was a bar during the logging days. After 1918 was used for a dance hall and social gatherings. One room was used as living quarters and the kitchen and dining room made up the other two rooms. The second floor was divided by a hallway with six rooms on each side for guests.

Jack Warner, who in later years operated the hotel, was stage driver on the *Beaver Lake-Damon* mail stage that went from there to *Luzerne* in the late 1800s. Contents of the old hotel were auctioned off in 1917-18.

O. J. Hickey, called "Limpy" by the residents, was a disabled Civil War veteran and postmaster until the early 1900s. He was also Township Supervisor. *Damon* had a post office from 1885 until 1912. After the post office closed, residents went to *Rose City* two or three times a week and picked up the mail.

125

Plat of "The Lost City of Damon" and principal buildings as described by Bruce McGregor who was born here in 1902. The one-time village was immortalized by James Oliver Curwood in his novel *Green Timber*, published after his death. Drawing by Roy L. Dodge.

About 1918-19 Edgar Waterman became rural mail carrier from *West Branch*.

Frank Ferry ran a sawmill on the flats, about 3 miles east in the early 1900s. He sold out to a Mr. Fournier in 1908-10. Some of the steam boiler and concrete foundations were on the site in the 1950s.

Another big building called the "Oil House" was on a side street in the rear of the Davison County store. It was used to store barrels of kerosene used for lamps and lanterns in the logging camps and homes in the area. Beyond the oil house was another huge building called the "Refrigerator." The upper part of the building had trapdoors through which cakes of ice were put in during the winter and packed in sawdust. The walls of the building were three feet thick. Dressed beeves were hung on hooks and kept cold during the summer to furnish fresh meat for stores and logging camps.

Bruce McGregor, former surveyor for the Conservation Department, lives in *Harrison* (1970) and was born in *Damon* in 1902. McGregor said Oliver Curwood, who created the story about the "Lost City of Damon," visited the village in 1911. "He talked to some of the residents and visited the school," McGregor said. A few years later his novel *Green Timber* was serialized in *McCall's Magazine* and after his death was published as a book. Thus the "Lost City of Damon" became immortalized.

The Davison Brothers timbered the last remains in 1912. In 1916 the warehouse and store was torn down and moved. One wing of the building was left for residents to use for a school. Mrs. Bruce McGregor, then Miss Gifford, taught school at *Damon* in 1920-22. The last of the buildings were razed in 1924.

After Curwood's book was published someone erected a sign which read the "Lost City of Damon" on the site of the former village.

A drive to the one-time village today is like a trip through the "twilight zone." Now a part of the Ogemaw State Forest, that was swept by a forest fire a few years ago, the vast expanses of grey, smoke-colored skeletons of pine trees cast a ghostly aura over the area. The only sound is the occasional chug-chug of an oil well engine from one of the many wells.

After World War II two houses were built near the village site by descendants of former families. One of them hung a sign near the site reading the "Lost City of Damon" and built a small replica of an old-fashioned grocey store. The old *Damon* cemetery is about ½ mile south and west of *Damon*.

———

EDWARDS–was a sizeable settlement and post office at one time. A church, school, and cemetery are on Greenwood Road, about ½ mile west of M-30 in

127

Edwards Township not far from *Frost Lake*, at one time a large Indian village. One of the first settlements in the county, many people in northern Gladwin County near the south county line, used to bury their dead in the *Edwards* cemetery and do their trading at *Edwards*.

1905 F. H. Wade, postmaster. Daily mail. Two general stores, two groceries, one ran by Joseph Fournier. 1917 RFD *Alger*, three stores in business. Post office open until 1928.

EYMER TOWN–was a store and settlement about 1919-20 on Skidway Lake in Mills Township.

GOODAR–in the early 1900s was one of the biggest logging operations in the county. Located near *Bean Shuttle Lakes*, 4 miles south of South Branch, the winter population approached 1,000. 1917 population (summer) 200. On the Robinson Lumber Company Railroad, a narrow-gauge, grade still evident. Mail to *South Branch*. Had a post office for one year, 1906. Lumberjacks took the train from *Emery Junction (National City)* to *South Branch* to the narrow-gauge train then on to camp.

Archie Berry of *Maple Ridge* in Arenac County said he and Angus Showers worked in the Robinson-Eastman camp at *Goodar* in 1918. *"Hawk Ash, a guy with long red whiskers was woods boss,"* Berry said, *"and was a tough guy to work for."* Pete Wishaun worked there that winter, and Frank Hull, son of the doctor in *Maple Ridge* was the doctor at *Goodar*, Berry said. The town was named after the township. There were remains of the village and grade in the 1950s.

Section 3, near Redhead Lake on Taber Road near the north county line.

GREENWOOD–in 1877: *"A new town in the midst of a pine and hemlock forest. Contains one sawmill and about 50 people. G. W. Hotchkiss, postmaster. Hotchkiss & Codding Lumber Company."*

1883 also known as *"Summit."* Settled 1873, Horton Township, on the M. C. Railroad. Forty or fifty camps operated in the area and employed 2,000 men. Logs were shipped down the Rifle River by millions of board feet each spring. 1883 population 100. *"There is a very desirable opening here for a physician."* Frank Horr, postmaster, general store, and township clerk. Also a hotel and other places, saloon, etc.

1905 a discontinued post office. Mail to *Alger*. Nothing remains. Some huge, virgin pine trees mark the spot near the new I-75 overpass and an empty, log building stands on the corner of Greenwood Road and Old M-76.

LOGAN'S MILLS–name changed to *West Branch* in 1875-76.

––––––––––

LUPTON–little remains of this one time village of 500 or more population in Rose Township near Rose City Road, about 5 miles east of *Rose City*. Post office established about 1895-96 and was laid out in about 20 square blocks. 1905 Joshua L. Rakestraw, postmaster and general store. 1917 population 150. Had a bank, post office, two hotels (one the "Hilton"), two general stores, school, meat market, livery barns, drug store, barber shop, sawmill, etc. Linton E. Cossand, postmaster.

Most of the streets are now overgrown to grass and weeds and only a few buildings remain. Is now the center of a large resort area. A supermarket is on the blacktop road leading from *Rose City*. A huge log building was erected near the corner in the late 1920s called the "Graceland Ballroom." During the day's of prohibition of liquor this was a speakeasy and hideout for the infamous "Purple Gang" of *Detroit*.

Lupton is one of the few post offices remaining in the county.

––––––––––

MALTBY–a post office in 1906. 1917 population 100. On the D. & M. Railroad, Goodar Township, 4 miles east of *Lupton*. John B. Gurley, postmaster, and general store. *Maltby* was noted for its mineral springs and had a bottling works that shipped the water in huge, glass jugs, called the "Ogemaw Spring Water Company." Was a post office until about 1928. A store and pallet mill are on the site today.

––––––––––

NESTER–named after Thomas Nester, a *Saginaw* lumberman who timbered much of Ogemaw and Roscommon Counties. Was a good-sized village during the logging days. 1905, on the Augres River, Logan Township. Tri-weekly mail. Mrs. Lillie Rose, postmistress. Two groceries, blacksmith shop, shoemaker, etc.

C. H. Prescott & Son operated a large shingle mill. 1910 RFD *Prescott*. Shown on 1969 highway maps, 6 miles north of *Prescott* on M-55. Nothing remains.

––––––––––

OGEMAW or *OGEMAW SPRINGS*–settled 1873. 1877, a post office and station on the M. C. Railroad, Ogemaw Township. Lumber is the only shipment. Population 40. Daily mail. William H. Toman, postmaster and general store. Ogemaw Lumber.

By 1884 permanent population about 200. The lumbermen in the village attempted to have the courthouse established here but failed. Most of the population moved to *West Branch* when it became apparent that village was to become the county seat. Old logging trails run through the country near the site, near Ogemaw Lake, and a railroad grade remains.

PIPER–was a lumber camp, later a village, 7 miles northeast of *Beaver Lake* and the terminus of the Beaver Lake Branch of the M. C. Railroad. Post office established in April of 1882. At one time had a baseball ground, roller skating rink, general store, church, blacksmith shop, and district school. Frank M. Thompson, first postmaster. 1887 population 125. In 1888 it was estimated that more than 50 million feet of lumber had been cut in the area.

In 1891 the Phillips-Jacob & Company had a saw and shingle mill, in addition to Thompson's shingle and planing mill. Post office discontinued in March, 1892. After that mail to *Beaver Lake*.

SAGE–1905 a post office in Cummings Township, 15 miles northeast of *West Branch*. Burton J. Corwin, postmaster and justice of the peace. 1917 mail to *Lupton*. Frank Lovewell, grocer; John M. Spooner, hotel.

1953 a *Sage* school was near *Twin Lakes* on Sage Lake Road.

SELKIRK–a post office in 1905, Churchill Township, 9 miles northeast of *West Branch*. Daily mail. Roy O. Carscallen, postmaster. The Carscallen brothers settled in the new village in the 1890s and had a general store and hotel. They came from *Omer* in Arenac County.

Selkirk was a post office in 1956. Not in 1964. Some buildings remain on State Road, about 3 miles east of M-33.

SLAYTON–in 1878 E. T. Slayton, of *Lapeer*, conducted lumbering operations in the area and formed the settlement. In Klacking Township, on the West Branch & AuSable State Road. Now called "Old State Road." 1883 Austin Abbott, postmaster and general store. Within a few years the area was timbered off and in 1885 mail sent to *Churchill*. The site is in Section 5, Klacking Township, in the Ogemaw State Forest, near Fairview Road and Rose City Road, south of *Damon*.

SOUTH BRANCH–a logging village and important station on the Rose City Branch of the D. & M. Railroad. 1905 population 175. Daily mail. A. F. Martindale, postmaster. Had general stores, two blacksmith shops, two saloons, barber shop, wagon shop, J. T. Guilford (sawmill), and Mrs. Martindale, grocery and boardinghouse. Has a post office today (1970).

130

WALKER'S CORNERS–see county history.

———

Other places during the history of the county were:

CORRIGAN–a post office in 1893.

LORANGER–on the M. C. Railroad just south of *West Branch.*

HARDWOOD LAKE–1910 on Hardwood Lake, Logan Township, 7 miles north-west of *Prescott*, RFD. South of M-55 on Henderson Lake Road (1970).

HAUPTMAN–on M. C. Railroad south of *West Branch.*

HUNT–a post office in 1893, north of *Clear Lake.*

LANE–1893 a post office on D.& M. Railroad between *Maltby* and *South Branch.*

SMITH JUNCTION–a flag stop on the Rose City Branch Railroad in 1910. Mail *South Branch.*

———

Chapter 15

OSCEOLA COUNTY GHOST TOWNS
AND THE HOME OF "THE OLD RUGGED CROSS"

This county was first named "Unwattin" after an Ottawa Indian chief in 1840. On March 8, 1843, the name was changed to Osceola, after a Seminole Indian leader during their second war against the United States. Some say the word means "black drink," others say "rising sun."

The land area was taken from Mason, Newaygo, and Mecosta counties. From 1859 to 1869 it was joined to Mecosta County with the county seat at *Leonard (Big Rapids)*. In 1869 the county government was organized, and included the east half of present day Lake County. The first-county seat was at *Hersey*. In 1871 the present half of Lake County was taken away, leaving 16 townships. In April, 1927, the people voted to move the county seat from *Hersey* to *Reed City*, where it remains.

The highest point in the lower peninsula is located near *Dighton*.

The home of the late Reverend George W. Bennard, composer of the hymn *"The Old Rugged Cross"* stands near Reed City. A large, wooden cross has been erected near US-31 west of Reverend Bennard's residence.

A historical marker was dedicated to his memory and is located at *Albion*, Michigan near the Albion College where he wrote the song, one of several hundred he composed.

RAILROADS

1890–the Toledo, Ann Arbor & Northern Michigan Railroad touched the northeast part of the county. *Marion*, 0 miles; *Park Lake*, 3 miles; then to *McBain* in Missaukee County. This railroad remains today.

1890–Grand Rapids & Indiana-Northern Division. *Reed City*, 0 miles; *Milton Junction*, 5 miles; *Ashton*, 7.3 miles; *LeRoy*, 13 miles; *Tustin*, 17.5 miles.

1906–Manistee & Grand Rapids Railroad. *Manistee*, 0 miles; *Riverbank*, 49 miles; *Tustin*, 55 miles; *Anderson*, 58 miles; *Dighton*, 61 miles; *Hartwick*, 68 miles; ending at *Marion*, 72 miles.

POST OFFICES

There were at least 20 post offices during the history of the county. Of these 7 remain.

GHOST TOWNS

ASHTON–settled November, 1868. 1872 population 100. Was the first station above the P. M. Railroad on the G. R. & I. in Lincoln Township. I. Joseph Ash, postmaster. Had three sawmills and shingle mill, two general stores, restaurant, saloon, and other places.

1877 population 125. F. Halladay, postmaster. I. P. Root, station agent.

1910 population 190. Seven miles north of *Reed City*. 1917, two general stores, a feed mill, and two sawmills remained. Many of the old buildings are standing. Shown on present day maps, east of US-131. No population given.

––––––––

AVONDALE–it is impossible to believe that the four-corners, 9 miles north of *Evart* in Hartwick Township, was once a booming logging village with stores, hotels, and saloons. In the 1880s George H. Erenbrock had a shingle mill and supply store. By the turn-of-the-century the population had dropped to 60. A. M. Grinnell ran the old general store that is still doing business (1969). Was a post office in 1890.

––––––––

CHIPPEWA STATION–was a station and settlement on the P. M. Railroad between *Farwell* and *Sears*, with more than 100 population. 1917 population 55, Orient Township, where Albertson Road crosses the Chippewa River. Herman Broker, postmaster and general store. Had sawmill, a doctor, and B. A. Seelye, fur buyer. Nothing remains.

––––––––

DEWINGS–on the G. R. & I. Railroad, LeRoy Township, just above *Ashton* in 1910. Population 55. 1917 RFD *LeRoy*. William Danielson, general store.

––––––––

DIGHTON–once a booming logging village and railroad center reached a population of about 1,000. As late as 1917 if was a busy town with 500 population,

Logging train of Dennis Brothers Salt & Lumber Company at a station near *Dighton* in the 1890s. This was a "Climax" engine made in Detroit, gear-driven but no match for the famous "Shay Locomotive," or Limey, as the lumberjacks called them. Photo from Fred Hirzel Collection.

on the Manistee Eastern & Western Railroad. Presbyterian church, a bank, and a huge, three-story brick school on a high hill overlooking the village. There were four teachers. E. C. Philapy, postmaster. Had a hotel and auto livery, four general stores, restaurants, livery and dray lines, Dennis Brothers Salt & Lumber Company (sawmills), hardware, dry goods, produce, and provision warehouses, blacksmith shops, Fay H. Webster (furs and hides.)

Many of the original houses and buildings stand today. Boarded-up windows of the schoolhouse overlook the one-time village. The railroad and station is gone. One store is in business and a TV repair shop. The old J. M. Curtice meat market and grocery store stands vacant with Curtice's name printed in bold, red-and-silver letters on the front window. Most of the former streets are overgrown to grass and weeds. *Dighton* is a real ghost town.

HARTWICK–was a village and post office in 1890, 10 miles north of *Evart* in Hartwick Township. 1917 population 55. Telephone. RFD *LeRoy*. I. G. Swander, general store.

HERSEY–figures and statistics fail to picture this frontier village of post Civil War days on the Muskegon River. Settled in 1851, after the county was organized, in 1869 *Hersey* became the county seat. Named after Nathan Hersey, first settler of the county in 1843, the village was founded by Delos A. (Doc) Blodgett, the first settler on the site in 1851. Richmond Township was the first formed in the county in 1861. Blodgett platted the village and inserted a clause that prohibited the sale of liquor or intoxicating spirits. When the big logging runs on the Muskegon started in earnest this clause was ignored.

Hersey produced two of the big names in the history of Michigan lumbering. W. S. (Winfield Scott) Gerrish, who ran a general store in *Hersey* in 1870, and D. A. Blodgett. Gerrish founded the first logging railroad in the world a few years later and went down in history. Blodgett's name became a household word in the State within a few years.

In 1918 the village still had a population of 300. After the last of the timber was harvested the population dwindled and in 1927 the county seat was moved to *Reed City*. What appears to be the old courthouse still stands, along with many original buildings. There are more vacant lots than stores in the business district. The once famed Hersey Roller Mills are idle, the depot and warehouses along the tracks have long since disappeared. The *Hersey* of today is a ghost of what it was yesterday and back in 1908 when old Bill Farrar had his shoe shop down across from the depot. Farrar erected signs all around the country advertising "Farrar's Shoe Repair - Down by the Depot." At the first signs of spring Bill grabbed a can of paint, jumped into his buggy, and visited each sign to replace the "De" in Depot, which boys had dobbed over during the winter.

INA–five miles east of *Dighton*, near M-115, was a post office in 1898 but not a village. 1917, Albert Kanouse, general store. A store and implement sales is about all the business the place ever had.

MCDONALD'S SWITCH–see *Orono*.

MILTON JUNCTION–1905 a station on the G. R. & I. Railroad. Postal name *"Orono."* See *Orono*.

ORONO–1877 a post office in Lincoln Township. Shipping point for lumber, tanbark, posts, etc. Settled 1875. Locally known as *"McDonald's Switch."* James M. Hawkins, postmaster.

1905 population 110. R. W. Brown, postmaster. Had general store; Reverend Price, Methodist; produce shippers; and Ward Wheaton, constable.

1917 population 50, 4½ miles north of *Reed City*. Ray M. Eichenberg, postmaster, general store, railroad and express agent. Had a coal and grain station. Not shown on today's maps.

PARK LAKE –during the logging days a lumbering center with hundreds of men in surrounding camps, and a population of more than 500. 1917 population 300. On the Ann Arbor Railroad, Highland Township, 4 miles northwest of *Marion*. Telephone. F. L. Eichenberg, postmaster, general store, and cord wood. Jesse L. West, hotel and livery. Today a four-corners.

PHELPSTOWN–name changed to *"LeRoy."* Was an extensive potato raising district in early days. Still has a business district, many old buildings standing, and is a post office.

————

RIVERBANK–1910 on the M. & G. R. Railroad and on Pine River. Is a geographic name. In LeRoy Township, Section 6 and 7, on the west county line. 1917 M. W. Marz, postmaster and general store. H. L. Seely, sawmill. Nothing remains.

————

SEARS–this village was confused in directories and maps with another village called *"Orient."* When the P. M. Railroad first came through in the 1870s, *Sears* was the post office for *Orient Station*, named after the township. At the same time another station about 6 miles east and on the Chippewa River, was called *"Chippewa."* This too was located in Orient Township, and the two villages, with three names, easily became confused.

During the logging days *Sears* had a population of about 500. A few years after it was founded, 1877, before the peak of lumbering, the population was 200. Daily mail. Nelson Ferguson, postmaster; sawmill; Jay C. Jenks, station agent; constable; National Hotel; Priest & Belfaur, general store; grocery; and Nels Willouhby, blacksmith.

1917 population 100, 3½ miles east of *Evart*. Nina B. Ferguson, postmistress. Had two groceries, general store, drug store, grain elevator, a doctor, and A. E. Roebuck, railroad and express agent.

The main street of *Sears* is visible to travelers on US-10 highway near *Evart* today. One of the only wooded trestle wagon bridges remaining crosses the railroad. The old, wood-frame, unpainted store buildings, most of them empty, stand overlooking the railroad tracks and look like a Hollywood movie set for a wild west movie.

Unpainted and weather-beaten, a tall, two-story building appears to have been the old hotel. Other buildings face a side street, one a former blacksmith shop with a board door hanging open on rusted hinges. Other side streets are grown to grass and weeds. Several houses are occupied, some modern and of recent vintage.

Passed up by modern day progress it is doubtful that either Mr. Sears, the founder, or Mr. Roebuck, the old station agent could revive the village if they were living today.

————

WINSOR–listed in 1884 as an unincorporated village. Old-timers in the area say *Winsor* was a village or settlement almost adjacent to *Evart*, a little to the southwest between the *Evart* city limits and the Muskegon River in Evart Township.

The village had a business district and 50 or more homes. It is said that the residents were levied with what they considered to be unjust and exorbitant taxes and the people moved into *Evart* or left their homes. The village disappeared and in 1968 was being subdivided for homes, although little progress had been made. One or two old abandoned houses stood on the site, that extends for perhaps ½ mile in width and nearly 1 mile long.

Other old-timers say that when excavation was made for the present Conservation Department equipment station on the outskirts of *Evart*, near the former village site, an old graveyard was dug into. Most of the area is planted to pine trees now 30 years or more of age.

————

One of a few remaining original log cabins in northern Michigan. Most log cabins became victims of forest fires or gave way to the elements. This log cabin, built in the late 1880s or 1890s is located near *Luzerne* in Oscoda County. Picture taken in 1968. Photo by Roy L. Dodge.

Chapter 16

OSCODA COUNTY GHOST TOWNS
AND THE STORY OF MCKINLEY

Oscoda is one of Henry Schoolcraft's manufactured names. He combined the Indian word "ossin," stone, with "muskoda" or prairie, to form Oscoda, meaning "pebbly prairie." It was called "Os-Ka-Do-Yawg," by the Indians, "Where the plains begin." Set off in 1840, *Mio* its county seat, was formed by lumbermen in 1880.

Established March 10, 1881. Prior to that time the county had been Comins Township attached to Alcona County. The land area was taken from Cheboygan, Alpena, and Alcona Counties. It was divided into three townships: Atherton, Mt. Pindus, and Comins. Since then there have been as many as nine. There are now six townships and no incorporated cities or villages in the county. Oscoda County is and always has been the least populated county in the State. In 1880 it was 467; 1950, 3,134; and 1960, 3,447.

The Act of 1881, setting off the county, designated *Union Corners*, in the southwest part of the county, as the temporary county seat and an election was held to pick a permanent site. After a couple of tries *Mio* was selected. There were other efforts to move the county seat but they failed.

It is said *Mio* was named after an early settler, Maria Deyarmond, who was called "Aunt Mioe." Eventually, it came to mean going to the settlement, whether or not a visit with Aunt Mioe was involved. A few years later the local printer, called Uncle John Randall, was short on type and in order to conserve his "e's" dropped the "e" from the name and it was shortened to *"Mio."*

Today most of the land is owned by State and federal government and Consumers Power Company. The Michigan lumberman has been immortalized in the National Lumberman's Monument on the site of the "High-Rollways," overlooking the AuSable River, 12 miles upriver from its mouth at *Oscoda*. It was dedicated in 1932 and is the only such monument in the State. It is the work of Robert Aitken, a New York sculptor and cost $50,000, donated by descendants of lumbermen.

Much of the history of the area has been preserved in a booklet *Their Yesterdays: AuSable and Oscoda*, written by Edna M. Otis, published in 1948. Miss Otis lives in *East Tawas* and is now past 90 years old (1970).

140

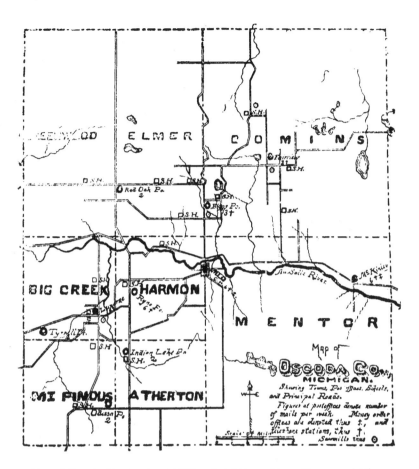

Map of Oscoda County about 1890 and eight townships: Greenwood, Elmer, Comins, Big Creek, Harmon, Mt. Pindus, and Atherton. Showing towns, post offices, schools, principal roads, and sawmills. Sawmills were located at *Fairview, Biggs, McKinley, Mio, Luzerne*, and one near the school in Comins Township north of *Fairview*. Map courtesy of Ruth W. Geister, *Roscommon*.

RAILROADS

1890–the AuSable & Northwestern, a narrow-gauge track that ran from *AuSable* and *Oscoda* at the mouth of the AuSable River on Lake Huron northeast to *Glennie* and over the Iosco-Oscoda County line to *Potts* (later *"McKinley"*) and back south to *Damon* in Ogemaw County.

1890–AuSable & Northwestern Railroad. *Lewiston*, 0 miles; *Red Oak*, 6 miles; *Maple Grove*, 9 miles; *Lymburn*, 16 miles; *Fairview*, 22 miles; *Twin Lake Junction*, 32 miles; *McKinley*, 34 miles.

1899–A. S. & N. Railroad. *McKinley*, 0 miles; *Twin Lake Junction*, 2 miles; *Flat Rock*, 8 miles; *Bamfield*, 12 miles; *Chevrier*, 15 miles; *Vaughn*, 17 miles; *Batton*, 19 miles; *Bryant*, 21 miles; back to *AuSable*, 40 miles.

1906–A. S. & N. Railroad. *AuSable & Oscoda*, 0 miles; *McKinley*, 40 miles; *Millen*, miles; ending at *Comins*, 53 miles.

1912–A. S. & N. Railroad. *AuSable*, 0 miles; *Hardy*, 39 miles; *Code*, 41 miles; *Curran*, 43 miles; *Byers*, 45 miles; *Beevers*, 50 miles; *McCollum*, 42 miles; *Miller*, 45 miles; *Dew*, 47 miles; and *Comins*, 50 miles.

POST OFFICES

During the history of the county there were at least 21 post offices. Of these 4 remain.

GHOST TOWNS

BIGGS–1893 a post office in Comins Township, 4 miles north of *Mio*. 1905 daily mail. Telephone. J. Randall, postmaster. Had a sawmill, flour mill, drug store, and Livingston's Orchestra.

1917 mail to *Mio*. In 1953 a Biggs School standing about 1 mile east of M-72.

COMINS–when *McKinley* folded, about 1902, the railroad was extended to *Comins*. About 1912 the railroad was widened to standard-gauge width and connected with the Detroit & Mackinaw Railroad and became the leading village in that part of the county.

An old building, formerly used for a day room and library for lumbermen in *McKinley*, was moved to *Comins* and used for a depot. In 1960 Mrs. William

Stone of *Comins* purchased the deserted building from the State and converted it into a home, for which it is used today.

For several years *Comins* rode high, with several stores, a post office, and lumbermen's supply warehouses. In the early 1920s livestock was also shipped.

1905 a rural post office on the A. S. & N. W. Railroad, 14 miles northeast of *Mio*. Daily stage to *Mio*. George Imlay, postmaster and general store. 1917 population 35. On the D. & M. Railroad, Clinton Township. C. E. Malott, postmaster and railroad agent. Had a hotel, planing mill, blacksmith, flour mill, Mrs. A. Seymour (hotel), and Henry Solomon (general store.)

Sometime in the 1920s, with the improvement of highway M-33, the railroad tracks were removed and the old grade is now grown to brush. Not much remains of *Comins* today. Perhaps one store, a gasoline station and some of the empty buildings.

———

HARDY–1917 a country post office on the D. & M. Railroad, 15 miles northwest of *Mio* (near Island Lake). Phillip H. Rose, postmaster.

———

HARMON–named after the township. First named *"Ryno"* and was a post office in 1894. 1910 mail to *Mio*.

———

KNEELAND–a small settlement 2 miles west and 1 mile south of *Fairview*. Was a post office from about 1906 to 1912-13. Had one or two stores and a farm implement store. Today the site of the former place is occupied by Kneeland Industries, a machine factory, which used part of the former Kneeland store for its present building.

———

MCKINLEY–on the AuSable River, 12 miles east of *Mio* on the north side of the river was established in the 1880s. In 1892. H. M. Loud & Sons lumbering firm of *Oscoda* purchased land from the Potts & Company. They extended railroad spurs to the site, built repair shops and roundhouses for the trains, and founded the village of *"Potts."* There was employment for more than 100 workers, plus lumbercamps in the area.

Most of the rails and rolling stock for the many narrow-gauge tracks that fanned out north and west of *Potts* or *McKinley*, were floated down the AuSable on rafts from *Grayling*.

Earl Steiner, *Comins* native and operator of an extensive logging and antique museum on M-33 near *Comins*, said in addition to many stores, depot, and saloons in *McKinley* there was a jail made of 2 x 4s spiked together flat side down, and covered with a layer of hardwood boards inside and out to make it escape proof. Tiny windows, too small for a man to stick his head through, were the only openings.

Another building connected with the depot was called the "Reading Room" and contained bunks and a library for use by lumberjacks. This building was later moved to *Comins*, he said, and is now a dwelling.

B. W. McCredie and his wife moved to *McKinley* from Canada in 1888 and operated a dry goods and clothing store there until the town folded up about 1902.

After the lumbering was completed, about 1890, the name of the village was changed to *McKinley*, in hopes the new name might bring new life to the rapidly dwindling village.

By 1905 the population was down to 50. *"Formerly known as Potts on the A. S. & N. Railroad, Mentor Township. Has a Methodist Episcopal church. John H. Fox, postmaster and general store; A. Gibbs, express agent; Reverend W. E. Ragen, M. E. minister."* In 1917 only 20 people remained and mail sent to *Hardy*. *South Branch*, nearest shipping point.

Steiner said after the buildings were removed, and the town was completely deserted, Calvin and Gertrude O'Brien owned the property. The Loud Company Store was moved to *Comins*, along with the library, and after that George Emily operated the store at *Comins*. Calvin O'Brien died and his wife married George Russell. When he died the estate went to nieces, Mrs. Arthur of *Rose City* and a Mrs. Madsen. They subdivided the property and it was sold for resort lots. A small lake in the area is named "O'Brien Lake" after Calvin O'Brien.

About 5 miles west of *McKinley*, bordering a narrow trail near *Comins Flats* on the AuSable River, is an abandoned cemetery shown on maps as "Comins Cemetery." About ten tombstones of various descriptions remain standing in the approximate three-acre plat now partially grown up with several 80-year-old jack pines and hundreds of tiny, 6" pine seedlings. Burial dates on the few remaining markers range from 1884 to 1906. Here many former residents of *McKinley* lie in undisturbed and unkept peace. Some of the families are Peter Caughy, his wife, son and other family members; Finch, and others. Two graves are piled with cobble stones for markers of for protection. Other markers have been destroyed completely, and here lies one of the most notable characters in the history of *McKinley*, George Davis.

144

George M. Davis was a Negro who came to the AuSable River during the logging days as a cook in lumber camps. During the spring logging drives he moved his kitchen to a floating raft (called a "wanigan") and followed the rivermen on the long journey down the river to the booming grounds at *AuSable*.

George Davis and his wife, Isabell, had three daughters and one son. One daughter was born crippled and died while still a young girl. The only son was drowned in the shallow waters of the AuSable someplace along the river near *Mio*.

There are several versions of the drowning. Some say he fell off the bridge at *Mio* and drowned; others say he accompanied his father on the spring drive and fell off the wanigan into the swift waters. The boy's body was never found. Davis built a small house or cabin on a point of the river below *Comins Flats*, and remained with the rest of his family after *McKinley* had disappeared and other residents had moved to *Oscoda* or *AuSable*, or went north with the lumber camps, in hopes that someday the boy's body would be found. The site of the cabin is known as *"Davis Point"* today.

Steiner said he remembers Mr. Davis when he drove a horse and buggy to *Fairview* or *Comins* for his groceries after *McKinley* folded up. Davis was a light-skinned Negro with sharp features and quite handsome. His daughters were even lighter in color. Mrs. Davis was somewhat darker. George wore a heavy, black mustache and was short and stocky, about 5 feet 6 or 7 inches. The boy towered above his father and appeared to be about 6 feet tall.

George M. Davis was born in 1884 and died at *McKinley* August 19, 1911, age 67 years, 8 months, and 16 days. His wife, Isabell, was born March 11, 1850, and died February 8, 1914, age 63 years, 10 months and 1 day. The crippled daughter died at about 14 or 15 and was buried in the old cemetery near the flats. Cora, the oldest daughter, moved to *Bay City*, married and raised a family. Some of the descendants live there today, Steiner said. Davis was highly respected and served as treasurer of Mentor Township for several years.

Natives say that as late as 1950 a small grave marker with the names and dates of death of the Davis family remained on the burial site. Today there are no remains of a marker. Deerhunters blasted it to bits in rifle practice. There are no traces of the markers in the tall grass, rotting fallen trees, and wild ferns covering the graves.

Since the 1940s *McKinley* has been built up with summer homes. In 1969 Edmond Bigelow, formerly of *Millington*, owned a store and gasoline station. Mrs. Bigelow said there were about 35 families in the area. A neat little church stands on the site, and the home of Claude Adams, U.S. Forester Fire Warden stands near the church and a log cabin used as a community hall. A crude sign near the road reads: *"This is the site of McKinley, a one-time logging town in 1880."*

RED OAK–was a post office in 1893 and in 1917, seven miles north of *Luzerne* on County Road 489. An empty gasoline station and grocery stands atop a high hill overlooking *Beaver Creek*. A dilapidated farm house, unpainted and weathered, and a fallen-down shed are all that remains of the village. A neat, wood frame church still stands. One family lives in a housetrailer on the site (1970). This is about all that remains. In recent years, a number of cottages have been built and a community hall erected north of the former village site.

Red Oak was at one time on the A. S. & N. Railroad. 1917 Samuel B. Randall, postmaster; George Richardson, farm implements; G. S. Griffin, George Ruth, and Lee Tubbs were livestock dealers.

WOOD–was a country post office, 9 miles west of *Fairview* in Elmer Township near *Red Oak*. Earl Steiner, who owns the museum at *Comins* has the original, handmade wood postal boxes from this post office. Each pigeon hole has a glass front with numbers from 1 to 40.

Steiner said there were about 30 people in the area in the late 1890s, so Mr. Wood applied for a post office and it was granted. He starved out trying to farm on the poor, sandy soil of the plains and moved away, Steiner said. Mrs. George Richardson then applied for the position of postmistress and was appointed. She was postmistress until about 1913 when *Wood* became RFD *Lewiston*. Listed as a post office in 1906 and in 1912.

Other places and settlements during the history of the county were:

DEW–1910 on A. S. & N. Railroad. Mail *Fairview*.

FITZPATRICK–a flag station on A. S. & N. Railroad in 1902.

HARDY–a post office 15 miles northeast of *Mio*. 1917 Philip Rose, postmaster. On the A. S. & N. Railroad.

HARMON–1910 mail *Mio*. Was *"Ryno."*

HICKS–1899 near south county line on railroad to *Luzerne*.

IMLAY–1899 on the A. S. & N. Railroad south of *Mio*.

INDIAN LAKE–a post office southeast of *Luzerne* in 1894.

KANE–1899 on A. S. & N. Railroad near *Red Oak*.

LALONE–1912 a settlement north of *Comins*.

LYMBURN–on A. S. & N. Railroad south of *Kane* in 1899.

MACK CITY–shown on 1899 railroad maps.

MCCOLLUM–a post office on A. S. & N. Railroad. 1910 mail *Fairview*.

MILLEN–1910 on A. S. & N. Railroad. Mail *Hardy*.

ODESSA–a post office in Mt. Pindus Township, just south of *Luzerne* in 1884 and on May 1, 1897.

RYNO–a post office in 1893 in Harmon Township, about 2 miles northeast of *Luzerne*. See *"Harmon."*

SPOOR–1910 mail *Mio*.

TONG–north of *Kane* on Railroad between *Kane* and *Red Oak*, 1899.

TYRELL–a post office near the west county line in 1893. On a branch of *Big Creek*. Section 33 or 34 Big Creek Township.

MARSH, HILLS, SNYDER, and *WIGGINS* were flag stops on the A. S. & N. Railroad in 1912.

Chapter 17

OTSEGO COUNTY GHOST TOWNS
AND THE FAMOUS "GLASS BOTTLE FENCE"

Otsego County was first named "Okkuddo" in 1840. The word is Indian, meaning "sickly." It was later named Otsego after a county and lake by that name in New York State. The county government was formed in 1875. The present county seat is *Gaylord*, which is located midway between the North Pole and the Equator. The land area was originally a part of Mackinac, Alpena, and Cheboygan Counties.

A historical marker in front of the courthouse in *Gaylord* tells the history of the county:

"First named Okkuddo when it was set off in 1840, this county was re-named Otsego in 1843 after a New York county and lake of that name. It is said to mean 'clear water.' Settlement did not begin until the late 1860s, when lumbering was started, Otsego Lake, the first village was founded in 1872 and became the county seat in 1875 when the county was organized. Gaylord was settled in 1874 and named county seat in 1877. Farming and the tourist industry are now the chief businesses."

Since this plaque was erected in 1961, many changes have taken place. New factories have been built in *Gaylord* and other villages, pulp wood is a major industry, and in 1970 one of the largest oil fields in the history of Michigan has been discovered with a rush of speculators bidding to lease land in the apparently rich oil fields.

RAILROADS

1890–Michigan Central Railroad-Mackinaw Division. Beginning at *Bay City*, 0 miles; *Waters*, 108 miles; *Otsego Lake*, 111 miles; *Bagley*, 115 miles; *Gaylord*, 119 miles; *Vanderbilt*, 127 miles.

1906–Boyne City, Gaylord and Alpena Railroad. *Boyne City*, 0 miles; *North Elmira*, 15 miles; *Mosher*, 17 miles; *Hallock*, 20 miles; *Hamilton*, 22 miles; and *Gaylord*, 27 miles.

1906–Detroit & Charlevoix Railroad. Beginning at *Frederic*, 0 miles; *AuSable River*, 2 miles; *Fayette*, 7 miles; *Deward*, 12 miles; *Manistee River*...; *Blue Lake Junction*, 15 miles; *Crooked Lake* ...; *Squaw Lake* ...; *Blue Lake* ...; *Mancelona Road*, 17 miles; *Lake Harold*, 21 miles; *Alba*, 25 miles; *Green River*, 31 miles; *Graves Camp*, 33 miles; *Jordan River*, 36 miles; *Wards*, 37 miles; and *East Jordan*, 44 miles.

> NOTE: Some of these places were not in Otsego County. The complete list of stations is given as this was the railroad referred to that was on land owned by David Ward.

1906–Michigan Central-Mackinaw Division. *Bay City*, 0 miles; *Waters*, 109 miles; *Otsego Lake*, 112 miles; *Sallings*, 116 miles; *Gaylord*, 120 miles; *Yuill*, 125 miles; *Vanderbilt*, 128 miles.

POST OFFICES

There were at least 20 post offices during the history of the county. Of that number 5 remain.

GHOST TOWNS

BAGLEY–see *"Salling."* Also "Other Places."

––––––––

BARNES–was the post office for *Gaylord* in 1875-76. In Livingston Township. *"It is in the northern terminus of the Mackinaw Division of the M. C. Railroad, and 10 miles north of Otsego Lake the county seat. Settled 1874. Population 50. The timber here is almost all sugar maple. The only shipment is birds-eye and curled maple lumber. William H. Smith, postmaster, general store, and land agent. A. M. Hilton, express and station agent; Reverend Thomas Neild, Congregational; N. L. Parmenter, homeo physician; A. J. Taylor, hotel proprietor."* The name was changed to *Gaylord* and is now a large city and the county seat.

––––––––

BRADFORD LAKE–settled 1873. In 1876 a post office and station on the M. C. Railroad, 3 miles south of *Otsego Lake*, the county seat. *"It is in a pine timber country, has one sawmill. Population 75. Daily mail. C. H. Davis, postmaster. A. M. Hilton, express agent; Wright-Wells & Company, sawmill, general store, and hotel."* (See *"Waters."*)

––––––––

149

This picture shows the few buildings left in the village of *Hallock*, north of *Gaylord*, in 1920. Kenneth Shue of *Harrison* bought the village in 1928 for $10 when all that remained were some foundations and grass blowing in the wind. *"I just let it go back again for taxes,"* he said. Photo from Roy L. Dodge Historical Collection.

Every village had at least one boardinghouse similar to the one above. Note the dining room in the house next door. The general store is the building in the far background on the left side of the tracks. This building was also a community hall and company offices. The village contained 6 rows of houses, 12 in each row, like these pictured, plus a row of larger houses for "white collar" workers and bosses. This ghost town was in Crawford County on the Detroit & Charlevoix Railroad and was named after David Ward. Only the old railroad grade remains. Photo courtesy Vlesta (Tousch) Irwin of *Ypsilanti* who lived there from 1909 to 1925, daughter of Albert Tousch, a worker in the *Deward* mills.

HALLOCK–Robert Moorhead of rural *Gaylord* taught school in *Hallock* in 1914-16. *"In 1914 Hallock was a thriving community,"* Moorhead said. *"At one time there were three stores; a large Gleaner's Hall, where recreation events were held: box socials, club meetings and even a piano recital given by Mrs. Joseph Theisen, a music teacher. Lumbering and farming were the industries. Many farmers worked in the woods during the winter."*

1917 on the Boyne City-Gaylord & Alpena Railroad, Elmira Township, 6 miles from *Gaylord*. Telephone. Some business places were; Badger Woodenware Company of *Boyne City*; Boyne City Chemical Company; N. C. Buckler, general store; I. L. Hatch, saw and feed mill; A. G. Kunkel, general store; Dwight Munn, grocery; in addition to potato warehouse, etc.

Kenneth Shue, now of *Harrison*, said, *"I bought the town of Hallock at a State tax sale in 1928. It was listed along with other unpaid tax lands. I bid $1 each for the ten lots described in the village and made a trip there to see what I had purchased."* All that remained on the site was grass blowing in the wind, Shue said. He in turn let the land revert to the State for taxes. *"At least I had the distinction of having been mayor, police chief, and any other offices required for a village,"* he said.

Moorhead said land for the small village was given by a farmer named Benjamin Hallock. In return the place was to be named after him. *"So it remains!"* he said. *"But only in the memories of the people as all the buildings are gone, except the old Ben Hallock home."*

———

OTSEGO LAKE–settled in 1872. In 1876 population 350, the former county seat. *"Contains one sawmill, a shingle and planing mill, a Congregational Church, two stores, two hotels, and a good schoolhouse. Stage to Mancelona and Elk Rapids weekly. Daily mail. Reuben Murray, postmaster."*

Located at the southern tip of *Otsego Lake*, the village was on the Old State Road leading to *Mancelona* and *Elk Rapids*.

David Ward made his home here in that year, and the area surrounding *Otsego Lake* and farther west in Mancelona County is "David Ward Country." Ward was an early timber baron in Michigan, having discovered a vast area of cork pine on the lake in 1854, which he described as the largest stand of this type of pine in the State.

In 1851, at the age of 29, Ward gave up his career as surveyor, timber looker, and schoolteacher to devote his time to lumbering the vast areas of pine timber he had laid claim to in the county. Thousands of acres of huge stumps standing almost at arms reach from each other, the old railroad grade, with ties intact in many places, and the remains of the ghost town *"Deward"* just over the line in Crawford County, remain in silent tribute to David Ward. Ward was only 5'5" and in poor health when he started his lumbering career. He died at his home near *Detroit* on May 29, 1900 at the age of 77, was a multi-millionaire and probably Detroit's wealthiest citizen.

A news item of March 6, 1891 said: *"The new branch of the Michigan Central Railroad has been graded from East Jordan to Frederic. This railroad runs 36 miles over David Ward land and is the longest railroad extending over land entirely owned by one man."*

———

SALLING–formerly known as *"Bagely."* 1910 population 52. Was a post office in 1906. 1917 on the M. C. Railroad, Bagely Township, 4 miles south of *Gaylord*. Telephone. RFD *Gaylord*.

———

WAH-WAH-SOO–1905 a summer resort on Otsego Lake, on the M. C. Railroad, Bagley Township, 4½ miles south of *Gaylord*. Ernest D. Byett, postmaster and general store; R. L. Dixon, physician and the Michigan Farm Colony for Epileptics. 1910 mail *Salling*.

———

WATERS–17 miles south of *Gaylord* on Old US-27 and on the Michigan Central Railroad has been established as a village, deserted, and re-established three times since it was founded 1872-73. First called *"Bradford"* or *"Bradford Lake,"* it was then called *"Wright's,"* after a lumbering firm, and finally *"Waters,"* as it is known today.

It was named *Bradford* after the name of one of the lakes it is situated on. In 1877 the Wright-Wells Lumber Company operated mills and owned a large general store and hotel in the village of about 75 permanent residents. Within the next ten years it became a bustling town.

After the big timber was harvested residents moved north with the mills and by 1890 only one store and post office combined remained. Henry Stephans,

Remains of the once-famous "Glass Bottle Fence," featured in Ripley's *Believe It Or Not* column. Erected in 1914 by wealthy lumberman Henry Stephans at *Waters* and became a historic landmark until ruined by vandals. Otsego County surveyor Wynn W. Wakenhut and helper Paul Schram, *Frederic*, surveyed and discovered the fence is on State highway property. Was moved in 1970. Photo by Roy L. Dodge.

Sr., formerly of *St. Helens* in Roscommon County, moved his operations here in 1891 and once again the village was booming.

1905 population 300. J. B. Johnson, postmaster; A. I. Bonnett, railroad and express agent; and Stephens Lumber Company, saw and planing mill.

> NOTE: The name *"Stephans"* had several spellings. Henry, Sr. used *"Stephens,"* the original spelling. Old-timers and residents spelled it *"Stevens."* Henry, Jr. spelled it *"Stephans."*)

1917 population 50. Charles Wright, postmaster, and R. Muscatt, railroad and station agent.

After remaining timber was stripped from the area about 1912, Henry Stephans, Jr. decided to make *Waters* his permanent residence in between his worldwide travels. His father died in 1884 and left the son his fortune made in lumbering. (See Roscommon County for the story). Selecting a site across from the depot, Stephans built a large two-story, frame house on the back of the lot and in 1914 dreamed up the idea of building a glass bottle fence as a monument to the roaring, hard-drinking lumberjacks who were never more to roam Michigan again.

Stephans offered local children a penny each for bottles and hired a cement contractor to erect the fence. Work on the fence progressed according to the supply of bottles. In their eagerness to earn money from the project, *Waters'* children robbed their relatives' pantries, dumped contents of sauce and ketchup bottles, and probably emptied the contents of their fathers' liquid refreshment cache, according to the number of whiskey and beer bottles used in the fence. Old-timers tell of boys who sold bottles to Stephans, sneaked back at night to pilfer the supply, then resold them to him the following day. Stephans was well-liked by everyone and purchased the same bottles over again with a chuckle.

When completed, the fence with a wrought iron gate in the center, spanned two city blocks bordering the main street that eventually became US-27. The shoulder high fence, capped with concrete slabs, was then finished off with letters 2 feet high that spelled out the owner's name, "Henry Stephans."

Stephans left *Waters* about 1917 in failing health. Within a short time the village that once covered a 40-acre area and boasted several streets lined with business places and homes, became deserted for the second time.

155

In 1927, Mrs. Edna Schotte, the matriarch of *Waters* and postmistress from 1930 to 1946, and her late husband, purchased 1,800 acres, including the village.

In 1935 the old Stephan home, then occupied by Harley Kennedy, was destroyed by fire. Most of the other buildings suffered the same fate over the years.

The Schotte's re-established the post office and when liquor was legalized in 1936, Mrs. Schotte and her husband were the first in the county to receive a tavern license. They built the "Glass Bottle Fence Gardens" tavern. In 1970 this old landmark also fell victim to fire and is now replaced with a new, concrete block building.

Vandals and thoughtless tourists, who came from all over the country to view the highly publicized glass bottle fence that was once featured in Ripley's *Believe It or Not* column, and also in Stewart Holbrook's *Holy Old Mackinaw*, tore most of it down.

The old depot was razed and for a time a lumberyard and warehouse did business on the site. These buildings are now empty. Mrs. Schotte said they set up a sawmill on the lake where they salvaged hundreds of deadheads (sunken logs), and made them into lumber.

In the early 1920s the Heart Lake Club, a group of land speculators, bought the old Stephans dairy barn on the edge of town and converted it into a hotel, lounge, and dining room. The enterprise folded up during the Depression and for several years stood vacant. With the start of the tourist boom in the 1940s the hotel was reopened as the "Wassir Hoff" and became known statewide. With the passing of the old bottle fence as a tourist attraction and the construction of the expressway that bypassed the town, the old hotel stood empty again for several years until late 1970 when it was again purchased and opened for business.

Many resort areas are being developed in the area and once more there are about a dozen business places in the village. Mrs. Schotte donated the site of the old Stephan home and the glass bottle fence to Otsego Township for use as a firehall and community building with a stipulation that the old bottle fence be restored. The remains of the fence were pushed to the back of the lot and to date nothing has been done to restore it. Perhaps the village will make another revival in the years to come.

WINDSOR–settled in 1877 and a few years later the name changed to *"Elmira,"* which remains today and has a post office and a store, Robert Moorhead said.

1917 population 300. On the G. R. & I. Railroad (now the Pennsylvania) in Elmira Township. Has Catholic, Free Methodist, and Presbyterian churches, and a bank. Winfield A. Gardner, postmaster and drugs; harness shop; two groceries; Otsego Hotel; Charles Partee, billiards; W. A. Waite, railroad and station agent; Weaver & Son, hardware; and the Elmira Bank of Buell & Wickett.

WRIGHT'S LAKE–see *"Waters."*

––––––––––

Other towns and places in the history of the county were:

ARBUTUS BEACH–1910 mail *Otsego Lake.*

BAGLEY–1877 a station on M. C. Railroad (see *Salling*).

BARNES–was the postal name for *Gaylord.*

BEAR LAKE–1890 the terminus of the A. S.& N. Railroad from *Oscoda.*

BERRYVILLE–was a post office in Corwith Township, 5° miles west of *Vanderbilt.* 1910 RFD *Vanderbilt.* School standing in 1953 and a Berry Lake, in Section 31. Now has a factory that manufactures inflatable mattresses for hospitals, etc.

BLUE LAKE JUNCTION–on 1925 railroad maps.

CHAMBERLAIN–1910 on the M. C. Railroad. Mail *Johannesburg.*

CROWLEY–1910 on the M. C. Railroad. Mail *Johannesburg.*

FAYETTE–1910 mail *Deward.*
      NOTE: Also a *"Fayette"* in the Upper Peninsula restored as a ghost town by the D.N.R.

HAMILTON–1910 on the Boyne City, Gaylord & Alpena Railroad. Mail *Gaylord.*

HAROLD–1910 on the M. C. Railroad. Mail *Vanderbilt.*

JOHANNESBURG JUNCTION–1910 mail *Salling*.

KLINGESMITH–a post office in 1893. 1910, discontinued in Chester Township, 7 miles east of *Gaylord*. Mail to *Quick*.

LOGAN–1917, six miles north of *Gaylord* and 2 miles south of *Vanderbilt* on M. C. Railroad. The station is known as *"Rogers."* RFD *Gaylord*.

MANISTEE RIVER–1910 mail *Deward*.

MOSHER–1910 mail *Elmira*.

NORTH ELMIRA–1910 on the B. C. G. & A. Railroad.

NUGENT–on the M. C. Railroad. Mail *Johannesburg*, 1910.

PRATTS–1910 mail *Johannesburg*.

QUICK–1910 population 20. A country post office, Chester Township, 9 miles east of *Gaylord*. Daily mail. Bartlett & Quick, general store; D. Schurer, sawmill and lumber.

ROGERS–see *Logan*.

SPARR–was a post office in 1926.

TROMBLEY–1910 on M. C. Railroad. Mail *Salling*.

TYRUS–1910 on M. C. Railroad. Mail *Johannesburg*.

YUILL–on north county line and on M. C. Railroad. Above *Vanderbilt*.

Chapter 18

PRESQUE ISLE COUNTY GHOST TOWNS AND THE COUNTY THAT HAD TWO COUNTY SEATS AT THE SAME TIME

Presque Isle is a French name meaning "almost an island." The county was organized in 1871 from land area taken from Mackinac County. A few years after the county was formed it was determined the original organization had been illegal, even though the county had functioned as a unit. In 1875 legal steps were taken and an election held. Even then *Crawford's Quarry,* which had erected a courthouse and claimed the county seat, refused to concede to *Rogers* and a long feud began between the two villages.

In 1877 *Rogers* was designated the county seat. Some years later the name was changed to *"Rogers City."* In 1944 it was re-incorporated as a home-rule city. In 1919 the population was 566. In 1969 it was about 5,000.

The region was first mentioned in 1837 when a traveller on a steamboat said they halted at *Presque Isle.* Only four people lived there. They were wood-cutters, who cut cord wood for steamboats.

In 1841 the county was part of Mackinac County; in 1853 attached to Cheboygan and in 1858 to Alpena. The land was considered worthless at that time.

About 1868 William E. Rogers, U.S. Commissioner of Surveying, came from *New York* to *Detroit* to make a geodetic survey of the Great Lakes area. He formed a three-man surveying party and reached Presque Isle County in that same year and decided to buy some of the unowned land and settle there.

In 1860 Frederick Burnham became the first settler and built a dock and boat landing in Presque Isle Harbor. Then Francis Crawford and his family came.

Henry C. Hoffman, County Clerk in 1969, said: *"In the 40 years following the coming of the first settlers, until limestone opened a new era in 1910, Presque Isle County was a lumbering center. Had Rogers City been alone to draw on the timber resources of the county, the forest era would have lasted for many more years."*

159

Three historical markers have been erected in the county. One commemorating the world's largest limestone quarry, discovered by Hanery H. Hindshaw, a geologist, in 1908-09. Purchased by Carl D. Bradley and the U.S. Steel Corporation in 1920, the company came under the sole ownership of U.S. Steel upon Bradley's death in 1928.

Another marker near *Rogers City* is dedicated to Lake Huron, the fifth largest lake in the world. *"Much of the shore is still as wild as when the Huron Indians were the only travelers on the lake,"* the plaque reads in part.

RAILROADS

1906–Detroit & Mackinaw Railroad, North Division. *Alpena*, 0 miles; *Polaski*, 17 miles; *Posen*, 19 miles; *Metz*, 25 miles; *La Roque*, 29 miles; *Bunton*, 32 miles; *Millersburg*, 38 miles; *Case*, 41 miles; *Onaway*, 47 miles; ending at *Cheboygan*, 73 miles.

POST OFFICES

Of at least 24 post offices during the history of the county 6 remain.

GHOST TOWNS

ADALAKSA–see *Shaw*.

———

ALLIS–post office in 1890, five miles east of *Onaway*. 1905 on the daily mail stage route from *Onaway* to *Cheboygan*. Mrs. Annie Petchell, postmistress. Had two general stores, a hotel, grocery, sawmill, Reverend B. F. Lewis, Methodist, and other places. 1910 RFD *Onaway*.

———

BELL (also known as *"False Presque Isle Harbor"*)–was established in 1884 as a lumbering village. William A. French, State Land Commissioner and former manager of the Chicago & Northwestern Railroad was a lumberman at *Bell* and furnished all the ties, fence, and car material for Chicago & Canada Southern Railroad west of the Detroit River. He served as State Representative in 1883 and for several terms.

1910 RFD *Alpena*.

CALCITE–see *"Crawford's Quarry."*

––––––––––

CRAWFORD'S QUARRY–in the early 1860s Francis Crawford and his family landed at *Burnam's Landing* on the Lake Huron shore. Crawford and his wife, Cynthia, established and platted the village. They came from *Detroit* and took up a large section of government land. They had three sons, Leonard C., Thomas, and Francis. Thomas and Leonard were in charge of cutting cordwood for tugs which were wood-burners at that time. Leonard died in 1881 and was buried at the *Quarry*. In 1875 Tom Crawford was County Treasurer and from that time on there was bitter rivalry between the village of *Crawford's Quarry* and *Rogers*. As the first settlers, the Crawfords assumed they had priority on the resources of the county and were determined to control the county at any cost.

A courthouse was built at the *Quarry*, and for several years both *Rogers* and *Crawford's Quarry* served as the county seat. Meanwhile a new treasurer was elected to replace Tom Crawford but he refused to turn his books and records over to his successor. Officers were sent to the *Quarry* with a warrant for his arrest and Tom escaped into the forest where he hid for several days. He finally escaped to the landing dock in town and took a tug for parts unknown. He never returned to the county and it is not known what became of him.

Francis Crawford, Tom's brother, became a schoolteacher and taught in *Rogers City*. He died there and is buried in the Rogers Cemetery.

In 1872 *Crawford's Quarry* had a population of 200. In Rogers Township, 2 miles east of *Rogers City*, the county seat. *"The county is mostly settled by Germans and Poles who have availed themselves of the government homestead law, and they are rapidly improving the country. Within the last two years (since 1869) about a thousand families have moved in, and still the immigration continues."*

L. C. Crawford, postmaster; Crawford Brothers, general store and dealers in lumber, wood, etc.; Crawford Brothers, wagon and blacksmith shop. Also had a hotel and saloon, general store, two shoe and boot shops, and other places.

1877 population 150. A Lutheran church and district school had been built. Weekly stage to *Alpena* in winter. Weekly mail. L. C. Crawford, postmaster; John Bruning, blacksmith; L. C. Crawford, sawmill and general store. Hotel and saloon, etc. Robert Francis, fisherman; William Hagen, general store; Mrs. Annie Marineau, telegraph operator.

After the lumber was depleted *Crawford's Quarry* became a ghost town. It came to life again in 1910 when the huge mass of high calcium limestone which lies along the shore from *Rogers City* to Presque Isle Lighthouse came into demand. The name was changed to *"Calcite,"* which became the home of the largest limestone quarry in the world. The place was then RFD *Rogers City*.

––––––––

GRACE–1905, also known as *"Grace Harbor,"* on the shore of Hammond's Bay in Lake Huron, Bearinger Township, 24 miles northwest of *Rogers*. Daily mail. Charles D. Bunton, postmaster, and superintendent of the Grace Harbor Lumber Company, saw, shingle mill, general store, and hotel. Also several fishermen and docks. Andrew Taylor, stage proprietor.

The Grace Harbor lumbering operation encompassed most of what is now *Huron Beach* and the *Hammond Bay* area. By building dams, the Ocqueoc and Black Mallard (Carp) Rivers conveyed millions of feet of logs to sailing vessels on Lake Huron for shipment. *Grace* had its own school, stores, infirmary, smithy shop, and many homes. More than 100 men were employed there. Remnants of the buildings still stand and for many years the mill was still there. There are many artifacts to be ferreted out in the remains of this one-time village.

In 1918 the lumbering was finished. Charles Shell, postmaster. Daily mail. A. E. Garden, lumberman; Sough & Masterson, sawmill, general store, and hotel.

––––––––

HAGENSVILLE–a post office in 1899. 1905 population 100. In Belknap Township, 7 miles south of *Rogers* and 5 from *Metz*. Telephone. Daily mail. Wilson Matthew, postmaster. Had three general stores, one run by Mrs. Gertha Hagen; farm implement store; school, August Grossmann, teacher; flour mill; smithy; saw and shingle mill, and other places.

1917 RFD *Metz*. Two general stores, saw and shingle mill.

––––––––

HAMMOND–a post office in 1899. 1905 population 30. On Lake Huron, Bearinger Township, 12 miles north of *Millersburg*. U.S. Life Saving Station. Daily mail stage. Mrs. C. Ventin, postmaster. Has two or three sawmills.

1910 population 60. 1917 population 42. Roy Berry, Lake Breeze Summer Resort; Spens Brothers, sawmill.

HAWKS–railroad name *"LaRouqe."* A post office in 1899 and in 1926. In Bismark Township, 11 miles southwest of *Rogers*, on the D. & M. Railroad. H. Horwitz, postmaster. Several general stores; Sorgatt & Mileke, hotel; August Kisloski, saloon; sawmills, etc.

1917 population 200. William Buchalter, postmaster, general store etc. Had two wooden bowl factories, LaRocque Manufacturing Company (lath and woodenware), shingle mill, two hotels, and other places.

———

METZ–although still a village and shown on maps today, became a ghost town when destroyed by fire in 1908. Before that time it was an extensive sawmill town, with several general stores, a saloon, hotel, two or three liveries, cigar factory, etc.

In October of 1908, after there had been forest fires all summer, strong winds forced the flames to *Metz* and *Posen*, and *Metz* was completely destroyed. Many residents boarded a logging train and tried to escape but the red-hot rails of the tracks melted and the train was derailed. Thirteen people on the train, plus two members of the train crew, perished. Other residents, who stayed in town, escaped to open fields and survived.

1917 had a hotel and livery, general store, wagon maker, dealer in ties, posts and house blocks. S. Konieczny, postmaster.

———

OCQUEOC–was not really a village. A post office in 1893. 1905 a country post office in Ocqueoc Township, on daily mail stage from *Millersburg* to *Grace*. Charles Glawe, postmaster and general store. 1910 population 26. 1917 William King, postmaster.

———

PRESQUE ISLE–1917 a country post office in Presque Isle Township. Joseph E. Kauffman, postmaster, summer resort, general store, and real estate.

The "New" Presque Isle Lighthouse was built in 1870 about 1 mile north of the Old Lighthouse. The present one is among 40 in Michigan still manned by resident Coast Guard personnel. A narrow road leads to the white conical tower, 109 feet high, at the north tip of the peninsula and is a popular tourist attraction. A historic marker is located at the "Old Presque Isle Lighthouse" built in 1840, and is now a historical museum.

Scene at Metz of the forest fires in Presque Isle...
The great steel rails were twisted and warped as though they had been straws.
Bradshaw C. Baker No 10.

Scene of the forest fire that swept Presque Isle County in the summer of 1908. Twisted rails of tracks at *Metz* where 15 persons lost their lives while attempting to escape by train. Note remains of sawmill on left. Photo courtesy of Neil Thornton, *Tawas*, Michigan.

SHAW–name changed to *"Onaway,"* but was first called *"Adalaska."* Settled in 1881. A lumberman constructed the first road between *Petoskey* and *Presque Isle* and was paid in acreage. His dream was to build a peaceful city, the ground was platted and finally named *Onaway*. From 1886 the village grew as a lumbering town. Incorporated as a village in 1899 and as a city in 1903. By World War I, the American Wood Rim Company was making bicycle wheels and steering wheels for autos, had cooper shops, sawmills, foundry and machine shop, shingle mill, etc. The steering wheel factory burned in 1926. The city that once had nearly 4,000 population became a home-rule city in 1920, and today is mainly a resort town with about 1,400 population.

————

Other places during the history of the county were:

AUSTINS–shown on 1906 railroad maps.

BIG CUT–1910 population 20.

BUNTON–1910 mail *Millersburg*.

CASE–1910 mail *Onaway*.

FISHER–a post office in 1893. 1918 on Lake Huron, 15 miles southeast of *Rogers*. Mail to *Presque Isle*.

GRAND LAKE–shown on 1893 railroad maps.

HOFFMAN–1905 a flag stop on the D. & M. Railroad, 25 miles by rail from *Alpena*.

HAMMONDS BAY–a post office in 1893.

HURST–1910 a station on the D. & M. Railroad, 34 miles by rail northwest of *Alpena*. Mail *Metz*.

LA ROUQE–post office name is *"Hawks."*

LISKE–1910 mail *Hagensville*.

MAY LAKE JUNCTION–1910 mail *Metz*.

MCPHEE–on 1899 railroad maps.

MOLTKE–1910 a discontinued post office 3 miles from *Rogers*, RFD.

NAGEL–1910 mail *Hagensville*. Was a new post office in 1905.

PACK SIDING–a station on the D. & M. Railroad in 1905, 46 miles northwest of *Alpena*.

POLASKI–1910 a station on the D. & M. Railroad. Mail *Posen*.

PROVIDENCE–1910 a discontinued post office. Mail *Millersburg*.

QUARRY–a discontinued post office in 1910. Mail to *Rogers*.

RAINY LAKE–1910 mail to *Atlanta*.

ROGERS MILLS–also called *"Rogers City."*

ROGERS CITY JUNCTION–1910 on D. & M. Railroad. Mail *Posen*.

SOBIESKI–1910 on D. & M. Railroad. Mail *Posen*.

SOUTH ROGERS–1910 mail *Metz*.

———

Chapter 19

ROSCOMMON COUNTY GHOST TOWNS AND THE HERMIT OF TREASURE ISLAND

Roscommon County was named "Mikenuqk," after a Chippewa Indian chief when set off in 1840. Its present name is taken from a county in Ireland. John Brink, an Irishman, surveyed the territory in 1838 and in his records called Houghton Lake *"Red Lake."* In 1839 Higgins Lake was called *"Forginson Lake"* by Brink as an expression of his sympathy to the Irish cause.

It is believed that Brink named *"Lake St. Helen"* after Baron St. Helens, a Britisher who was raised to the Irish peerage with that title.

The county was chartered in 1880 and land area taken from Cheboygan and Midland Counties. In 1874 Midland County relinquished Roscommon County, which also included the west half of present Gladwin County. An agreement couldn't be reached with Roscommon for a settlement as to the exact land area involved in the transaction. Several lawsuits followed between the two counties and finally in 1883, it was agreed that Midland County pay them $6,000.

Until about 1879 *Houghton Lake* was the county seat. Settled in 1870, in 1877 had a population of 20. Lumbering was the only industry. H. H. Woodruff was the first postmaster and in 1878 was elected Chairman of the County Board of Supervisors when it was voted to move the county seat to *Roscommon*.

RAILROADS

1912–Grand Rapids & Indiana, Missaukee Branch. *Missaukee Junction*, 0 miles; *Reedsburg*, 31 miles; *Michelson*, 32 miles.

The Michigan Central, Mackinaw Division served *St. Helen, Moore*, and *Roscommon*.

From 1890 until 1898 a branch of the Michigan Central Railroad extended from a point 1 mile north of *St. Helen* west to within a few miles from the southwest tip of Houghton Lake. Two stations, *Lone Bridge* and *Williams Junction*, were located on this line.

Most of these old grades can be followed, although in some places they cross private property.

Just below *West Branch* at *Hauptman*, another branch of the M. C. Railroad, extended west into Nester Township and a settlement called *"Fortesque"* was located there. At the end of the Hauptman Branch of the M. C. Railroad was a place called *"Barker City"* at the terminus of the line in Nester Township, due north of *Meredith. Fortesque* was about 10 miles south of *Roscommon* and at this point the tracks swung north to *Pine Ridge*, about 6 miles south of *Roscommon* in 1893.

A sawmill town named *"Achill"* was just north of Sugar River on County Road 500, north of M-18 that goes through Nester Township to *Maple Valley* on M-55. M. J. Willing of *Royal Oak* now owns 3,000 acres bordering Gladwin County in Sections 26 and 35 of Nester Township which includes the townsite of *Achill.* He changed the names of Hoister Lake to *"Achell"* and another un-named lake to *"Willing Lake."* They are designated as such on current county maps.

Willing said the old mill pilings remain in the lake. A large, weed-grown basement of the former general store and several foundations remain. This and the old railroad grade are all that is left of the town. *Achill* is shown on 1890 and 1893 railroad maps and listed as a post office April, 1893.

Some of these old grades can also be followed for several miles by driving south from *Camp Nakomis* south of M-55. Part of the trail has been marked by the D.N.R. at intervals. One of the first plaques notes that the Houghton Lake State Forest was planted in 1914. It lies in a vast area at one time covered by virgin pines. The stumps from the logging days remain and this is the only plaque ever dedicated to stumps. This trail extends for about 5 miles and was lined with telegraph wires and some poles left from the 1890s.

One plaque bears a picture of an old farm house and a windmill and marks an abandoned farm site. During the lumbering days a sawmill was located in the clearing. Later the stumps were cleared and a man called "One Armed Pete" farmed here. He was struck by lightning and killed about 1900 and the farm buildings abandoned.

Other old railroad grades are strung along in the *St. Helen* area, most of them built by Henry Stephens, pioneer lumberman in the area. In 1882 he orga-nized the Henry Stephens & Company with his two sons, Henry, Jr. and Albert L., founded the village of *St. Helen* on the M. C. Railroad a short distance north of where the present business section lies along M-76. During a 14-year period, from 1882 to 1896, Stephens cut more than one billion feet of lumber in the *St. Helen* area. In 1891 he started operations at *Waters* in Otsego County and by the turn-of-the-century *St. Helen* was a ghost town until the Carters moved in and made a resort around the lake.

POST OFFICES

Of at least 18 post offices in the history of the county only 6 remain.

The building of a new mill town. Company houses under construction and the beginning of the new village of *Michelson* in Roscommon County, 1910. Note school house on left; man with team and plow digging up tree roots for roadway; mills and spark deflectors on sawdust burners in background; and neat rows of "outhouses" behind each row of houses. Photo from Fred Hirzel Collection.

Lumber piled at the *Michelson* sawmills ready for shipment. Sawmill burned in July, 1911 and was rebuilt. Mills lasted until 1924. Last child was born here in 1926. Now planted to pine trees, site is marked by Conservation Department. Photo from Fred Hirzel Collection.

GHOST TOWNS

ACHILL–see railroad history.

_____

COY–1917 a post office in South Branch Township, 8 miles east of *Roscommon*. Daily mail. Oliver B. Scott, postmaster.

_____

EDNA–a post office in 1877. Name changed to *"Prudenville."* Settled in 1871. 1877 population 50. Logs, furs, and fish are shipped. Mail stage to *Farwell* and *Roscommon*. Clara J. Denton, postmistress. A. A. Denton, hotel; Denton & Rowe, store and lumber. An original log cabin is still standing in good condition between M-55 and the landing near the main corners.

_____

GEELS–a flag stop on the M. C. Railroad, 8 miles southeast of *Roscommon* in 1917. Mail *Roscommon*. Section 6, Richfield Township.

_____

HERBERT–1905 a country post office, Richfield Township. Frank Kirkland, postmaster. 1918 RFD *Keno*.

_____

KENO–six miles north of *St. Helen* in Section 15, Richfield Township. Was a post office.

_____

KIRKLAND–post office in Backus Township, Section 20, on Denton Creek, about 4 miles east of M-l8 and 1 mile south of M-55. 1917 J. A. Huntley, postmaster; C. Becktold, railroad express agent. Remains of some buildings standing in 1949-50. 1953 schoolhouse still standing.

_____

LOXLEY–shown on 1969 highway maps, 1910 a post office in Roscommon Township. Mail tri-weekly. Frank Kirkland, postmaster. Located near the south US-27 expressway exit between Old US-27 and the expressway, south of Houghton Lake State Police Post.

1917 population 200. Mail tri-weekly. Edwin G. Gowen, postmaster; John R. Bowman, hotel; N. L. Gage, grain; J. W. Gowen, general store; E. D. Haines, saw and flour mill; Oster, meats; William Patterson, shingle mill; John Reed, sawmill; and Bert Ritenburg, general store. Was a post office until about 1918-19.

_____

This large house was built by a timber baron in the 1880s for a farmhouse and to accommodate visitors. It was purchased by Charles Lyon of *Roscommon* who founded the Lyon Manor post office and used the house for a hotel. Lyon froze his legs one winter and had one leg amputated. The mansion was torn down in 1958 and a ranch-style home built in its place by the present owner. Photo from Fred Hirzel Collection.

172

MICHELSON–each year in August people from Michigan and other neighboring states meet at the State camping grounds near Reedsburg Dam to talk over the old days when *Michelson* was a booming mill town.

Lauren Vanettan of *Cadillac*, now 77 years old, and his wife, Ruth, who taught school there, described the village at its peak.

"To begin with, when Michelson was a town, this flood waters didn't exist," Vanettan said with a sweep of his gnarled hand towards the endless miles of stump-filled water.

"When we put up logs here it was a nice wide stream of fast-running, clear water. Just above the town is the mouth of the Muskegon where it comes out of Houghton Lake. Most of our logs came through there. They were floated in rafts across the lake from camps ran by what we called 'Chin-Whiskered Jobbers.'

The Michelson mills were steam-operated and the stacks towered above the highest trees. The main street was half-a-mile long with houses on each side in straight rows all painted white. They were rented to men with families. I came here in 1912, just three years after the town was built, and my wife came here in 1919 to teach school. Schoolteachers didn't last long here!" he said with a chuckle. *"The men outnumbered them about two hundred to one!"*

Vanettan said there were three sections of town. The main street, which ran under the high tramway of the shingle mill, and the company-owned houses were called *"Shingle Town."* Near a large clearing where logs were piled, peeled, and sorted, other cabins and shanties were built. This was called *"Post Town."* The business section and where the boardinghouses were located was *"Michelson."*

"I started out peeling logs for 1¼ cents a piece," he said. *"There was a big peeling crew. Herm Bowerman was yard boss, and I remember a colored man, who worked there for several years, named Tom Ford."*

Some of the people who lived there were David, Ryass and Leandas Stout; several Powers brothers; and Glenn Robinson, now nearing 80, is one of the few remaining in the area. He lives on a farm near the town site and at one time ran the general store.

Alec Erickson and Marshall Picard were rivermen. Paddy Whalen, who had two brothers, Mike and Ben, were river hogs on the Muskegon for 40 years. Paddy settled down at *Michelson* when he was nearly 85 years old and stayed on to be near the river until his death.

Henry Slingerland, John Grover, and Levi Houghton worked in the mills. Levi's son runs the Houghton Rexall Drug Store in *Clare* (1969). Joe Lee was mill boss. Henry Lord was foreman and filer. Everett Estelle was blocker and sawyer. Lon Spink, now operator of the Reedsburg Store lived there and started driving team at age eleven.

Grace Greishammer was the first person to drive to *Star City* for the mail that came from *Lake City* after the trains quit coming. She drove a pony on a two-wheeled cart. In later years Fred Edwards hauled the mail, then Tom Wilson.

A big man of Turkish descent with a long, handlebar mustache and a uniform-type suit with brass buttons came through town each summer with a horse-drawn van. The horse had a harness with high hames and a large bell hanging between the hame knobs that could be heard long before he could be seen coming down the road. The Turk was called "Happy George, the Peddler" and carried knicknacks, needles, bolts of cloth, novelties, and tinware.

A sign was erected on the site by the Conservation Department that reads: *"Site of Michelson, once a thriving lumber town of over 500 people. The Michelson family founded a large saw and shingle mill, which operated here from 1909 to 1924. Pine and cedar logs came from the vast dead stream swamp, now a part of Houghton Lake Forest."*

Mrs. Martha Nurenberg of *Port Sanilac* was a niece of E. H. Sorenson who operated a general store and lived over the store. She remembers: *"Learning the ABCs forward and backwards, getting my hair washed in kerosene to get rid of lice gathered at school, the day we had a merry-go-round and a carnival that came to town. I can still feel the excitement of that ride."*

Vanettan said, *"The town has been dead and buried now for over 40 years, but it seems like only yesterday that the whistles were blasting, saws echoed across the river, and people got married and babies were born here."*

Old foundations remain and rows of giant trees, along with one-time streets, but the entire area is now covered with pines planted in the 1930s that are 15 or 20 feet high.

1917, E. H. Sorenson, general store, hardware, etc.; C. H. Lilly, express agent; Everett O. Estelle, hotel; Vernon Murray, confectionery; James Oliver, lumber; Glenn Robinson, dray; Mrs. G. Robinson, milliner; Edward Sorenson, livery and garage. Also a Mrs. Devore ran a boardinghouse.

MICHELSON MILL–1910 mail *Michelson*.

NELLSVILLE–1905 population 70. Roscommon Township, 4 miles east of *Michelson*. Mail tri-weekly. J. F. Bailey, postmaster.

The only store remaining, just west of the M-55 overpass near I-75, closed its doors years ago and has a "For Sale" sign in the window. The streets are only tracks with grass grown up between. Perhaps 15 or 20 small houses remain in the area. Large lumber camps were in the area, one on the southeast side of the expressway where a milk company or creamery stood before the new road was built.

Probably the last big event in *Nellsville* happened on Labor Day, 1922, when Sam Johnson, a black boy from *Stittsville* and only son of his parents, was killed in the eighth round of a boxing match between Johnson and a professional boxer called "Dummy" Maxon, a white deaf-mute. The referee counted Maxon out on a foul blow in the first round, but Maxon's handlers refused to accept the decision and the crowd pressed to have the fight continue. *"Johnson had a local reputation as a rough-and-tumble fighter and it was the desire of many to find someone 'who could take the conceit out of him,'"* one local paper stated. There was a furor over the fatal boxing match and it is doubtful if another was held for at least another year.

The Johnson family was the only family of blacks in Missaukee County, Fred Hirzel said, and were well-liked by their neighbors.

———

LYON MANOR–today the modern post office on the southeast side of Higgins Lake stands across the road from the site of the former three-story house built by an early lumberman and later purchased by Charles Lyon, former owner of the Great Northern Hotel in *Roscommon*. Lyon made the old house into a summer hotel and named it "Lyon Manor," after which the post office took its name. After he finished farming in the area he subdivided the land into lake resort lots. Some of the streets bear names of members of his family.

In 1918 population 30. Anton W. Elgas, postmaster. The old house, a combination store and post office, still stands with the yard overgrown to weeds across from the present day Lyon Manor Store. Lyon Manor Hotel was torn down in 1958 and an expensive summer home stands on the lake shore in front of the former site. Huge trees surrounding the manor were also cut down and the area is now lawn.

———

MARKEY–in Markey Township, about 2 miles north of Houghton Lake (Markey) Airport and weather bureau, on a blacktop road, had a population of more than 300 people in 1917. Daily mail stage to *Roscommon*. Mrs. Elizabeth DeWitt, postmistress, three sawmills, meat market, feed mill, two hotels, general store, and other places. Two large sawmills remain today.

The one-time flourishing village was named by DeVere Hall, land speculator and State legislator in 1890, who founded the village and named it after his
real estate partner, D. P. Markey, ex-speaker of the State House of Representa-
tives.

NOLAN–1905 population 80. Sixteen miles northwest of *Gladwin*, to which
place it is connected by daily mail stage route. E. A. Coan, postmaster; Coan
Lumber Company, sawmill, shingles etc. 1910 population 70. Mail to *Butman*.
Was a post office May 1, 1897. Located in Section 19 on an old railroad grade
that runs from Clear Lake south to Coan Mill Pond, on the east side of County
Road 500 near present-day "North of The Border Tavern." In 1953 the Eggleston
School and Nester Town Hall was standing near the site.

TREASURE ISLAND–is the name of a small island of about 30 acres that lies off
Point Comfort on the southwest side of Higgins Lake. Legend relates that before the lumbering days an old trapper built a dugout on the island and made this
his winter headquarters. After the logging days Felix Flynn owned the island
and erected a rough, clap-board hunting cabin. From the late 1890s until the
1920s the island was called *"Flynn's Island."* As the land around the lake was
developed for summer homes and resorts, some developer changed the name to
"Treasure Island."

For many years (nobody seems to know the exact length of time but before
the turn-of-the-century) a man named Israel Porter Pritchard settled on the island
and became known as the "Hermit of Higgins Lake." Lloyd L. Harman, in 1929,
said Pritchard lived on the island prior to the building of the hunting cabin. *"He
occupied the cabin for many years but suddenly disappeared and the cabin was
found vacant when the campers arrived the following summer,"* Harman said.

Fred Hirzel of *Moorestown*, several miles west of Higgins Lake, said
Pritchard had a son living there and he remembers when the old man came there
and stayed for one winter. *"I can't remember too much about him,"* Hirzel said,
*"but he only had stubs for fingers. They appeared to have been frozen and
dropped off,"* Hirzel said. The old man came to the store in *Moorestown* and
bought tobacco a few times and before spring disappeared from there.

According to Harman the hermit returned to the island and discovered the
cabin had burned during his absence. That was about 1898 or 1899, as his body
was discovered by campers in the dugout in the summer of 1902-03. Officials
were called to the scene and his decaying body was carried to a boat, using the
board door of the dugout for a stretcher.

Harmon said Pritchard isolated himself from the world because he had been
a "bounty jumper" during the Civil War. It was not unusual for a man to accept

the bounty (bonus) paid by different states for enlisting and then desert and enlist again in another state to collect their bounty. *"As I heard the story,"* Harman said, *"Pritchard had collected the bounties in seven states."*

Others say the old man hid out on the island after the accidental death of his wife, who many people believed he had murdered.

Today several expensive summer homes occupy part of the island and none of today's residents remember when the hermit lived there.

Charles Lyon of Lyons Manor used to visit the old man and take him cast off clothing and food. Lyon tried to induce him to move off the island but he refused and stayed there until his death.

––––––––

Other towns, places and flag stations during the history of the county were:

ACKLISS–in Higgins Township, Section 30, 4 miles south of *Roscommon* near Robinson Lake.

CROOKS–Section 3, Lake Township, ½ mile north of *Houghton Lake* on the Dead Stream.

MOORE–a station on the M. C. Railroad, Section 26, Higgins Township, about 5 miles southeast of *Roscommon*, east of M-76.

PRICES–Section 18, Higgins Township, 2 miles south of *Roscommon*, on the west side of M-18.

SHAYS–Section 33, Gerrish Township, near present south Higgins Lake State Park.

TIERNEY–1910 mail *St. Helen.*

VERNCROFT–shown on 1925 maps near Atchel Lake in Section 26 or 27 Nester Township near the south county line.

––––––––

Chapter 20

WEXFORD COUNTY GHOST TOWNS AND THE "BATTLE OF SHERMAN"

This county was first named "Kautawaubet" after a Chippewa Chief who was a friend of Governor Cass and Henry R. Schoolcraft. First set off in 1840, the name was changed to Wexford, after a county in Ireland in 1843. Organized in 1866 as Wexford Township, Manistee County, an act of March 30, 1869 set it off as a separate county with the townships of Hanover, Wexford, Colfax, and Springville.

First settlement was made at *Sherman* in 1863 and this village was the first county seat. *Clam Lake (*now *Cadillac),* settled a few years later, coveted the distinction, and a county-seat war of unusual duration and bitterness, lasting for a decade, was waged. In 1881 the county seat was moved to *Manton*, but later that same year the records were removed by force to *Cadillac*, which became the county seat in 1882.

The census of 1870 recorded a population of 650 for the entire county. From 1875 to 1884, during the peak of the lumbering era, population rapidly increased, reaching its peak of 20,769 in 1910. From 1910 until 1930 it decreased to 16,827. The 1960 census recorded a population of 18,466 and today (1970) it is about the same as in 1910.

Most of the land area consists of high hills, lakes, and swampland. Once the timber was removed nothing remained in most areas but stumps and blowing sand.

In the early 1900s *Cadillac* became a major industrial center and for a time was the home of nationally known 'Acme Trucks." With the advent of the automobile and tourist trade the county became a center of resort business. In the 1940s *Cadillac* became famous for the manufacture of Chris Craft pleasure boats and yachts. About the same time, some of the high hills were converted into ski slopes, and tourism, both winter and summer, is now the major industry of the county.

The city of *Cadillac* will celebrate its centennial this year (1971) with a month-long celebration and festival planned for the month of July.

RAILROADS

1890–Grand Rapids & Indiana, Northern Division. Beginning at *Richmond, Indiana*, 0 miles; *Grand Rapids*, 233.8 miles; entering the county at *Hobart*,

325.8 miles; *Cadillac*, 331.6 miles; *Missaukee Junction*, ...; and *Manton*, 352.6 miles.

1890–Cadillac & Northeastern Railroad. Beginning at *Cadillac*, 0 miles; *G. R. & I. Crossing*, 1 mile; *Beckett's Crossing*, 8 miles; *Mitchell's Crossing*, 10 miles; then on to *Komoko*, 11 miles; and *Lake City*, 14 miles.

1900–Ann Arbor Railroad. Beginning at *Toledo*, 0 miles; entering the county at *Cadillac* from *Lucas*, 227 miles; *Millersville*, 236 miles; *Boon*, 238 miles; *Harrietta*, 245 miles; *Yuma*, 249 miles; *Sherman*, 254 miles; *Bagnall*, 258 miles; and *Churchills*, 262 miles.

1900–Grand Rapids & Indiana Railroad, Northern Division, between *Cadillac* and *Mackinaw*. *Mackinaw City*, 0 miles; entering the county from the north at *Haire*, 112 miles; *Manton*, 116 miles; *Missaukee Junction*, 124 miles; *Cadillac*, 128 miles.

POST OFFICES

There were at least 28 post offices during the history of the county. Of these 7 remain.

GHOST TOWNS

ANGOLA–1900, a post office in Henderson Township. 1905, seventeen miles southwest of *Cadillac*. On the daily mail stage from *Thorpe* to *Cadillac*. In Section 29, on Downing Creek, and in the home of F. O. Wait, postmaster. 1910 population 50. Mail *Hoxeyville*.

———

BAGNALL–formerly known as *"Farnsworth,"* on the Ann Arbor Railroad. Wexford Township, 3 miles west of *Sherman*. C. W. Flinn, postmaster, general store, and telephone manager; Bagnall Lumber Company, sawmill; Clare Powell, railroad and express agent; and Phillip M. Farnsworth, grocer. About a dozen loggers were listed, two ginseng growers, a nursery, Stone & Flinn (canthook makers), blacksmith, Fick Durand (drayman), and several other businesses.

1910 population 100, and 1917 population 50. *Mesick*, 3 miles distant, was the nearest bank. D. J. LaGoe, postmaster. Bellaire & LaGoe, general store and telephone company.

———

BAXTER–1917 population 40. Greenwood Township, on the M. & N. E. Railroad, 25 miles northwest of *Cadillac*, and 8 from *Buckley*. Herman Marvin, postmaster, general store, and real estate. Fred Muth, produce.

———

179

BENSON–a post office in 1890. 1905 Cherry Grove Township, 8 miles southwest of *Cadillac*. On daily mail stage from *Thorp*. Swan Benson, postmaster. 1910 population 30. Charles A. Benson, general store.

BONDS MILLS–1877 a post office in Haring Township in the central part of the county. Also a station on the G. R. & I. Railroad, 6 miles north of *Clam Lake*. Has one sawmill. Settled in 1872. Population 40. Frank Kysor, postmaster. Bond & Kysor, sawmill and general store. Not listed as a post office in 1890. 1910 mail to *Gilbert*.

BUNYEA–1905 a post office on the Ann Arbor Railroad, 8 miles northeast of *Cadillac*. Drayton Seaman, postmaster; Sturtevant & Bunyea, sawmill. 1910 RFD *Cadillac*.

CLAY HILL–post office established July 20, 1870, Thomas S. Henderson, first postmaster. Henderson built a huge tavern and inn with about 20 rooms for stage coach travelers in 1870, when the Old State Road was extended through the county. For many years this was the only building on the site and was later known as the "Brant Half-Way House." Hundreds of travelers stopped overnight in the 1880s and were sometimes stacked clear to the eaves. The attic even had pallets on the floor for people to sleep on.

1877, a post office in Henderson Township, 15 miles south of *Sherman*. Lumber and some farm products are shipped. It is on the mail route from *Woodville* to *Sherman*. Weekly mail. Thomas Henderson, postmaster.

On April 25, 1891, the name of the settlement was changed to *"Hoxeyville"* by the post office department. Residents of the place, which still has a post office, celebrated their centennial in 1970 and are using the profits to establish a historical museum.

ELEANOR–the railroad name for *Hoxeyville* (see *"Clay Hill."*) 1905 daily stage to *Cadillac*. Edwin B. Brooks, postmaster and general store. 1918 population 22. South Branch Township. Thomas Mitchell, general store; and Russel Wilmarth, general store.

ELTON–also spelled *"Alton."* Clam Lake Township, near Stone Ledge Lake. 1905 a country post office, 8 miles southeast of *Cadillac*. A. S. Cassety, postmaster and general store. 1910 population 30. RFD *Cadillac*.

FARNSWORTH–name changed to *"Bagnall."* See *Bagnall.*

GILBERT–on the G. R. & I. Railroad, Cedar Creek Township, 4 miles south of *Manton*. 1905 population 200, has Swedish Lutheran Church. Daily mail. Jacob Larson, postmaster, general store and wood. Had blacksmith; J. Carlson, pianos and sewing machines; produce warehouse; L. L. Lane, railroad and telegraph agent. Had a constable, deputy sheriff, and justice of the peace. Reverend Norleen, Lutheran minister.

1918 population about 30. Telephone. J. Larson, postmaster and general store; H. E. Blue, express and telegraph agent; Freeman Brothers; and Moseley Brothers, warehouses.

All that remains is a church and cemetery (1953).

HAIRE–1890 a station and post office on G. R. & I. Railroad. Liberty Township, 3° miles north of *Manton*. 1918 population 37. Telephone. RFD *Manton*. Horner & Crawford, grocers.

HANOVER–see *Wexford.*

HARING–1877 a post office and 50 population, Haring Township. A station on the G. R. & I. Railroad, known as *"Linden."* Three-and-one-half miles north of Clam Lake. *"It is in a pine forest, but little more than a lumber camp as yet. Settled in November 1872."* Daily mail. Ephiram Shay, postmaster, groceries and lumber; W. S. Dove, eavestrough manufacturer.

Ephiram Shay, the postmaster, experimented with using a steam engine to haul his timber from the woods, beginning in the winter of 1875 using wood rails. After several years experimenting with different types of rails and engines he invented a new concept in steam locomotives which became known worldwide as the "Shay Locomotive." He sold his patent for the gear-driven engine to the Lima Engine Works of *Lima*, Ohio for $10,000. Famous in Michigan during the logging days, the small engines were used all over the State on narrow-gauge tracks. Bearing the "Lima" trademark and name, old-timers nicknamed them "Limeys."

Shay moved to *Elk Rapids* near *Traverse City* where he became manager of the water works in later years. While there he patented several other inventions, including a motorboat and an all-steel, collapsible building. He was also one of the first automobile owners in the area.

The famous Shay locomotive has been the subject of many railroad stories and at least two books. One of his engines is on display at the city park, near the former depot, in downtown *Cadillac*.

What appears to be an old, two-story, wood-frame hotel and dance hall stands near the railroad crossing on the site of the former village.

––––––––

HARRIETTE (also spelled *"Harrietta")*–was incorporated as *"Gaston"* in 1891, amended and named *"Harietta"* in 1893. Although still an incorporated village, on the Ann Arbor Railroad, 18 miles northwest of *Cadillac*, the town had a population of five or six hundred at one time. Today there are only 50 or 75 people living in the village and two or three business places.

1918 population 400. Methodist and Peoples Union Churches, a graded school, and a bank. C. W. Barry, postmaster, drugs and general merchandise; B. A. Addison, station agent; Bank of Harriette; general stores; livery stable; hay and feed store; hardware; saw and stave mill; Dr. John McIntosh; Mrs. Minnie Southwick, telephone manager; W. H. Westerman, manager State Fish Hatchery.

John A. Barry, proprietor of the bank, was born July 29, 1848 in Livingston County, Michigan. Barry worked in lumber camps when he was a young boy. At age 18 attended medical school and became a doctor and druggist. In 1899 he moved to Harrietta and went into the drug business with his brother and a man named Curtis. Barry was Village President, justice of the peace, Supervisor, and in 1906 was elected to the State Legislature.

Only a few buildings remain in the once-thriving village. Most of the original streets are overgrown to grass and weeds, and there are many foundations and basements of former buildings. The depot, bank, hotel, and main buildings have long since disappeared.

––––––––

HOBART–in 1873 listed as *"Summit Station."* 1877, a station on the G. R. & I. Railroad, Clam Lake Township. Settled in 1871. Ships lumber, tanbark and shingles. Daily mail. William H. Cushing, deputy postmaster and general store, sawmill.

At one time population over 100. 1905 population 60. Six miles south of *Cadillac*. J. G. Cooper, postmaster; S. Anderson, school commissioner; B. E. Boyce, blacksmith; C. A. Boyce, feed mill and wagon maker; Nels Parsons, blacksmith; Simon L. Rouse, general store; Henry Gilbert, justice; Charles Swanson, potato buyer.

1918 population 80. Telephone. Mrs. Grace Lood, postmistress; A. M. Lood, general store; had feed mill; pickle station; and potato warehouses. S. P. Otteson, railroad agent.

All that remains of *Hobart* is a church, what appears to be a former townhall, and a potato-storage building. Two very nice homes are near the site of the one-time village. An expensive, redwood sign, similar to those erected in State Parks, stands on a front lawn of one house and reads *"Hobart."*

————

HOXEYVILLE–has a post office and shown on maps. See *"Eleanor"* and also *"Clay Hill."*

————

LINDEN–railroad name for *Haring*. See *Haring*.

————

MEAUWATAKA–1872 on the old stage route between *Clam Lake* and *Sherman*. *"A steam sawmill has just been built here and settlers are coming in rapidly."*

1877 a post office in Colfax Township, 8 miles west of Bonds Mills, on Meauwataka Lake, covering about 200 acres, and from 60 to 75 feet deep. The name is Indian, signifying "half-way." The place has a sawmill, planing and gristmill, Methodist church, and a good free school. Settled in 1867. Mail weekly. E. C. Dayhuff, postmaster.

1905, daily mail by stage from *Cadillac*. Elijah Smith, postmaster. Had Adventist, Free Methodist, and Methodist Episcopal ministers, stores, barber shop, Remington sawmill, blacksmith shop, Smith & Roode, general store, etc.

1918 no population given, but only a few people lived here.

————

ROUND LAKE–1884 an unincorporated village on Round Lake and on present day Pennsylvania Railroad, 4 miles east of *Missaukee Junction*, Haring Township. Population 273.

————

SHERMAN–this village and its history is probably the most spectacular of any town in the county and the so-called "Battle of Sherman" in a long, drawn-out dispute over the site of the county seat is a subject of conversation even today.

Within the past two or three years a historical marker has been placed in the remains of *Sherman* next to highway M-37 and it reads as follows: *"FIRST WEXFORD COURTHOUSE - Wexford County was organized in 1869. The law organizing the county also specified that the county seat should be located*

Post office at *Sherman*, first county seat of Wexford County. Note old courthouse in background, used for a school until 1937. Fires destroyed most of the buildings in the village that once boasted two main streets one-half mile long and lined with business places. Picture undated, probably about 1890 near the Fourth of July. Note the Negro boy, far right, dressed in his Sunday best. He was a member of a family who lived here. Nearly every village had at least one family of Blacks. Photo from Fred Hirzel Collection.

This marker was erected in 1968-69 on the site of what remains of *Sherman*. Reads in part, *"First courthouse completed in 1872* (see courthouse on previous page) *was located about 200 feet west of this market and was used for a schoolhouse until about 1937."* Another historical marker has been made telling the story of the battle for the county seat of Wexford County. Photo by Roy L. Dodge.

185

'at or near what is called Manistee Bridge,' where the Newaygo and Northport State Road crossed the Manistee River. In 1870 the village was platted just south of the bridge. The first county courthouse, completed in 1872, was located about 200 feet west of this marker. After a heated controversy, the county offices were transferred in 1881 to Manton, a small town in the eastern part of the county. The dispute was finally settled in 1882 when Cadillac was chosen as the county seat of Wexford County. The old courthouse in Sherman was used as a school until 1937."

In 1872 the population of Sherman was 400. Situated in Wexford, Hanover, Antioch, and Springville Townships on the Manistee River, 27 miles northwest of Clam Lake. It contains two hotels, some stores and mechanic shops. Daily mail. J. S. Walling, postmaster. Had two hotels, "Grant House" and the "Sherman House"; William Mears, general store; Austin-Hanna & Lyman, builders and undertakers; drug store, and several other places.

By 1877 the town was booming. Had two churches, a weekly newspaper (The Pioneer), two or three flour mills, hotels, lawyer, doctor, and professional men, and several sawmills.

Sherman had been a growing village for five years or more, was the county seat, and all it lacked to make it one of the largest cities in northern Michigan was a railroad. During this time Manton, founded in 1871, and Cadillac, which was settled as Clam Lake about the same time, engaged in a controversy over which place should be the seat of justice. The county had erected a new, two-story courthouse in Sherman in 1869, supposing the matter to be settled. About 1880 most of the business section burned to the ground. In 1881 the court records and county seat was moved to Manton, which by this time had outstripped Sherman in size and population. In April of 1882 an election was held to decide the location of the county seat, and by what was called a "rigged election," Cadillac won.

The people of Sherman went about rebuilding the village while the other two towns fought over the site of the county seat. In 1882 stages ran to Manton, Traverse City, and Manistee semi-weekly. J. H. Wheeler, postmaster. Mrs. Gladys Nisewander, niece of J. H. Wheeler, is still living at age 83 in Buckley, not far from Sherman. "Uncle John wrote the history of Wexford County, had it published, and is in the libraries," she said.

Mrs. Clark Corning of Grawn, Michigan, was born in Sherman in 1892 where her father ran one of the hotels. "My father, Edwin Milliman, purchased the "Exchange Hotel" when Sherman was a thriving village in 1895. I started to kindergarten in what was once the courthouse," she said.

"There were five mills in the area, a bank, jewelry store, two drug stores, two hardwares, two general stores, two doctors, several saloons, a printing *shop, a shoe cobbler, and in spring there were always the men who were called 'river drivers' who rode the logs on the river. There were two main streets. Two churches (one remains now), a millinery shop, and this lady was kept busy making ladies hats, and a jail which we kids were afraid to even walk by."*

Mrs. Corning described the hotel as: *"A 37-bedroom, three-story hotel with two housekeeping suites, two large display rooms where traveling men came and displayed their goods, and merchants came to be entertained and place orders. There was a large dining room, always with white linen cloths, large office, public and private sitting rooms. He ran a livery barn in connection and met the Ann Arbor train in Mesick twice daily, with a fancy horse drawn bus."*

Mrs. Corning still has a trunk her father kept when some man failed to pay his board bill.

"M. J. Clagett and wife were steady boarders at our hotel," she said. *"He had a stave and heading mill 1 mile west of Sherman and the gathering of houses there was called 'Claggetville,' then it was changed to 'Glengary.' Now nothing remains except a few summer cabins on the Manistee River."*

The courthouse was purchased by the village in 1885 and used as a school. The following year it became a graded school with four schoolteachers.

In 1904-05 another fire burned all the buildings on the other main street except the "Exchange Hotel," and the next day Milliman sold out to Fred Cooper.

The last census for *Sherman* was recorded in 1920 and it remained an incorporated village with no population, and probably no elected officials, until 1940. Shortly after that year the village was unincorporated.

The 12 or more streets that once divided the city blocks are grown to grass and weeds. Many old houses remain in a state of neglect. One or two appear to have been hotels. Trails wind through the underbrush of some of the streets. Part of a picket fence remains standing near a vacant lot, weather-beaten and forlorn. Giant Lombardy poplars, some over 100 years old, stand dead and stripped of most of the bark, silent sentinels of the town that once was.

A grocery store and gasoline station were in business in 1968 on M-37 that goes through the former village. One church remains and each year in August former residents hold a "Pioneer Picnic." Last year (1969) Mrs. Corning said over 80 people attended and most of them came long distances to attend.

———

187

SPRINGDALE–1877 a post office 6½ miles due south of *Sherman* in what is now Springville Township. Weekly mail. Andrew J. Green, postmaster.

———

UMITILLA–1877 a recent settlement of 50. Boone Township, 10 miles west of *Linden (Haring)* on the G. R. & I. Railroad. Settled in March, 1876. Stage to *Linden* and *Clam Lake* tri-weekly. Marilla D. Johnson, postmaster; William A. Johnson, hotel; Johnson & Company (William A. Johnson, Sarah C. Mather, and John M. Dennett), lumber manufacturers.

> NOTE: This may have been changed to *"Boon"* which is in about the same location.

———

WEXFORD–1871 was a stopping place for stages between *Sherman* and *Traverse City*. Grew to be a good-sized village. Colfax Township, 6 miles north of *Sherman*. Daily mail. The village is known as *"Hanover."* J. A. Foust, general store and postmaster. A list of business places is almost identical to those a few years later in *Sherman*. William Mears, general store; John Wheeler, sawmill; E. Gilbert, hotel; had sawmill, etc.

1877 population 20 and in Hanover Township near the north county line. Weekly mail. Israel Foust, postmaster. In later years became quite a town with a bank, drug store, etc. 1884 population 52.

1918 population 150, 1½ miles west of *Buckley*. Telephone. D. W. Connine & Son, bankers; Freeman Shaver, hotel; Frank Sheriff, hotel and livery; William Sanford, grocery and dry goods; George Cornell, shoes,baker, and general store; George Furtsch, grocery; Connine & Blackhurst, hardware; and several other places.

Some of the buildings burned and the last hotel was torn down about 1920-22. A schoolhouse, church,and cemetery remained in 1953. For many years a grocery operated and was called *"Wexford Corners."*

———

WHEATLAND–1872 a post office 9 miles southeast of *Sherman*. Eight miles west of *Manton Station* on the G. R. & I. Railroad. Jonathan West, postmaster. Named after Jonathan Wheat, justice of the peace.

1877–Jonathan Wheat, postmaster. Not listed as a post office in 1890.

———

YUMA–was a post office in May, 1897, and is listed for about 65 years. At one time the population reached nearly 400. 1917 population 150. On the Ann Arbor Railroad, Springville Township, 5 miles south of *Mesick*. Telephone. Minnie E. Rose, postmistress. R. E. Hamilton, general store; H. Slater, restaurant; Frank Tosier, meats; and F. S. Tubbs, blacksmith.

Shown on present day maps. Post office discontinued about 1960. Now RFD *Mesick*.

————

Other towns and places during the history of the county:

AXIN–1918 a post office in Cherry Grove Township, southeast corner of Section 17, five miles northwest of *Hobart*. Daily mail. A. J. Morgan, general store.

CLAGGETTS–named after a lumberman who owned the mills. On the Ann Arbor Railroad. 1910 mail Mesick. See *"Glengary,"* also *"Sherman."*

CLAM LAKE–in the 1870s a large village on Clam Lake. Both the town and lake are now *Cadillac*.

CUTLERS–1910 mail *Harriette*.

DAKE'S MILL–1910 on the M. & N. E. Railroad. Mail *Buckley.*

DERRY–1910 on Ann Arbor Railroad. Mail *Harrietta.*

DIGGINS–on a spur of the Ann Arbor Railroad, a lumber camp and settlement made by the logging firm of Cummer & Diggins, who along with Louie Sands and Mitchells of *Cadillac*, owned much of the timber lands in the county, had their own railroads, etc.

DUFORTS–1910 on the Ann Arbor Railroad. Mail *Harriette.*

FAYS–on the Ann Arbor Railroad. 1910 mail *Harlan* in Manistee County.

FLAIRITYS–1910 on the M. & N. E. Railroad. Mail *Baxter*.

GARDINER–1910 on the Ann Arbor Railroad. Mail *Bunyea*.

GASSERS–1910 on Ann Arbor Railroad. Mail *Harriette*.

GASTON–name changed to *"Harriette."* See *Harriette*.

GLENGARY–1910 a sawmill town on the Manistee River near *Sherman*, Springville Township. Formerly *"Claggetts."* 1910 on the M. & N. E. Railroad.

HACKER–a station on the Falmouth Branch of the Lake City-Cadillac Railroad. Two miles from *Round Lake Junction*.

HASKINS–1910 on G. R. & I. Railroad. Mail *Walton*.

189

HENDERSON–on G. R. & I. Railroad. Also see *"Hoxeyville."*

LINDEN–the name for *"Haring."* See *Haring.*

MCPHERSON–1910 on the Ann Arbor Railroad. Mail *Boon.*

MILLERSVILLE–1910 on the Ann Arbor Railroad. Mail *Boon.*

MINERS ROLLWAY–1910 on the M. & N. E. Railroad. Mail *Yuma.*

MISSAUKEE JUNCTION–on G. R. & I. Railroad. Mail *Cadillac.*

MYSTIC–on Buttermilk Lake, Liberty Township, about 5 miles northwest of *Manton* was at one time a village. 1910 population 18, RFD *Manton.* A school and cemetery remain on the site.

PERUES–1910 on the Ann Arbor Railroad. Mail *Yuma.*

RUMBO–1910 on the M. & N. E. Railroad. Mail *Buckley.*

SAUNDERS–1910 on the Ann Arbor Railroad. Mail *Harrietta.*

SELMA–1910 mail *Cadillac.* On the Ann Arbor Railroad near Mud Lake just north of Lake Mitchell.

SOPER–1918 a discontinued post office. RFD *Manton.*

THORP–1918 in South Branch Township, 14 miles north of *Luther.* Mail to *Hoxeyville.*

WALLS–was a settlement. A church, school, and cemetery was on the site as late as 1925.

WEST SUMMITT–1872 a post office and station in Wexford County, 6 miles south of *Clam Lake*, on the G. R. & I. Railroad. Name changed to *"Hobart."* See *Hobart.*

WHITESANDS–1910 mail *Cadillac.*

WILLIAMS–1910 on the Ann Arbor Railroad. Mail *Boon.*

————

ABOUT THE AUTHOR

Born at Lansing, Michigan, November 11, 1918, a descendant of Michigan pioneers, Dodge started investigating Michigan ghost towns in 1954. He was a member of several Michigan historical and genealogical societies. Mr. Dodge was a well known freelance writer and many of his articles about ghost towns and logging in Michigan appeared in leading newspapers and several magazines in the State.

In addition to writing his family history book, published in 1967, he also authored a series about northern Michigan towns published in the *Bay City Times* from 1968 to 1970.

In 1970, Dodge authored a book called *Michigan Ghost Towns, Volume I.* We were all surprised by the popularity of this volume. In 1971, another book called *Michigan Ghost Towns, Volume II* was published. These two volumes covered the Lower Peninsula of Michigan. In 1973, the last of Dodge's series was published called *Michigan Ghost Towns, Volume Ill.*

Roy was severely wounded while serving in the Armed Forces during World War II. However, Roy did not allow his debilitating disability dissuade him from tenaciously pursuing the historical information he needed to write this unusual history of his beloved state. Sometimes, wracked with pain, he stoically traveled to the various locations in the State to meet with the numerous senior citizens who provided him with pictures and anecdotes of "Michigan, the way it was."

Before he passed away, Roy wrote a couple more volumes on particular periods and areas of Michigan. However, his legacy to us and the people of the State of Michigan is his work covered in *Michigan Ghost Towns, Volume I, II, and III.*

To continue his legacy and meet the never-ending requests for his books while considering today's economics, we have taken the liberty of combining Volumes I and II, covering the Lower Peninsula. We are titling this reprint, *Michigan Ghost Towns, the Lower Peninsula.* Embracing this unique State with two peninsulas will be two volumes, one for the Lower Peninsula and *Michigan Ghost Towns, the Upper Peninsula.* We think Roy would approve our move.

The Publishers

ACKNOWLEDGMENTS

To compile a book of this type would be impossible without the cooperation and assistance of literally hundreds of persons. Most of the research for compiling these former towns and places was conducted at the Michigan State Library in Lansing, the State Archives Records depository in Lansing, and from my private library of more than 100 books and booklets about Michigan.

During a four-year period I drove at least 10,000 miles in the State visiting ghost town sites and cemeteries, in both Upper and Lower Michigan. Many hours were spent in libraries all over the State, correspondence with historical societies, and visits to many museums, both private and public.

As in any historical work there is a wide margin for inaccuracy. Most dates in these volumes are taken from Michigan Legislative Manuals for the years 1890 through 1969, and Michigan Gazeteer and Business Directories for various years. Other dates are taken from courthouse records, newspaper accounts of the period, original plat maps, either at the State Archives or from town and county records.

It is with regret that I could find no published or compiled history of most of the 33 northern Michigan counties covered in this book: Volume I and Volume II of *Michigan Ghost Towns.*

Although it is impossible to mention all the people interviewed, those who wrote letters with information about former towns in response to a series of 220 towns published in the *Bay City Times* from 1968 to 1970, and others who provided information, I want to thank Kenneth Priestly of Vassar; Fred C. Hirzel of Moorestown; Virginia Keebler, Dennis R. Bodem, and others for their kind assistance at the State Archives. Ralph Strobel of Saginaw; Cal (Calvin) Ennes of Au Gres; ladies of the Gladwin, West Branch, Clare, Harrison, and Evart libraries. The Manistee County Historical Society, which gave me information about their area otherwise unobtainable; the Fife Lake Historical Society; and the kind assistance of personnel at the Michigan State Library, Grace Dow Memorial Library of Midland; Anthony L. Tominac, Michigan Department of Commerce who furnished much information on Lake County; Mrs. Clark Corning of Grawn, Michigan who volunteered firsthand information about Wexford County and the Grand Traverse area; Rollin D. Yorty of Higgins Lake, friend and historian; Ruth W. Geister of the abstract office in Roscommon; Mrs. Christel S. Dillenback of Big Rapids, and many others. I offer my humble apologies for omitting the names of many other nice people who helped me with the book, as the list is nearly endless.

Roy L. Dodge